WOMEN IN THE SANCTUARY MOVEMENT

In the series

WOMEN IN THE POLITICAL ECONOMY
edited by Ronnie J. Steinberg

WOMEN
in the
SANCTUARY
MOVEMENT

Robin Lorentzen

TEMPLE UNIVERSITY PRESS

PHILADELPHIA

Temple University Press, Philadelphia 19122
Copyright © 1991 by Temple University. All rights reserved
Published 1991
Printed in the United States of America

Library of Congress Cataloging-in-Publication Data

Lorentzen, Robin, 1949–
    Women in the sanctuary movement / Robin Lorentzen.
      p.   cm. — (Women in the political economy)
    Includes bibliographical references and index.
    ISBN 0-87722-768-3 (alk. paper)
    1. Sanctuary movement—Illinois—Chicago.
  2. Women in church work—Illinois—Chicago.
  3. Church work with refugees—Illinois—Chicago.
  I. Title.   II. Series.
  BV4466.L67   1991
  261.8′32—dc20   90-11132
                                                      CIP

CONTENTS

ACKNOWLEDGMENTS

I wish to thank many people who helped make this book possible. Kathleen McCourt and Judith Wittner of the sociology department and Susan Ross of the theology department of Loyola University of Chicago offered plentifully their good ideas and unflagging support. The special interest of Stephen R. Warner, University of Illinois in Chicago, prompted me to seek a publisher. The insights and suggestions of Ronnie Steinberg and Michael Ames at Temple University Press, as well as those of Gregory Wiltfang, and the skilled copyediting of Patricia Sterling helped transform the manuscript into a book. Finally, I am deeply grateful to the twenty-nine women I interviewed in the Chicago sanctuary movement for their extraordinary generosity and willingness to share their experiences. Their accounts make up the book's heart, and I dedicate it to them.

WOMEN IN THE SANCTUARY MOVEMENT

I

INTRODUCTION

This is a study of women's participation in the sanctuary movement, a religious-based political movement originating in the early 1980s among church and lay workers in response to growing numbers of Central American refugees at the Mexico-U.S. border.[1] A striking feature of the movement is that women outnumber men by about two-thirds at all levels of organization, and by about one hundred to four in the Chicago Catholic Sanctuary. While the media have conveyed an image of sanctuary leaders and spokespersons as male clerics, women actually predominate. The movement's chief actors are housewives and nuns; its main work is done by volunteers who mobilize family, church, and community resources to reconstruct refugees' lives.

Contrary to one leader's claim that the movement "runs by itself, on faith,"[2] the study shows that homemakers and women religious literally produce the movement through local and national woman-based groups in religious and community settings. Women's activism is rooted in a network of local sanctuary sites, "peace and justice" organizations, and a larger coalition of movements opposed to U.S. policies in Central America. Comprising movement organizations pursuing similar goals, these "social movement industries"[3] provide structure and meaning to women's political identities. For most, even before they enter the movement, their personal experience and knowledge contrast sharply with official viewpoints about the refugees' situation; involvement in sanctuary enhances their sense of "cognitive liberation"—new ways of thinking about social conditions and change.[4] In Meadian fashion,[5] women reconstruct the movement out of collective experience and action, developing the movement and their activism.

Sanctuary activists generally assist Central American refugees seeking political asylum in North America and protest U.S. policies perceived as creating the refugees. Caretaking activities involve using family, church, and community resources to support refugees in sanctuary; protest activities include going to outreach events, demonstrating, being arrested, and traveling to Central America on "personal witness" and "repopulation" missions. These activities have given rise to two orientations in the movement.[6] The humanitarian approach grew out of early discreet efforts to help undocumented refugees enter the United States; it tends to view supporting them as an end in itself, and it justifies illegal acts of transporting and sheltering them as "civil initiatives" upholding basically good but inadequate amnesty laws. The political approach developed out of later efforts to build a national solidarity movement with the refugees; it views sanctuary as a way to educate the American public about their situation, and it calls for acts of civil disobedience—protest, arrest, and "turning the railroad around" (that is, accompanying the refugees home)—against laws perceived as unjust and unjustly enforced.

Deeply rooted, this division is an important source of tension and change in the movement. Linked to the structural conditions of participants' lives, it characterizes their ideologies and activities across region, time, and gender. Although humanitarian-oriented male religious in Tucson led the movement early on, politically oriented women religious in Chicago have increasingly shaped its development. The division reappears in Chicago women's rhetoric identifying themselves as politically oriented and movement men as humanitarian and paternalistic. It also distinguishes two groups of women at two local Catholic sanctuaries. While most women fell somewhere between the two orientations, laywomen and women religious at the two sites tended to represent the extremes, providing "ideal types"[7] for understanding women's participation in the movement. Rooted in their contrasting life structures, striking differences appear in how the two groups construct a sanctuary, care for the refugees, perceive the issues, and view themselves as agents of human liberation.

The purpose of this book is to provide a better understanding of women's roles in social movements. Social science research has somewhat obscured women's historical participation in movements; until quite recently, women have been invisible in most accounts except in relation to the home and family. Gendered perceptions in social science are now recognized as such as new studies grounded in women's situations and experience identify them as important historical actors. An important corrective for women's unnoticed history is to ask, "Where are the women?" in previously uncharted areas of social experience.[8] Moving beyond deterministic, functional views of social behavior, new studies make connections between women's roles in society, social movements, and larger spheres of change. However, no complete and valid descriptions yet exist of women's activism in all its historical, cross-cultural forms,[9] and there is no developed paradigm representing women's activism. Studies suggest that in their long history in movements, they have rarely and only recently organized on their own behalf and have been divided on many issues. Their experience, often frustration, in movements has often radicalized their views of gender, but the conditions giving rise to "incipient feminism" remain unclear.[10] This study focuses on the ideological and structural conditions in which women transform sanctuary from a woman-based network into a feminist movement, and in which "female revolt" becomes a part of their activism.[11] Assuming that gendered patterns in the movement are a function of basic structural issues, it develops two models for understanding women's activism based on the contrasting social locations in the world of laywomen and women religious and the relative costs and contributions of their "hidden work" in the movement.[12]

SANCTUARY AS A WOMEN'S MOVEMENT

Sanctuary shares much with other woman-based moral reform movements originating in the "free spaces" of religious institutions in the past two centuries, such as the abolition, temperance, and peace movements.[13] These have generally been religion-based movements in which primarily white, middle-class women have played active if not dominant roles. Recruited through their usually deep religious involvement, women in these movements often revolted against religious orthodoxy, male clergy who tried to confine their activism to the family sphere, and the constricted opportunities available to them as middle-class women.[14] Varying widely, these movements have given women a sense of spiritual equality, if not more equal opportunity to participate in religious affairs. Their prominence in these activities has been linked to their lack of access to formal channels of power. After women won the vote, political parties failed to include them as equals, encouraging them instead to use their organizational skills at the grassroots level. Their vote now matching men's, women still predominate in community-based movements.

Much of women's activism has been rooted in the tradition of congregations as caring communities.[15] The United States is especially dense in religion-based social organizations—its most common form of associational membership—and many mass movements have been organizationally rooted in churches.[16] The institutional free spaces of churches are "complex, shifting and dynamic" and "partial in their freedom and participation," giving rise to democratic movements such as the abolition, Catholic Worker, and civil rights movements, as well as reactionary, backward-looking ones such as the Ku Klux Klan, American Nazi Party, and New Right. "Parochialisms" of class, race, gender, and other biases rooted in broader social environments have often characterized these movements, undermining democratic tendencies by imposing different sorts of values.[17]

The concept of sanctuary itself constitutes a free space. Participants use family, church, and community resources to create free space in which to reconstruct refugees' lives. They also protest U.S. policies perceived as causing the refugees' situation, using institutional free space to shelter and legitimate their activism. Free space is a prerequisite and a product of the movement, providing sanctuary for all participants.

The roles of women in the movement also constitute free space. Largely because of their predominantly white, middle-class status, their deviance is generally overlooked and made invisible, their activism met with benign indifference or special consideration by public officials who look the other way. Women's deviance is unapparent partly because they are defined as socially unimportant; consequently, they are much less likely than men to be assaulted, arrested, or jailed for their activism.

The twenty-nine Chicago women interviewed for this study (see the Appendix) expressed an awareness of their predominance in churches and of the importance of institutional free space to their activism. They generally noted that "churchgoers are mostly women," a fact that "creates a network among them." Identifying "the doers in the church" as "mostly women active in the day-to-day nuts and bolts," they saw "a natural connection between churches and women": "women keep churches going."

Another kind of free space is created by participants' claims of religious precedents for harboring refugees.[18] Identifying with other movements legitimates and shapes this movement and enhances its members' sense of cognitive liberation. Interpretations of history from the standpoint of the movement point to such ancient traditions as the Old Testament custom of refuge cities and altar sanctuary and the Greek, Roman, early Christian, and Anglo-Saxon versions. More familiar precedents include sanctuary for fugitive slaves by means of the nineteenth-century "underground railroad" and the sanctuary of the "confessing church" that harbored Jews during Europe's Nazi occupation.[19]

Women have articulated these historical parallels by pointing out similarities between refugees aided by sanctuary and other groups. For example, one woman interviewed quoted a Vietnamese boat person who told a refugee in sanctuary, "I came by water, you came by foot. We don't speak the same language, but together we'll help each other." Another quoted a board member of a "small, poor" Japanese-American church endorsing sanctuary: "Wouldn't it have been wonderful if they'd had sanctuary at the beginning of World War II for displaced Japanese-Americans?" Some saw connections between sanctuary and other struggles for human rights. Participants used historical parallels to claim legitimacy for sanctuary. Several compared sanctuary to civil rights, civil disobedience, and Nazi resistance movements; one compared refugee detention centers at the border to concentration camps.

Some women made these connections in more personal terms, their ethnicity enhancing their sense of identification with the refugees. For example, a black woman said, "Even though we were brought here against our will, there formed an underground railroad to help us." A Jewish woman said, "We were in Egypt, oppressed in the land of bondage, and were let go, so maybe we have an understanding of sanctuary." All Jewish women named the Holocaust as motivating their sanctuary involvement. As one put it, "Jews who survived the Holocaust were given sanctuary. Because we have been the recipients, it compels us to do so."

SANCTUARY AS A POLITICAL PROCESS

The sanctuary movement is a part of larger political processes that have developed out of macro-organizational conditions and events. Its background includes the histories of Spanish colonization and U.S. hegemony in Central America, the conditions and dynamic forces in that region leading to the emergence of grassroots opposition movements, and the refugees' exodus to the United States, where immigration policies shape their lives. Political instability and institutionalized violence in the refugees' home countries led to the development of increasingly polarized and violent factions, as religious and political institutions shifted their positions toward one another and the refugees. Last, North American church workers' illegal contacts with the growing numbers of refugees at the U.S. border spawned the movement.

Lacking precious metals, Central America played a minor role in the Spanish American empire. After the Spanish conquest, the church became a powerful source of authority in the late seventeenth century. Led by Creole landowners, conservative elites upheld Hispanic institutions—especially the church—and were suspicious of reform. Supported by the middle class, liberal elites who favored restricting the clergy and abolishing slavery triumphed in the late nineteenth century. The church, stripped of power, declined as a key actor until the 1960s. Military and police forces used by liberals' "republican dictatorships" to intimidate and suppress the opposition became forces in their own right. Land suitable for producing coffee was farmed primarily by Indians tilling communal lands or by small peasant producers. As coffee exports became crucial to local economies, elites cashed in on export opportunities, taking over their lands through fraud, coercion, and state power. Elites controlled laborers—Indian and Ladino peasants—with private armies, later using national militaries to create a repressive state apparatus. Export strategies led to heavy dependence on the United States, and direct U.S. investment mushroomed from the 1950s on.[20]

While elites continued to block land reforms, economic decline in the late 1970s and early 1980s made the situation worse. In many areas the Catholic church began shaping the urban and rural poor into a new social force. Two events mark a shift in the church's role: the Second Ecumenical Council of the early 1960s (Vatican II), and the 1968 conference of Latin American bishops at Medellín, Colombia. The bishops called for increased education, social awareness, and the creation of "base communities" to organize local community self-help groups, cooperatives, peasant organizations, Christian-oriented unions, and other popular organizations. Important changes also took place among the urban working and middle classes, who sought to organize reformist political movements. These patterns of deprivation and growth exerted enormous pressure on Central American societies as new social forces mobilized to push for justice and reform. Backed by increasingly strong U.S. support, elites have continued to meet reform efforts with brutal repression.[21]

U.S. policies have helped to differentiate this pattern in Guatemala and El Salvador. The United Fruit Company (UFC) became Guatemala's first transnational corporation in 1901, and overt and covert intervention has since helped maintain U.S. influence. A 1954 CIA-backed coup crushed a reformist government that had confiscated and begun redistributing uncultivated UFC land. The coup reversed land reform, producing a long period of political instability and deep divisions in the military, unhealed by new leaders. The army has killed tens of thousands of people and displaced over a million from their homes. By 1989, civil war had caused over 100,000 deaths and 40,000 disappearances and created about 200,000 orphans.[22]

In El Salvador, the military has ruled for more than fifty years except for two brief periods of civilian rule totaling less than a year. Reform movements of the 1960s culminating in 1972 electoral victory, were crushed by the army and right-wing death squads. During the 1970s, violent anti-Catholic sentiment developed toward liberation theology, a movement by church workers attempting to form base communities in which peasants could improve their economic conditions. As those labeled Communists were arrested, tortured, and murdered, several guerrilla movements and broad-based peasant opposition groups organized. Civil war escalated along with the U.S. role; in the 1980s the United States became the "principal architect, financier, and strategist" for the Salvadoran government and armed forces.[23]

In 1980, Salvadoran Archbishop Oscar Romero asked the United States to stop military aid to El Salvador; he was murdered a month later by right-wing terrorists as he said mass. Some fifty popular organizations formed the Revolutionary Democratic Front, and the Farabundo Marti Liberation Front became the umbrella for five guerrilla organizations. The army killed hundreds of peasants and raped and killed four U.S. churchwomen. The United States stopped military aid but resumed it a month later; the Catholic Church documented 12,000 murders and no indictments. By 1989, about 75,000 people had died, 150,000 had been wounded, and one and a half million had been forced to leave the country or relocate in urban shantytowns—in a country of only six and a half million people. The United States had spent about $50,000 per guerrilla and $300 per civilian; after years of deepening U.S. military involvement, government forces were far from victory as guerrilla forces adapted to continual isolation.[24] This pattern is a part of a larger strategy in the region; since 1983 the United States has conducted almost continuous military maneuvers in Central America and the Caribbean, and by 1984 it was engaged in an invasion of Central America "neither officially acknowledged nor publicly recognized."[25]

As for those fleeing such conditions, in 1982 about 300,000 Central Americans were registered at refugee camps in Mexico, Honduras, and Costa Rica, and an undetermined number were in these countries illegally. About 100,000 have entered the United States illegally each year since 1980, a fifth of the total annual illegal population in this country. By 1987, up to 750,000 Central Americans, and a tenth of the population of El Salvador, had entered illegally in what the *New York Times* called "one of the most determined and concentrated migrations of any national group to the U.S. in recent history." Over two-thirds were arrested before or upon entering.[26]

Although in 1981 the Immigration and Naturalization Service (INS) began to enforce alien and asylum laws "with a new vigor," many Central Americans have successfully entered and settled in the United States. Having been tortured or imprisoned, or having watched loved ones being tortured or murdered, many arrive with deep emotional scars and unaddressed health needs. Women make up 53 percent of these refugees; often alone, jobless, and undocumented, they constitute a growing segment of those unqualified for amnesty.[27]

U.S. immigration policies are a function of U.S. foreign policies, and how the government interprets and applies international treaties and national laws compounds the refugees' problems. Since 1980, annual resolutions have urged Congress to give extended voluntary departure (EVD) status to Salvadorans, allowing them to remain in the United States until their country stabilizes. The State Department, however, has maintained that El Salvador and Guatemala have not suffered the same widespread levels of violence as other countries. Government policies are clearly biased, spokespersons' arguments obscuring both the distinction between economic and political refugees and Salvadoran and Guatemalan refugees' actual circumstances.[28]

Some studies point to inconsistencies in the U.S. asylum process, questioning its rationale for systematically denying amnesty to Salvadorans. Others contradict the government's views of human rights abuses in Central America. As for refugees' risks if deported, government claims that abuses have decreased in their countries are contradicted by Amnesty International, Americas Watch, and the Washington Office on Latin America. For some, deportation is fortunately a lengthy process.[29]

Some observers consider "transparent" the government's view that most Salvadorans and Guatemalans in the United States are economic refugees: to acknowledge "political" refugees from countries whose governments it "enthusiastically supports" would raise "embarrassing questions";[30] the refugees' presence might bring unwanted "public exposure of its covert and overt military activities in Central America."[31] The government has gone so far as to give the Salvadoran government information on suspected leftist refugees, thus increasing their risks if deported.[32]

Since 1986 a new law has jeopardized the jobs and threatened to force the return of tens of thousands of refugees. Formerly the Simpson-Mazzoli law, the Immigration Reform and Control Act offered legal status to refugees applying within one year who could establish that they had entered the United States before January 1, 1982, and had resided here continuously. Fear of being declared ineligible and deported kept the rate of applicants low. Acquiring proper documentation was a serious obstacle, making entire un-documented communities dependent upon past employers. Other obstacles were application costs and the possiblity of broken families. Soon after the law was passed, about 6,000 refugees, mostly Salvadorans, went to Canada.[33]

The sanctuary movement developed out of church workers' response to the refugees' growing presence at the border more than to their perceived conditions at home. About two million Central Americans fled violence and civil war between 1980 and 1983, constituting the largest human displacement in the Western Hemisphere in modern history. Refugee workers first tried raising bond for those detained by the INS and helping them apply for political asylum under the 1980 Refugee Act. After exhausting their resources in the "most massive bailout" in INS history, they next tried improving the refugees' chances for asylum by bringing them clandestinely into the country. Beginning with "evasion services" at the border and then the establishment of refugee camps in southern Mexico, they constructed an underground railroad to bring the refugees in illegally. When this failed to win more asylum cases, they decided to try to build support for the refugees within their national churches.[34]

Two religious men in Arizona first conceived of public sanctuary and became the movement's early leaders. Since the 1970s there had been a strong grassroots movement in Tucson, concerned with environment and urban growth issues, in which local churches and synagogues were taking the lead. Rev. John Fife of Southside Presbyterian Church had been in active in these campaigns. Fife first encountered Central American refugees in 1980 when he met with twelve survivors of a group of twenty-four Salvadorans led into the Arizona desert by Mexican smugglers who apparently lost their way. The meeting changed his view of refugees: until then he had believed that they crossed the border "for the same reason as Mexicans—to get jobs." A weekly prayer vigil for Central Americans began at Fife's church, which soon became a place for the refugees to meet with immigration lawyers and discuss their problems.[35]

Retired rancher and Quaker Jim Corbett became involved in 1981 when a Salvadoran hitchhiker, whom a friend had picked up near the Arizona-Mexico border, was arrested. Corbett was struck by the complex immigration procedures concerning refugees and began actively helping Central Americans apply for asylum. He and other Quakers in the area were soon filling their homes with refugees, and he asked Fife and other members of the Tucson Ecumenical Council (TEC) to do more. At first, refugees were introduced during worship services at Southside, and members of the congregation volunteered to take them home. Later, they were transported away from the border, then from the border to the church, and finally directly from across the border, until the decision to declare sanctuary publicly "became inevitable."[36]

In 1981 the TEC created a task force on Central America (TECCA) to respond to the growing number of refugees' needs, raise funds to bond out those in detention, and support the asylum process. As major contradictions became evident between legal guarantees for refugees and INS practices, the Tucson group began to give up on the legal route. Turning increasingly to evasion services, it deepened its involvement with the refugees through the underground railroad. On March 24, 1982, the second anniversary of Archbishop Oscar Romero's assassination, the Southside congregation formally declared itself a public sanctuary in a letter to the U.S. attorney general.[37] Southside became "the cradle of the loosely structured sanctuary movement." Dozens of similar declarations across the country followed.[38]

As awareness and concern for the refugees grew, the movement spread rapidly along a network of religious affiliates. Growing nationally and denominationally, its membership increasingly overlapped with that of a larger coalition of movements opposed to U.S. foreign policies. By the mid-1980s an estimated 42,000 Americans had pledged to resist U.S. policies in Central America, and sanctuary had became the largest grassroots civil disobedience movement in North America since the 1960s.[39]

The sanctuary network extends into thirty-four states. The state of New Mexico, some twelve to twenty-seven cities, about five hundred individual churches and synagogues, and thousands of organizations have officially declared themselves sanctuaries. The illegality of harboring and transporting undocumented refugees prevents an accurate count of how many people have participated in the movement. Estimates are 70,000 North Americans and 2,000 to 3,000 Central American refugees—a fraction of the half-million entering the United States illegally each year.[40]

As the job of creating the movement grew, the Chicago Religious Task Force on Central America (CRTFCA) offered to become involved. Organized in 1980 in response to the four churchwomen's deaths in El Salvador, it had focused on ending U.S. support there. The agency agreed first to Corbett's plan to conduct a refugee to a Chicago church, then to becoming the national coordinator for the underground railroad. Like the Tucson group, its steering committee was made up mostly of nuns, priests, and ministers who were well informed through the churches about conditions in Central America. Far from the border, CRTFCA developed a closer connection when Sister Darlene Nicgorski, who had lived and worked with refugees in Guatemala, joined the CRTFCA staff and began working with the Tucson group.[41]

The agency initially sent organizers to help with every declaration. As requests for assistance grew, it produced manuals to teach interested groups how prospective sites could become sanctuaries; these, along with the examples of earlier declarations, spurred the movement's development.[42] In two years the agency had assisted over two hundred sanctuaries, published and distributed more than 30,000 copies of manuals and pamphlets, and generally "refined the concept of public sanctuary" in which church-sponsored refugees tell their stories to the American public.[43]

In 1982 the Tucson group debated whether evasion services were weakening the capacity of conventional social service agencies to assist refugees. Corbett responded by criticizing conventional services as a paternalistic method of preparing refugees to provide cheap labor; he called sanctuary "a way out of the bog of condescen-

sion" created by such programs.[44] Another debate that year produced a far greater division in the movement. When Tucson sent
Chicago two refugees who had "no understanding" of the political
conflict in Central America and were "therefore not useful," they
were returned on a bus. Fife denied that Southside refugees were
required to be politically useful, and Tucson stopped sending refugees to Chicago. As this split widened, sanctuary developed as two
movements: a national grassroots resettlement effort, and a national
network of antiwar activitists.[45]

The split is rooted in the two groups' relative distance from the
border, with its massive supply of refugees and close INS scrutiny.
While border workers were attempting discreetly to meet refugees'
immediate needs, Chicago activists became involved in "conscious-
ness-raising," persuading church communities around the country
to become more active in the campaign against U.S. policies in
Central America. Although both groups opposed U.S. policies supporting repressive regimes, their contrasting approaches to sanctuary "contained the seeds of future trouble" as Tucson pursued a local
grassroots initiative and Chicago tried to coordinate a national
protest movement.[46]

The conflict between humanitarian and political impulses is
both inherent in the movement and produced by its detractors. The
INS began secret surveillance and wiretapping of Texas and Arizona
sanctuary activitists in 1984, then moved publicly with lawsuits in
1985–86. Relying heavily on quotations from CRTFCA newsletters
that described sanctuary as civil disobedience against unjust laws,
INS agents and other critics tried to use this division to prove that
the movement was not humanitarian and was working with refugees
to serve its own political ends. The implication that the movement
was primarily political "seriously undermined the Arizona activists'
legal position," contradicting their claims that their actions merely
upheld the 1980 Refugee Act. The government's attempt to suppress
the movement ultimately backlashed, however, creating enormous
interest in sanctuary and prompting its greatest period of growth.

Beginning with the trial in Tucson of eleven church workers in 1985, the media gave wide coverage to the movement and related issues.[47]

Whether sanctuary is a political movement against U.S. policy in Central America or a humanitarian effort to assist its victims remains an unresolved question; however, border workers and Chicago activists have not been as ideologically divided as their detractors have portrayed them. Most supporters reject altogether the humanitarian-political debate. They point out that sanctuary is not against the law; that the government has gone after religious, not political, activists; and that sanctuary churches actually represent a wide continuum of political positions.[48] In their view, the debate itself is part of a government strategy aimed at "creating splits and exploiting different perspectives within the movement."[49]

Other disagreements surround the movement. Government officials claim that sanctuary promotes the opening of borders, which the U.S. has a right to protect. Sanctuary spokespersons respond that sanctuary promotes ending U.S. policies in Central America designed to target civilian populations and create refugees. They add that human life is sacred and should be treated as such, that the movement stands for making the refugees' own countries sanctuaries so that they can return home.[50]

Government officials have accused the movement of luring Central Americans to the United States, where they take jobs from citizens and burden the social service system.[51] However, a Chicago woman who conducted her own study refuted this claim. She contacted twenty-two sanctuary cities and asked whether they had experienced any negative repercussions from sanctuary: had they been besieged by refugees or heavy demands on city resources? Half responded, all affirming "no discernible increase" in refugees or demands.

Sanctuary spokespersons contend that the government drives the refugees to the United States by supporting covert wars in Central America and that it uses the movement and the refugees as scapegoats for unemployment. They claim that undocumented workers contribute more than they take because they pay social security taxes yet receive no tax refunds or social security benefits. They argue that undocumented workers have historically taken jobs that U.S. citizens don't want, constituting a source of cheap, uncomplaining labor whose low wages have increased profits and lowered consumer prices. They suggest that the real causes of unemployment are the numbers of corporations that have left the United States for cheap labor markets in developing countries.[52]

Critics claim that sanctuary workers are well-intentioned but naive persons led by political dissidents and opponents of U.S. policies. Women who were interviewed for this study strongly rejected the suggestion that followers are "dupes" carrying out leaders' hidden agendas. For example, Geselle, a nun who had traveled extensively and lived in Central America, indicated that her previous experience was merely reaffirmed by Corbett's and Fife's early statements: "My own experience and reading had already informed me. They simply reinforced it." Eva, a homemaker, also rejected the idea of wide differences between leaders and followers: "People without other responsibilities tend to be active—people with time and money."[53]

Whether the sanctuary movement is humanitarian or political, government action toward it has been based on the belief that its members are politically subversive. Over the course of its existence the movement has operated under surveillance and harassment by government agents.[54] The women I spoke with were understandably concerned about their vulnerability to government surveillance, and some were hesitant about being interviewed; three mentioned the possibility that I might be a spy.

Most of the women indicated that prior to their sanctuary involvement, their personal knowledge about the refugees' situation contradicted government claims. They had already been exposed to everyday realities that contrasted sharply with official views; over time their experience became a base from which to examine old ideologies and forge new definitions. Several described meeting refugees in their communities, listening to their stories, and piecing together their own views. Some made this connection through their children's schools; for example, one approached her son's school-mate's mother to ask whether the woman's Salvadoran husband, who had started a local refugee center, would speak to her church group. She was surprised to learn that he had been "killed on the streets of Chicago" by a Honduran who first befriended and then shot him, was jailed and released on bond, and subsequently skipped the country; his widow believed that "the CIA did the job." Another woman had invited a Chilean boy's father to speak to her students. A teacher at the time of Allende's overthrow, the man had been suspected, imprisoned, and tortured; this is how she "began to piece together what was going on." Others reported making similar connections at their churches, synagogues, prayer groups, and libraries and through reading and conversation.

Women often indicated how they judged the truth about the refugees. One recalled asking herself, "Why would peasants come here and say these things if they weren't true?" Women's knowledge is rooted in their personal experiences with the refugees and with others whose experience they trust. As one put it, "I listened to the people I respect." Another described meeting a missionary with "firsthand experience" who told her, "I was down there—I know what the Reagan administration says is a lie."

Seventeen of the women I interviewed had lived or traveled in Central America, where their experiences contradicting government claims about these countries often came as a surprise. "We were traveling in a state of siege," said Geselle of Guatemala in 1967. "People were disappearing and being held for no reason. . . . These were my first exposures. It was a shock." She first heard about death squads in a village where an abandoned truck remained in the town square for weeks; its driver had been shot to death by the *mano blanco*—the white hand—and his truck left there as a warning to others. She also learned that landowners privately hired the army to kill those who complained about working conditions. In 1985, traveling in Nicaragua with a university group, she viewed the damage where the CIA had mined a harbor in 1984. Touring a shrimp-freezing plant that exported primarily to Canada, she found that "the rest of the world does business as usual with Nicaragua." At a refugee camp half-filled with Salvadorans fleeing the civil war in their country, she noted that "people there were very busy trying to better their lives . . . the camp was a sort of grassroots democracy." In comparing her perceptions of Guatemala and Nicaragua, she indicated the sharp contrast between her experience and government claims:

> Both are terribly poor, but the atmosphere is totally different. In one the government is against, in the other, for the people. In Nicaragua people aren't afraid of the soldiers and government. In Guatemala people felt safe only in the parishes. They didn't trust the government. People always acted guarded, always afraid to be stopped by the police. In Nicaragua people were very free, said anything to anyone. They weren't guarded. I saw a lot of casual interaction on the streets between people and the military. There was a lot of hope among the people. Much faith. It was evident in their activities. They were improving things with very few resources.

Lori, a young minister, visited El Salvador and Nicaragua in 1985 as a seminary student. She too described new realities that contradicted government claims:

> In Nicaragua there's lots of soldiers and guns, but I felt very safe. We never had any trouble. But in El Salvador the guns are pointed at you. That's how I felt. . . . [At] night by about 7:15 the streets are very deserted . . . we could hear gunshots. . . . No one's out past seven; cars, past eight; taxis, past nine. And these aren't even official curfews. . . . Things go on at night. People get killed and bodies get dumped. We drove by a car accident where the driver was shot in the head. . . . It was very scary. . . . In a cafe I learned not to sit with my back to the door. Nobody does. In case somebody starts shooting or if a bomb goes off, you can save yourself.

The fear is so evident in everyday life. People don't speak on the streets or buses. . . . The war's a way of life. You can never escape the war in Nicaragua—there's nothing to buy—but you can be in Managua and feel affected by the war but not be a part of it. . . . It's mostly on the front where the contras are. In El Salvador the whole country's a war zone. In some ways I hated El Salvador. . . . We went back to Nicaragua and said, "Thank God! We're back in freedom now!" We felt giddy, happy, overjoyed to be in Nicaragua.

In sum, large-scale political processes help explain the sanctuary movement's emergence, divisions, and viewpoints, including women's distinctive experiences and understandings. Assuming that social movements are politics by other means, political process theory provides an encompassing, macro-structural account of the movement, focusing on relationships within and between movements and between movements and institutions in surrounding societies.[55] Viewing the movement's development as a response to ongoing processes of interaction within larger political environments, it portrays sanctuary as a nationally based movement organization; its context, the modern centralized state. The state, a frequent target of political movements, characteristically attempts to "control, channel, repress, or facilitate" them.[56] The sanctuary movement has clearly targeted the state as the cause of the refugees' problems. State agents have in turn prosecuted sanctuary activists, spied on movement operations, passed immigration laws confusing the refugees' status and requiring their deportation, and repeatedly looked the other way when illegal government activities occur.

A movement's emergence requires existing opportunities for change; political instability enhances dominant groups' and institutions' vulnerability and the likelihood of collective action. Regime crises and contests for political dominance increase the political opportunities of organized challengers by undermining the hegemonic position of previously dominant groups. The collapse of states as repressive agents may set in motion widespread collective action.[57] Political conditions in Central America and the recent flood of refugees to the United States have contributed to growing opposition to U.S. policies, helping to launch a loosely organized national coalition of "peace and justice" movements that are increasingly overlapping and politically oriented.

State repression may spur collective action by provoking movements to grow in size and commitment or force them underground by making even nonviolent protest impossible. As political opportunities expand and improve the bargaining positions of challenging groups, movement opponents are more likely to use restraint, even with increased threats to their interests.[58] In the movement's early history, the government's attempt to repress it by prosecuting refugee workers and secretly monitoring their activities backfired, creating enormous publicity for the movement. While covert surveillance has continued, no formal sanctions followed the Tucson trial, even as movement activities became more political and participants more outspoken.

Even when dominant groups are vulnerable to pressure, giving subordinate groups the potential to organize, collective action depends on how people think about their situation. When prospective participants question authorities' legitimacy, assert what they perceive as their rights, and believe that they can bring about change, cognitive liberation may occur.[59] This study shows women combining their personal experience and knowledge about the refugees' situation with their growing consciousness as women to build a national protest movement. Cognitive liberation occurs with their identification with "underdogs," their desire to act, and their involvement in small woman-based groups at social action churches and synagogues where they learn politicized biblical rhetoric and become active on the refugees' behalf.

Although a movement's life cycle may develop independent of objective reality,[60] macro-organizational conditions clearly explain sanctuary's emergence. Recent sociopolitical events—disruptions in U.S. and world economies, the United States' becoming a debtor nation, Japan's usurping world power—have decreased the global hegemony held by the United States since World War II. These shifts are related to struggles over U.S. control in developing nations, which enhance worldwide opportunities for opposition movements. The Iran-contra affair, government involvement in drug trafficking, and other events have contributed to political instability, helping to build opposition to U.S. foreign policies and transforming the ways people think about conditions and change.[61]

"Suddenly imposed grievances"—dramatic, highly publicized, often unexpected events that increase public awareness of and opposition to particular grievances[62]—also account for the movement's popularity. For example, the assassinations of Oscar Romero and the four churchwomen, the refugees' growing presence at the border, and their "good" stories heard by "good churchgoing folks" have helped mobilize movement support. Government surveillance of sanctuary activists and other opponents of U.S. policies, and lawsuits against Texas and Arixona sanctuary activists, have also increased public awareness of the issues.[63] The judge in the Arizona trial, calling inconsistencies in the government's asylum policy "irrelevant," banned testimony about persecution in the refugees' countries and the defendants' motives in providing sanctuary.[64] In so doing, he created enormous interest in the movement and prompted its greatest period of growth.

Political opportunities have come from both "bottom up" and "top down" for the movement. Political leverage has been enhanced by broad political, economic, and demographic changes outside participants' direct control, and by widespread support and sponsorship from local and national religious organizations. Taking the moral high ground in a larger protest movement, sanctuary has also benefited from "radical flank effects": that is, the presence of "extremist" organizations within the same movement industry, which increase more moderate groups' appeal.[65]

As a religious arm of the peace movement, sanctuary is part of a growing coalition of movements opposed to U.S. foreign policies. A study of movement linkages indicates that many activists identify their participation as a continuation of "the Movement" that developed out of the civil rights movement in the late 1950s and eventually extended into welfare rights, anti-Vietnam, feminism, environment, gay rights, antinuclear and other issues. That sanctuary is strategically allied with this larger group, successfully challenging "not just one immigration law, but a whole pattern of exploitation," explains why it "appears dangerous to the government."[66]

II

A NATURAL HISTORY OF THE CHICAGO MOVEMENT

Much of the sanctuary movement's "extracurricular mobilization"[1] takes place among members of social action committees at traditionally active churches and synagogues. These small woman-based groups are made up of informal friendship networks whose members have already mobilized to distribute resources to outsiders and have possibly cooperated in previous actions.[2] A natural history of the Chicago movement examines women's roles in its origins and development and in three stages of institutional involvement marked by particular activities and tensions coinciding with the refugees' arrival, stay, and departure. It locates the dynamics of change in how law-abiding citizens learn to translate their personal response to the refugees into collective illegal action.[3]

ORIGINS AND DEVELOPMENT

Chicago's becoming an early center for the national movement provided much of the impetus for the local movement's development. After the initial involvement of the Chicago Religious Task Force on Central America (CRTFCA), the movement emerged formally in 1982 when Washington Church declared itself the city's first sanctuary. By 1987 about sixteen churches and synagogues had followed suit. Divided among the city and its suburbs, these "sites" are loosely linked by six coalitions that tend to cut across neighborhood and religion: Northside, Westside, Northshore, Southside, Catholic, and Jewish sanctuaries.[4]

A citywide network emerged out of the interaction of sanctuary sites, coalitions, social justice agencies, and support organizations that make up the Chicago movement. Donna, a coalition staff person, called the local movement "very sporadic" until separate groups decided to organize to discuss common projects they could work on. In 1986 a citywide "umbrella group" formed—the Intercity Sanctuary Alliance (ISA)—its steering committee made up of representatives from each constituent group, meeting every few weeks; ISA, Donna pointed out, includes those with "broader vision of how to do outreach work in the community."

Though Chicago is not officially a sanctuary city, Chicago's leaders have informally supported the movement. Before his death in 1987, Mayor Harold Washington declared that no city officials, including police, would assist INS agents in enforcing policies regarding undocumented refugees. Jesse Jackson and Operation Push have also supported the local movement. Two Chicago suburbs have undergone the process of becoming official sanctuary cities, one successfully. Members at sanctuary sites in Oak Park began articulating a proposal in 1986, supported by the Council of Churches; after public debate, however, the Community Board rejected it on the recommendation of the community relations committee, despite supporters' continued picketing and pressure for the proposal's passage. Evanston did officially become a sanctuary city in 1988 after an intensive six-month outreach effort by members at local sites. Although the mayor opposed it, the Evanston City Council passed the proposal sixteen to two.[5]

Several social justice agencies have been instrumental in bringing the sanctuary movement to Chicago, sustaining it, and forging links between religious and secular groups and with a larger coalition of movements opposed to U.S. policies in Central America. As noted, CRTFCA began coordinating the national movement in 1982, serving as its clearinghouse until 1987, when it turned toward more outreach and "accompaniment work."[6] Although other agencies have placed refugees at various sites, Donna remarked that CRTFCA has done it "so well" that she'd be "suspicious of any sanctuary group not willing to work through them."

Women religious at another local "peace and justice" agency were catalysts in forming the Chicago Catholic Sanctuary (CCS) in 1986, enlisting about one hundred women from seventeen local religious orders to defy church authority and support sanctuary. The agency helped organize a conference in 1987 for the purpose of creating an ad hoc committee and agenda for the national movement. Another "antiintervention" organization sharing staff members with local social justice agencies has helped coordinate many "actions" that members take part in: group acts of nonviolent civil disobedience at public demonstrations. Most of the women I interviewed indicated that they were members of this organization.

The local sanctuary network links diverse denominations and coalitions citywide. For example, when a refugee family's relatives arrived unexpectedly at St. John's, a Catholic site, members of nearby First Street Church, a Protestant site whose refugees had moved on, began helping to support and house the extended family. When the family's main wage earner became ill and unable to work, Temple Israel, located across town, provided support for six months until declaring itself a sanctuary and preparing for its own family's arrival. This pattern of participants supporting sanctuary elsewhere before declaring it at their own churches and synagogues is typical, especially for Catholics. For example, six of fifteen Catholic women reported participating at other sites before CCS existed. Several indicated that they often attended their own church mass, then went to sanctuary events at sites declared by Protestants—"the only ones willing to go out on a limb."

Small, homogeneous Protestant churches of about one hundred families tend to be the most successful in declaring sanctuary. Women indicated that consensus is easier to reach in "small communities with a tradition of social action"; small congregations are "ideal" for these issues. Nine Protestant sites in the Chicago area have congregations of about this size.

In contrast, the large size, heterogeneity, and conservatism of most Catholic parishes tends to hinder their becoming sanctuaries. For example, Charlotte, a Catholic active in sanctuary at First Street Church who otherwise attended a "traditional" parish church, reported that the person who led the movement to ban handguns in her community and the person who led the opposition both belonged to her parish. She explained that most of its 2,500 members "are just not open to Central American issues, the nuclear arms race, and so many things that require a world view."

Two local Catholic groups—St. John's and the CCS—have overcome these obstacles. St. John's, a small "church within a church," unofficially became a sanctuary in 1985, enabled largely by its small size and autonomy within a larger parish; it has its own budget, priest, and lay officials. About fifteen of its 120 families belong to both congregations, "straddling the fence" with the "big parish," which has about 2,500 members.

An obstacle deterring Catholic groups from more openly declaring sanctuary is the archdiocese's position. Cardinal Joseph Bernardin supports existing legislation, maintaining that parishes may discreetly assist undocumented refugees but not publicize or politicize their situation.[7] Josie, a nun active in CCS, remarked that the archbishop "probably has more refugees in his archdiocese than he has any clue to." Official disapproval and the group's inability to use church property spurred the nuns to form CCS publicly, independent of a parish. As Dawn put it, the group was helped by "the Cardinal saying it's illegal and forbidden, galvanized by the asininity of the hierarchy." Kim noted the spirit of defiance in which CCS was formed: "Our point is that people have to know about the Central American war, and the U.S. role. He said he doesn't have time to meet with us. The idea of the nuns who began CCS is, we don't need his approval."

Synagogues face similar obstacles to becoming sanctuaries: large size, heterogeneity, and conservatism. Women at Temple Israel and Temple Zion indicated that synagogues aren't often sanctuaries "because the concern isn't for Jews—it's not a Jewish cause." An important difference, however, is that the national organizational hierarchy—the Union of American Hebrew Congregations (UAHC) and the Central Confederation of American Rabbis (CCAR)—supports the sanctuary movement.[8] Four local synagogues have overcome these obstacles and become sanctuaries.

Small Protestant churches may face other kinds of obstacles. For example, one woman reported that 60 percent of the congregation at a church in a Hispanic neighborhood were undocumented refugees, which greatly influenced its decision not to declare itself a sanctuary.

Dina, active at First Street Church, reported that sanctuary was defeated at her own church (of the same denomination) because the congregation feared that the church would suffer damage to its image and lose financial support as a historical landmark; further, its officials reportedly claimed that taking a stand on political issues would go against denominational philosophy. Yet officials at First Street Church, located nearby in a less affluent neighborhood, used the same philosophy to justify its openness to sanctuary. Eva, a member of First Street Church, expressed this contrasting interpretation: "The great covenant . . . is to live in peace, find truth, and love and help one another. Beyond that there's no religious dogma. [This church] is beyond Christianity. It encompasses all faiths, prophets, and saviors . . . there are no crucifixes—instead, murals of Confucius, Buddha, Camus, and Tubman."

A congregation's decision to declare sanctuary is often accompanied by disagreement and, at times, the loss of the more conservative members. For example, Alicia, a member of Temple Israel, reported that when the rabbi made the initial announcement in the temple bulletin, two members—both lawyers—quit:

> The first said . . . this was not a Jewish issue and shouldn't be a high priority. . . . The second man . . . was really upset. . . . He brought a whole law casebook on immigration. He was opposed to taking any kind of illegal action. . . . He accused these people of just wanting a better life. . . . He said, "This is

not a Jewish issue. Let someone else do it. What do they mean to us? Why are we doing it?"

A congregation's failure to declare sanctuary may also be accompanied by disagreement and the loss of the more social action–oriented members. For example, Dina indicated that about half of the group of twenty who originally worked on bringing sanctuary to a vote at her church left when it was defeated, more "because of the attitude of the congregation not wanting to know about it . . . than because of the vote." Newly declared sanctuaries often attract these dissatisfied members from nonactive churches and synagogues; when First Street Church declared itself a sanctuary, several "movement people" from Dina's congregation transferred to this "little poor church." Similarly, Christine, a clergywoman at Westminster Church, noted that "several dynamic, justice-minded folks" had joined her church because it was the only "progressive" one in the area, and "the ecumenical community is pleased" that it exists.

Losing more conservative members allows social action churches and synagogues to strengthen and homogenize their ranks. As Jackie put it, Westminster Church had been "broken open to these issues" ever since the pastor went to Selma and participated in the civil rights movement in the 1960s. As a result, "half the congregation left, and the folks left behind became the core of the folks who branched into the women's movement, the civil rights movement, sanctuary, and the gay rights movement."

All eight of the sanctuary sites I studied have similar histories of social action on behalf of other social causes. These are special churches and synagogues dedicated to a wide range of issues. Over time, members have used institutional free space to support causes often unpopular in their communities, providing arenas in which members can collectively express social concerns and take social action.

Westminster, a small Protestant church that became Chicago's second sanctuary in 1983, is a typical social action church. Its pastor involved the congregation in open housing and other issues in the

1960s. The church housed the community's first women's liberation group and created an alternative school that "effected long-term change in the community schools." It opened the first day-care center in a community that was strongly opposed; church members "had to fight to offer it." In the early 1970s, Westminster offered an LSD rescue service, using vitamin therapy, at a time when community hospitals were helping to prosecute those seeking emergency treatment. Besides becoming a sanctuary and operating a day-care center, in the 1980s the church had a homeless shelter, housed a "gay church," and declared itself a "nuclear-free zone."

University Church, another small Protestant sanctuary church, in the 1960s opened its parish hall to university students for political meetings not allowed on campus. It also established a "multifaceted community center" with programs in job counseling, tutoring, adult literacy, and English as a second language, staffing the center with "students, neighborhood, and church people." Its congregation includes an "intentional community" that buys, repairs, and lives in old buildings in the neighborhood. The church became a nuclear-free zone in 1985, the same year it became a sanctuary. It had also held a fund raiser for Mayor Harold Washington, had sponsored a study task force on South Africa, and was offering six-week classes on sanctuary, nuclear war, arms control, and homosexuality. Finally it was in the process of becoming an "affirming church" for gays and lesbians.

Despite facing greater obstacles, the synagogues and Catholic parishes that have become sanctuaries share this profile with social action churches. For example, Temple Israel, a sanctuary since 1987, is known as "the free synagogue" because of the rabbi's "freedom of the pulpit." Women described the founding rabbi as "an unusual man" who went to Selma during the civil rights movement and the new rabbi as "also very socially active." Early concerns at Temple Israel were gun control, open housing, homeless shelters, and an interfaith housing coalition; Jewish issues were Israel, Soviet Jewry, and the Shalom Project "on the nuclear and peace issue."

St. John's, the small social action church within a large traditional parish, became a sanctuary in 1985. A separate church since 1972, its early issues were "poverty, justice, war, and soup kitchens." According to members, the congregation includes "a lot of old civil rights liberals from the 1950s," "divorced Catholics, ex-priests, and ex-nuns." One called it "the only place where ex-Catholics can go"; another noted its informality: "They let the kids take their shoes off and run around the gym" where the congregation holds its services and meetings.

Sanctuary churches and synagogues are organizationally distinct from their traditional counterparts. Whether intentionally or not, they tend to be structured like a Latin American "base-community" church.[9] Geselle called this "a real grassroots self-help movement by indigenous people which transforms their whole perspective of their situation." Gloria said of St. John's: "It's patterned like the base communities of Central America. Families know each other, help and do things together. Lay persons take turns at services." Ginny, a divorced mother of four who had difficulty maintaining housing, recounted how the St. John's community had helped her family: "For a while we moved a lot . . . we were barely scraping by. . . . One day the priest asked somebody, 'Why [does this family] have to move so often?' When he heard the answer, the church raised $4,000 . . . so we wouldn't have to keep moving."

The base-community concept is more characteristic of but not unique to Catholic sites; for example, the rabbi's "freedom of the pulpit" at Temple Israel is somewhat similar. Christine related that a visiting Panamanian bishop familiar with the writings of Paulo Freire introduced the concept at Westminster Church in 1977; thereafter, it became the church's established format:

> We've pulled up the pews in the sanctuary and put them in a circle. We have a sermon, usually by [a co-clergywoman] and me; then we regroup and talk about the sermon, argue or disagree. Once a month somebody else preaches. Sometimes very personal responses are made to the sermon—this allows the community to know one another. We pray in a circle before

and after the sermon. "Designated enablers" is what [we] are called, not leaders.

The chance to address social issues is a significant part of women's attraction to social action churches and synagogues; they characterized such opportunities as "a plus," "certainly appealing," and "the right match." A laywoman active in CCS, Jeannine recalled leaving her traditional parish because it had no discussion of social issues: "There was no challenge there—nobody wanted to be controversial." Jackie, a minister's wife, spoke of always having to "live a double life" because of her "uncommon beliefs and dedications" until her husband was assigned to Westminster Church, where her "public and personal persona were integrated" and her political activism was "affirmed, understood, and celebrated." For some, the opportunity for social action is more important than denomination. For example, Andrea, active at University Church, claimed that her "denominational loyalty" was to "whatever church is doing social action": "Faith without action is not faith to me. . . . If we ever moved somewhere else and the most active church were Roman Catholic, I'd go there. Denomination means nothing. . . . I'd go to a synagogue, although that would be difficult because I'd need to learn a lot about Judaism."

In most cases, only a handful of members of these churches and synagogues actually participate in social action. A socially concerned few join special social action committees that function generally outside the congregational majority's interest and awareness. Women indicated that "it's usually just a committee of hands-and-feet folks who do all the social concerns," something of a "fringe group" in the congregation. As noted, these committees are made up mostly of women, who outnumber men by 98 percent in CCS and by three to two in all the other groups, including social justice agencies involved with sanctuary. Women also predominate at about two hundred host churches that make up the Overground Railroad, a parallel but unrelated "legal" sanctuary operation headquartered in the Chicago area.

STAGES OF INVOLVEMENT

When this study was made in 1987, one of eight sites—Temple Zion—was in an early stage of becoming a sanctuary; five sites—Washington, University, and St. John's churches, Temple Israel, and the Chicago Catholic Sanctuary—had assisted one to four sets of refugees; and two previous sites—Westminster and First Street churches—had moved on to other forms of support (neither had ceased participating altogether, although two women who experienced "burnout" were no longer involved).

I describe these sites on the basis of women's activities across three stages of involvement. In the "pre-refugee stage,"[10] congregation members first learn about sanctuary, go through the process of formally declaring their church or synagogue a site, and prepare for the refugee's arrival. Social action committee members discuss the issues among themselves, hold meetings with the congregation, and make proposals to declare sanctuary. After a favorable vote, activities shift as committee members begin marshaling resources for the refugees' care. They do this primarily by soliciting goods and services through informal local networks, a process similar to much of the hidden work that women perform as volunteers in communities.

Initiation to sanctuary occurs in a variety of ways that affect the character and duration of subsequent institutional involvement. Generally, the more openly the idea is introduced to the congregation and the more institutional support it receives, the more widespread, committed, and enduring participation will be. For example, at Washington Church, Chicago's first sanctuary, the congregation was gradually introduced through witnesses' firsthand accounts of conditions in Central America, of the refugees' plight, and of the newly declared sanctuary church in Tucson. An ordained minister in the congregation reportedly returned from Central America and told a church council meeting that "some really bad stuff [was] going on," and that a church in Tucson was "taking in refugees with bullet holes in them who are fleeing El Salvador." At subsequent meetings, members learned "more and more." Eventually John Fife visited the church after a local social justice agency reportedly recommended it as a prospective site. Women found him a credible witness—"not a fire-and-brimstone minister" but a quiet and "well-balanced man" with a sense of humor who "spoke gently about his experiences."

In some cases, congregation members became interested in sanctuary because denominational leaders of national organizations endorsed it or were associated with national sanctuary figures. For example, Christine explained that her denomination is "all in favor of sanctuary at the national level—it's the grassroots level that's not there." Women at Temple Israel and Temple Zion indicated that knowing about a Tucson rabbi who was "friends with Corbett and Fife" and "big" in two national Jewish organizations that were endorsing sanctuary made the difference between "talking about it" and "deciding to look into sanctuary."

In other cases, congregations were introduced to sanctuary through the efforts of energetically committed members who facilitated the decision to declare sanctuary. For example, women at First Street Church called one man "instrumental" in the drive to make his community a sanctuary city and in "introducing the issue and forming a small sanctuary committee" at the church. Previously uninvolved in Temple Israel's social action committee, Lena joined precisely when its interest in sanctuary was waning. The committee chairwoman described her as an "irritant" who "dug things out and presented them and wanted to know why [no one had] done things yet," indicating the critical difference she made in the sanctuary process: "The whole thing would have died at that point if she hadn't come on board. . . . I put it all in her hands, and she's carried the ball . . . she's gotten things done."

Lena claimed to have been "very dissatisfied" and "about to resign" because the synagogue wasn't "doing jack shit" about sanctuary. She "saw other churches getting active" and was "searching around literally for some reason to stay." Then she attended her first social action committee meeting and confronted its members: "I said, 'What are you guys doing about sanctuary?' 'Well, we've been trying to move in some direction and haven't gotten off the ground.' I heard constipation." When the committee brought the resolution to the board six months later, she declared, "That's not enough—why don't we just make [our suburb] a sanctuary city?" and led the successful effort to do so.

In most cases, congregation members were introduced to sanctuary by the example of other local sites. Attending another site's declaration ceremony was a "real impetus" for many to get involved. Sanctuary participants, along with members of social justice agencies, often solicited official endorsement and material support from other churches and synagogues. Acting as catalysts and role models, they also encouraged new sanctuary sites. One woman related how agency members had sold the sanctuary idea at Westminster Church: [Church and agency people] came out and spoke with us . . . and said how great it'd be for the third anniversary of Oscar Romero's assassination [to have] a new sanctuary site opening." Another recalled the agency members' pitch: "We need more sanctuaries to open, to bring the situation in Central America to the attention of the media and the American people."

At Washington Church, agency members not only "helped with the nuts and bolts of the family once they arrived" but also answered lingering questions and helped define the group's orientation. When asked, "Why can't we just care for a family and not do the public things?" they reportedly provided this rationale: "The family is actually safer this way. This publicity may protect them from government harassment. Also we're making a public statement to help raise U.S. consciousness. The family is putting itself at risk for this. The truth has to be told."

Members of University Church, which is located within a cluster of theological seminaries near a large university, learned about and initiated their own involvement in sanctuary independent of national figures, special catalysts, agencies, or other sites. The congregation includes about thirty seminarians and ministers and has widespread participation in social issues; half its members are involved in "home and class study groups." Leslie, a clergywoman, recalled that the congregation was "definitely aware of what was happening in Central America" because there was "a good size core of people in the church and community . . . committed to sanctuary." Denying that outside social justice agents had prompted the church's involvement, she claimed that committed church members had brought the issue "to the attention of the whole congregation."

Once sanctuary has been introduced, the process of becoming a site usually occurs over a period of months, during which time social action committee members set up a task force to learn about and discuss the issues. Participants "do their homework" at this point in order to decide "the best thing to do": they talk to lawyers, "study the issues," and consider all the "ramifications—legal, moral, energy, everything." They must "figure out how to feed, house, and support a refugee family" and have "all the information" when it "comes time to present" their proposal. Congregations voting on sanctuary proposals sometimes initially acquiesce in limited ways. Pam noted Temple Israel's tentative early involvement: "We passed a proposal that we wouldn't have site sanctuary but would support any refugees fearing for their lives. We would accept site sanctuary only with board approval on a case-by-case basis." Eva described the original limited commitment at First Street Church: "The congregation was not enthusiastic but did grant a policy of sanctuary for four months as part of refugee stopover only—an overground railroad."

Although members often disagree over the decision to declare sanctuary, those opposed seem to end up participating anyway. For example, Pam described a woman at Temple Israel who was "very cautious and would never commit herself" yet "eventually agreed" and "took it up as her cause." Christine noted that those who'd been opposed at Westminster Church were often "the first to volunteer"; Jackie said that the "four against" were "primarily folks who didn't think we had the energy to do it—they weren't opposed philosophically, ideologically, or politically. They were just worried about being tired. . . . All four helped eventually."

However, opposition may be more serious; for example, Westminster committee members considered housing the refugees in the church basement where they would share a bathroom with nursery school children, until some parents objected that the refugees might pass on parasites.[11] Discussion ended when a doctor said he was "more concerned about some right-wing nut throwing a bomb into the basement." In the end, the nursery school lost two families and gained four over the decision to declare sanctuary.

Participants at Washington Church faced other problems as Chicago's first sanctuary: procedures were not yet institutionalized, and there were no other sites to serve as role models. Becoming a site early on was a more risky, tentative process, given the uncertainty of the government's response. Like other deviant groups engaged in illegal activities who must learn the technique firsthand,[12] early participants were not sure whether and how to get involved or what the consequences might be. The "big question" concerned "breaking a federal law": that is, committing a felony. Belinda, then chairwoman of the social action committee, recalled her role in this process as "perfect": she was "meant to be there then." Her narrative of how law-abiding citizens come to break the law illustrates the sense of protection from legal reprisals that women's middle-class backgrounds provide:

> I'm a middle-class homemaker selling vitamins. I wouldn't even litter. I'm a law-abiding citizen. Yet I wrote the letter to [the U.S.] Attorney General . . . [saying] we're going to declare ourselves a sanctuary. I was scared, but I didn't believe that jail would happen. We joked about that—me, a staunch member of [my suburban community], two kids, dogs, hauled off to jail in a peach suit. I wasn't radical, a Communist, subversive. No matter how the government tried to portray the sanctuary movement, I wasn't it. . . . My dentist called the night when it was on the ten o'clock news [to say] "I'll bring you a cake with a file in it."

The turningpoint came when members of the congregation met the refugees, heard their stories, and "had to decide." They had to "listen to what people were saying and weigh it against what the government said." This illustrates how the refugees' presence forces people to choose between being "law-abiding" and acting on their personal knowledge of the refugees' situation. A young Salvadoran catechist's testimony had a great impact on Belinda, largely because the woman did not fit the image of a terrorist:

> I'll never forget her. She was a little tiny thing. . . . She very quietly, respectfully told us, "We were helping the poor through the church to build homes and establish farms, but the government called us subversive." We thought, "Wait a minute—how could anybody call her a subversive?" Any jerk could see she wasn't a Communist looking to overthrow the government. She was a young girl, maybe twenty-one, acting on her faith.

Belinda reported that the refugee's presence appealed to instinct, not facts, to help members "know the truth": "She wasn't angry. She didn't even talk about injustices. It was her presence. Humans know when people are telling the truth or lying. We know. Now what do we do?"

The next step was a congregational meeting to discuss the issue. They "began with Bible study," then asked a lay minister and "the lawyers" in the congregation to "instruct" them as to what their faith and the law "required them to do"; they "were frightened." At the deciding moment, two special catalysts—"conservative" matriarchs in the congregation—spoke of a "higher law" and doing "the right thing," helping to rationalize law-breaking to the group. One reportedly said, "I don't see that we have any choice. Clearly these people are being persecuted. The U.S. is clearly in violation of international law. We have a higher law that we must obey." The other, "not a boat rocker, chair of the Sunday school for a hundred years," lifted the group's collective courage by saying, "I'm really scared to do this, and . . . I don't know yet how I'll vote, but I feel it's the right thing to do." Others "immediately . . . stood up and supported them." As Belinda put it, "There were these love messages that were so beautiful."

The congregation's final consenting vote is another turning-point for social action committee members, who then shift their attention from whether to how to become a sanctuary. At Washington Church, seventy voted in favor, two abstained, and none were opposed. Belinda reported that afterward they "knew what [they] had to do—a lot of work" to prepare for the refugees' arrival. Preparations usually necessitate reassessing an institution's commitments and reallocating its resources. There are hard decisions and, in some cases, hard feelings—as there were among those at Westminster Church who feared that allowing the refugees to share a bathroom with the nursery school would pollute the children. Other conflicts were more agreeably resolved; for example, the Westminster Women's Center codirectors were reportedly "very concerned" that the publicity of sanctuary "would hurt the privacy of lesbians" but later conceded that since the church had "given them sanctuary," they "wouldn't stand in the way of giving it to others." At Washington Church the committee needed permission to adapt as the refugees' apartment a locker room being used by "the junior high folks"; the young people not only consented but "even helped get it ready."

Social action committee members perform a great deal of work preparing for the refugees' arrival: fundraising, cleaning and painting living quarters, and soliciting furniture, food, linen, clothing, and cookware. At the same time, they often have difficulty enlisting help from the congregation; turnout at educational events is reportedly quite low. For example, Alicia recalled "less than enthusiastic response" at Temple Israel; only one person responded to the rabbi's appeal—a doctor who gave $100. To make matters worse, committee members often have little time to make these preparations. Since the refugees often travel in adverse circumstances, their arrival is difficult to anticipate, putting a strain on the committee. In the rhetoric of crisis management and demonstrating her considerable skill at it, Alicia described the "bombshells," "hysterics," and "flukes" that accompanied final preparations at Temple Israel, listing the myriad tasks that committee members perform in this phase, often under duress. Her narrative reveals on a very small scale how sanctuary is literally produced by volunteers at churches and synagogues across the country. It also characterizes much of the hidden work that middle-class women perform as volunteers in their communities:

> Juan called and dropped a bombshell . . . the women and two kids were blocked behind the border and couldn't get across, but there was a family in Kansas who needed help. The family consisted of seven people arriving in ten days. We had $800. I promptly had hysterics, called everyone I knew to raise money, put desperate notices in the [temple] bulletin. It was one fluke after another. I started a telephone campaign . . . [for] contributions. I called everyone who owed me one. It was a time to collect on favors. . . . We finally got to a point where we had enough [furniture and clothing], and I asked for money. There were two weeks of hell—five or six hours on the phone every day trying to raise money. I neglected my work for two weeks. . . . Everything that could . . . went wrong.

Once these preparations are under way, the group enters the second and most demanding phase—the "refugee stage," in which the congregation formally receives the refugees and hears their moving stories, which inspire and fuel members' subsequent involvement. Committee members initially locate refugees through social justice agencies, religious leaders, and other congregation members. The congregation at Washington Church reportedly "never knew the behind-the-scenes stuff; [an agency] arranged it." At Temple Israel an immigration lawyer with "tremendous connections in the Spanish-speaking community" located the refugees.

The refugees' arrival is usually accompanied by much fanfare and publicity, with processions of cars traveling to meet them and public speakouts along the way. Refugees frequently "give witness" at formal declaration ceremonies where they meet members of the congregation and describe in moving detail their torture or imprisonment by government agents at home. For example, the CCS held a large declaration ceremony at a local parish on December 2, 1986, the sixth anniversary of the deaths of the four churchwomen in El Salvador. Women attending the ceremony found it "very powerful" and "moving"; "the church was packed." After a liturgy on the churchwomen, one refugee, who had reportedly been involved with Oscar Romero's work and "had to leave," told a "powerful story"; some noted that "she cried in the middle of it."

First contact with the refugees is a highly charged, impelling experience that stimulates the subsequent activism and commitment of newcomers to sanctuary. Meeting the refugees and hearing their stories often represents a cathartic high point, a moment of "collective feeling" that produces dedication to the tasks ahead.[13] Ginny wept profusely in describing her initial encounter with the refugees at First Street Church as the point when she became personally involved:

> When the family came, there were many church people there. The family had handkerchiefs over their faces, even the babies. . . . Cameras were there, so the babies couldn't take off the kerchiefs. The littlest drank a bottle under the kerchief. . . . I just got in the reception line and introduced myself. . . . The next day I asked how to say, "I'm the church secretary and if you need anything, please call me."

Similarly moved by their bandana masks[14] and compelling stories, Jeannine reported feeling "very distressed" the first time she encountered the refugees; the meeting was an "eyeopener" that created an immediate shift in her perspective:

> It was very disturbing to see people with bandanas on their faces. . . . They talked about what was happening in El Salvador—what the government was doing, and why they had to leave. They were pleading with us to please do something. They really had me then, putting those refugees in front of me. All of a sudden I felt responsible for our government's actions.

Others also indicated that the refugees' deeply impressing stories played a critical role in spurring them to action. Women's accounts illustrate how they shape and make sense of the stories in their own terms:

> Rafael is forty-seven, a Quiche Indian. He grew up in the highlands of Guatemala. He started working on coffee plantations when he was eleven. He can remember planes flying overhead spraying pesticides. Many children died from this. He became active with the church as a lay-catechist, and this was the beginning of his political activism. The people he was working with were "disappeared" so he left ahead of his family and came to Mexico. He's very gentle, lacking any bitterness. He's an exceptional person.

> The father fled Guatemala. He worked with an electrical engineering program, and the government looked at anybody like that who worked with the peasantry as a threat. The priests warned him that he was on a hit list. After he fled, the army came to his house and threatened his family.

> He was a middle-class person—very young, emotionally immature. The army was after him to join. We took him to a doctor who said, "He's like a little flower"—a delicate, sensitive person. I'm sure his mother knew he couldn't survive in the army, and he fled [El Salvador]. He's definitely here illegally—scared, harassed, threatened.

> Juan's family belonged to a Christian base community. His father was a small farmer [who tried] to help peasants get their own land and be self-sufficient. [The father] and his brother were involved. The [Salvadoran] government repressed any kind of sharing or cooperative. Juan's uncle was murdered. Juan's brother was chased and caught by the military. He'd been hung on a tree with his heart cut out. Juan found him and felt he'd be next. . . . He was eighteen.

> Rudy was twenty—a middle-class kid. I can't remember why he was being sought by the [Salvadoran] army. They came to

kill him. He wasn't there, so they killed his mother and left
her there in the house for him to find. He felt if he'd been
there, he'd have been killed, and it was his fault that she died.
He was very emotionally disturbed and felt deep guilt.

Anna was arrested in El Salvador and [her daughter] was with
her at the time . . . she was handcuffed to Anna while she was
tortured and abused in prison. . . . For a while [the daughter]
had nightmares. The guards would clap their hands when they
were beating people so others wouldn't hear. After that,
whenever [the daughter] heard clapping, she'd get very frightened. . . . Anna escaped off the back of a truck with [her
daughter], who was seven or eight. They were with other pris-
oners on the back of a moving truck . . . being transported
somewhere. She asked herself, "Is there nothing I as her
mother can do to save this child?" So she took a moment
when the guard was distracted . . . and pushed [the girl] and
herself off the truck. They were unconscious when they
fell . . . already physically in very bad shape. . . . She was a
catechist, working with Romero. She knew the four martyred
missionaries . . . they were very much at risk.

Several women indicated that they had failed to anticipate the
refugees' difficulties fully; as Ginny put it, her "problems were nothing compared to theirs." Some were particularly troubled by the
refugees' fears and the debilitated state in which they frequently
arrived. For example, Belinda remarked, "They were afraid they'd
see tanks coming down the street the first night, and every night
after. That's when we realized their level of fear."
    Josie recalled that some CCS women had difficulty with the fact
that a refugee was a sexually active single parent: "Now we have
these three children. . . . What are we going to do with them? We
now have a woman who's sexually active, has emotional and psychological needs, is heavily traumatized, is a single parent. Their
medical needs are tremendous."
    After the refugees' arrival, committee members begin the work

of providing for their total needs. At first they "monitor" the refugees' safety and adjustment "around the clock," spending a great deal of time and energy establishing the procedures of sanctuary. Eva explained that this "constant company" was needed because "the family speaks no English and they're in culture shock." Donna said that monitoring was necessary because they and the refugees feared being "harassed" by "INS and FBI agents"—"whoever." Jackie described the group's early security system at Westminster Church, the city's second sanctuary: "In the early days, we had signs posted everywhere about what to do if INS or FBI came: [the minister] first, [the clergywoman] second, me third."

There were some "crank calls," but no women reported government intervention at any site. The Westminster congregation reportedly "had a real good relationship with the local police." Committee members "went to them and told them" about the refugees in sanctuary. The police allegedly responded, "It's not a local issue; it's a federal issue," and "Hey, we're not going to bother you." This is characteristic of the kinds of unofficial support the movement receives within a system that officially condemns it. Instances of clergy, judges, and police who look the other way indicate that the involvement of officials in the social world of the refugees is different from what most people might expect. Jackie indicated that the group relied on this tacit tolerance in their early, potentially risky operations:

> It got easier once we knew we weren't in imminent danger. We got threatening calls from people who said they'd blow up the church—crank calls left on the answering machine. We did a lot of media things because we wanted everyone to know. We were early. We got a lot of hostile stuff. That's another reason we told the police.

Committee members ease the work by allocating tasks among themselves, arranging for the refugees' total care—housing, education, employment, legal aid, health and dental care, speaking engagements, social outings, and translating. As Jackie put it, at first "all" tend to do "everything":

We brought food in and someone to eat with him for two weeks. There was a grocery store down the street and we taught him to shop. We divided the task force into areas— living space, contacts for speaking, legal stuff, physical care like medical and dental. I was involved in all of it. . . . We all did everything. We all had a zillion meetings and were busy with everything.

In time, procedures become somewhat institutionalized. For example, Christine indicated that early participation at Westminster was "widespread"; "later, there was more specialization," and "now, a formal committee does the work." Donna reported that since receiving its second family, the group at Washington Church had "instituted a committee" that holds a weekly "prayer vigil and business meeting." Leslie, a clergywoman at University Church who worked very closely "in the early days . . . overseeing people," spoke of "cutting back" after they "got settled." Her greater involvement with the first family—because it was more important when sanctuary was "brand new" that "the pastor . . . know what's going on"— illustrates how her clerical position supported the gradual routinization of procedures.

As a step in a larger process of seeking amnesty, the refugees typically stay at one sanctuary for six months to a year, then move on to other sites, regions, and activities. Constant turnover provides committee members a chance to rest, renew resources, and select their next activities; however, they also disrupt their personal attachments to particular refugees. For example, Jane's group at Washington Church didn't realize that a refugee would be there only temporarily; she recounted how they "cried and cried" the day he left, "talked about experiencing grace," and "felt the spirit was present." This typifies many participants' emotional and religious orientation.

When refugees leave, most sites take in others, sometimes also continuing to support those who have moved on. For several months, Jackie's group at Westminster Church supported a refugee who "chose to drop out of the limelight": "We found him an apartment and subsidized rent for a while. We found him a job and set him up with furniture, sheets, as well as we could. He had a job downtown in . . . a restaurant."

Like the women religious at CCS who struggled with a "sexually active" single parent in sanctuary, Jackie's group struggled with this refugee's personal choices:

He was twenty. He got married to a forty-two-year-old North American woman. We were very worried about it . . . that he was being used, that she was a very needy person to be doing this. They moved to California where her family is and got married. Or so they said.

Her portrayal of the next two refugees at Westminster Church shows that those with "good" stories aren't necessarily "good" refugees. Juan—his uncle allegedly murdered and his brother "hung on a tree with his heart cut out"—turned out to be an exemplary refugee, "a joy":

He made contacts with Salvadorans all over the city. His room was always filled with Salvadorans, eating, watching TV, talking. He was a really expansive person. . . . He decided he could no longer stay at the church . . . he'd done what he could, and went to New Mexico to work with Salvadoran refugees at a settlement camp. . . . He was here almost a year.

Rudy, on the other hand, who said his mother had been killed by the army and left for him to find, was "emotionally disturbed," "unhappy," "damaged":

He was very introspective—a big strong person but very fragile. I took him to a counseling session with a pastor who spoke Spanish. He went a couple of times but said he didn't want to go back. He became very withdrawn. When Juan had all his friends over, [Rudy] would come to our house and just sit. He sulked a lot. He did speaking engagements for a while

but dropped out. . . . We didn't know how to help, what to
do. . . . In January [he] said he wanted to go to Tucson and
then back to El Salvador and get his two sisters out—he felt
they were in danger. We said, "Fine." We bought a one-way
air ticket to Tucson and gave him a bunch of money. We had a
communion service in his room and drove him to the airport
with a coat over his head. We put him on a plane.

What happened next illustrates the broad range in middle-class
women's abilities to influence legal processes, activate networks of
support, and raise large sums of money fast. It is also another
example of officials' tactic compliance with the movement; in this
case, those who otherwise formally prosecuted refugees informally
helped support someone in sanctuary:

We were real nervous about him hanging around in Tucson.
We got a call in the middle of the night . . . he'd been arrested
for driving without a license . . . someone in the Tucson sanctuary had lent him a car, and he didn't know how to drive.
Bail was $7,000. It was the local police. We called a sanctuary
lawyer in Tucscon and . . . negotiated him out in twenty-four
hours. We got a loan from two or three people in the congregation and wired it down there. He was out. We filed for a
change of venue to get the trial here. The lawyer got him to
start asylum papers. I did all the legal stuff. Our lawyers
worked together—we got them to say he was a resident of
Chicago. . . . The judge ruled that the bond was too high and
reduced it by $2,500. We got him back here and contacted a
lawyer to begin the asylum process. They wanted documentation for everything. We got together a lot of sanctuary information on the issues and put that with his papers. The lawyer
said, "When his case is called in two weeks to seven years, if
he shows up, you'll get the $5,000 back." We [told Rudy],
"It's so unsure you'll get asylum status, we feel you should just
take off." He was happy to get away. He's still in the Chicago
area. We made several attempts to stay in touch and he didn't

return it. . . . He never really clicked in the movement—he
was too unhappy, too damaged.

These accounts reveal the considerable work committee members do in constructing a life for the refugees and the way refugees'
problems complicate their adjustment; both exhaust participants.
For example, after First Street Church had supported a family for a
year, Eva remarked, "I don't think we can afford to take on another
refugee."

When the last refugees leave and the group's resources are
depleted, the site enters the third or "post-refugee stage," and committee members move on to outreach and educational efforts: they
demonstrate, travel to Central America, and help support the refugees in other sanctuaries.

As noted, at the time of this study two of eight Chicago sites
were no longer sanctuaries, although they continued to support the
movement through other activities. Both were small Protestant
churches that had been sanctuaries for about two years. Christine
reported that when the last refugees left Westminster Church, committee members "decided to put their energies into getting new
sites"; their activities had been directed "more into systems change
than direct services" and "educating other churches rather than
being a site." Some members also "did a lot of demonstrations";
others were involved in the process of making their community a
sanctuary city. Committee members at First Street Church had also
moved on to other forms of support after the last refugees left. Those
who were Catholic became involved in CCS when it emerged or
helped support the extended refugee family in sanctuary at St. John's
Church. Others turned toward educational outreach, demonstrating, and travel.

Though all sites continued their institutional involvement at
some level, two women reported experiencing "burnout." For Jennifer, who had integrated her family life intimately with the refugees'
day-to-day lives at St. John's, sanctuary became an all-encompass-
ing, exhausting experience—"something you can only do once":

> The involvement was so intense—you can't do it again. I'll
> know other refugees again and I'll always give what I can, but
> I know I'll never do this again. . . . If anyone knew what they
> were getting into at the beginning . . . they'd never do it. I
> wouldn't. I'd gladly go to the basement, get snowsuits, mit-
> tens, whatever they need when the clothes drive comes around
> and give that way. "Here, need more? Back to the basement!"
> Because that way of giving is a whole lot easier.

After more than two years of intimacy with the refugees, her own
family had "pulled back" when its personal boundaries were over-
run by the arrival of the extended family. Pressure mounted until the
family entered therapy to determine what was "causing this stress"
on the "family system." Her son's outburst about the refugees'
intrusive presence spoke for them all and helped them address their
problems. Yet even as they withdrew from their previous intense
involvement, her family remained quite close with the refugees: "We
give what we can, and the kids are still over a lot, but we've had to
establish boundaries and rules to protect our family life."

The other woman reporting burnout was Belinda, who had
chaired the social action committee at Washington Church years
earlier when it became Chicago's first sanctuary. She situated her
involvement clearly in the past, calling it "a very significant time . . .
looking back"; though she was "not active now," she still supported
sanctuary financially through her church. In the rhetoric of stress
management, which she taught, she explained that "you can't sustain that level of activity," naming several self-help maxims by
which she had "balanced" her life and justified withdrawing from
the movement:

> At the end of the year . . . I felt at peace . . . no matter what,
> everything would be all right. . . . You control those things
> that are within your control and let go of what you can't. It's
> a much healthier way to live. It doesn't mean you ignore Cen-
> tral America. You keep working for change but keep it in per-
> spective. Otherwise it's too frustrating. . . . I have to do the

best I can. Bloom where you're planted. I gave up "type A"
behavior for Lent . . . some things you can't control. . . . I
teach . . . wellness as an attitude. . . . My life's very balanced
right now. I'm grateful for the experience of sanctuary. It's
been a growing experience for me and for the church.

As long as some committee members continue to participate in
sanctuary activities after the refugees leave, cases of individual burnout do not seriously affect continued involvement of non-site sanctuaries or the overall level of support for the local movement. Strong
support by a large number of committed individuals increases
the likelihood of continued institutional involvement. University
Church is a good example of a sanctuary likely to remain involved
over a long period of time: it is located within a cluster of theological
seminaries; its congregation includes many seminarians and ministers; and more than half of its members are involved in educational activities. Leslie felt certain that sanctuary would "continue
strongly" because the group remained active "between families";
further, "a good core of people" were "very involved" in the national
movement.

The overall account provided by these participants shows the
diverse, multidenominational network of sites, coalitions, and agencies that make up the local movement and the kinds of traditionally
active churches and synagogues that provide sanctuary. It describes
their participation in terms of particular activities and tensions surrounding the refugees' coming and going: the risky, tentative stage of
becoming a site and receiving the refugees, the massive work of
supporting them, and the transition to other activities after they
move on. It indicates women's special attraction to these sites, their
predominance on social action committees, and the close fit between
sanctuary work and their volunteer activities in their communities.
It also shows how officials often informally support the movement.

Locating the "real action" of the movement at an intermediate
level between individuals and broad contexts, this account shows
how macro events are translated into micro mobilization in small

group settings where processes of collective attribution are combined with rudimentary forms of organization to produce mobilization for collective action. Social action committees at local sanctuary churches and synagogues constitute these settings, which represent "structures of solidarity incentives" for the movement and provide the interpersonal rewards on which much social behavior depends. These small woman-based groups and associational networks make up the basic building blocks of the movement and the "cell structure" of collective action.[15]

III

IDEOLOGICAL SPLITS

Conflicting humanitarian and political impulses dividing the sanctuary movement are rooted in the structural conditions of participants' lives. Ideological splits characterize the orientations and activities of Tucson and Chicago leaders, local men and women, and laywomen and women religious. Distance from the border and its inherent risks account largely for regional differences. Norms prescribing gendered behavior account for but fail to predict sex-typed roles in the local movement. The positions of laywomen and women religious in, respectively, families and religious orders helps explain their contrasting styles of activism. Women's perceptions of these divisions are related to the gendered struggles they have experienced in the movement and other social spheres.

TUCSON AND CHICAGO LEADERS

As noted, early leaders were religious men in Tucson who favored a local grassroots approach to the refugees' situation, which conflicted with the approach of later leaders, primarily Chicago women religious, who stressed protest activities and a national movement. Both cities were important sanctuary centers early on, differentiated by orientation and distance from the border. In Tucson, sanctuary developed chiefly as an emergency response to the great flow of refugees and their immense needs. In Chicago, where "good" refugees were carefully selected and recruited on the basis of their moving stories and desire to speak out, sanctuary developed more as a means for making a movement.

Chicago women, particularly women religious, tended at first to idealize Tucson leaders as "charismatic gurus," only later perceiving and rejecting the men's stand against a national movement. Some expressed a sense of disappointment and deception: one nun said of Jim Corbett, "It was very difficult to see him fall from his pedestal"; another said of Fife, "It's like being deceived by somebody you really trust." Some spoke of "the big split" when Chicago returned some refugees on a bus to Tucson because they lacked "good" stories. A minister's wife claimed that Fife begged her to try to heal the rift, an effort she called "probably hopeless." A nun noted that the "Fife/Corbett group" was unrepresented at a national meeting.

Chicago women characterized the regional division in terms of localism and caretaking versus nationalism and activism. They did recognize that sanctuary issues were different at the border, where operations were riskier and required more autonomy and secrecy. For example, in comparing the risks of caring for undocumented refugees with those of making a movement on their behalf, one woman noted that Tucson activists would likely be "hassled" by the government for "harboring and transporting," whereas the charge in Chicago would likely be "conspiracy"—two or more people conspiring to break the law. Others claimed that Tucson wanted "a loose-knit movement, not an organization at all," that Tucson was "solely religious," whereas Chicago was "also political."

"Good" refugees became a divisive issue early on: Tucson tended to give sanctuary to those in need; Chicago sought out those who had been repressed at home. Women expressed their awareness of the importance of "good" refugees to the Chicago movement, describing them as "good speakers with good stories," "articulate," "very political"; people who "understand immediately that sanctuary work isn't just charity but changing American public opinion and government policy," and recognize that they "can help stop the war and change U.S. policies"; "a different caliber of people—politically oriented," "appealing to liberal people in the community." In contrast, refugees lacking good stories and a political outlook were perceived as "just interested in getting by."

While actual differences between the Tucson and Chicago movements are arguable, each of the two orientations does appear to have characterized the movement at different times. In its natural history the political tended to become its end; the humanitarian, its means. As one woman noted, "At first people just wanted to help those refugees here. After a while, they began bringing them in clandestinely." Perhaps initially an expressly humanitarian act, sanctuary became more intentionally political in response to government and media attention. The movement's growing politicization refutes the notion that participants had either a humanitarian or a political orientation exclusively. Ironically, those exercising their right to protest have more legal ground than those caring for illegal refugees, a fact reflected in the government's prosecution of religious rather than political activists.

As noted, growing linkages and overlapping memberships with religious and secular justice groups help explain the political direction the movement soon took. All the sanctuary sites studied had supported prior social action, and all the women interviewed had been previously active on other issues. Twenty-four had taken part in civil disobedience actions, eight had been arrested, seventeen had traveled to Central America, and most belonged to large national "peace and justice" organizations. Women also indicated increasing levels of commitment and involvement in the movement's organizational survival. They linked the importance of membership in other "solidarity" groups to their activism: "I didn't do civil disobedience until I joined;" "when I joined . . . I signed a pledge to do what I can"; "I've been more politically oriented because I'm a member."

As the gap between Tucson and Chicago widened, women denounced the movement's male leaders, aligning themselves with women leaders and a more political approach. Their views of regional male and female leaders contrasted sharply: although some saw Fife as a "flamboyant mover-shaker type," "well-liked," and "a very friendly guy," more described him as "a glamour boy—very smooth," "paternalistic," and "cocky." Corbett fared worse: they termed him "a megalomaniac," "arrogant" and "patriarchal," having "the social analysis of a five-year old," a "macho rancher" or "local wheel" or "lone coyote type," a "gruff old rancher who ordered his wife around."

In contrast, they viewed women leaders as important models for their own participation, portraying them as "powerful" individuals with something to say about the movement. For example, one recalled realizing when she first got involved, "Gee, it's not a male bastion." Another called writer Renny Golden "intellectually and spiritually gifted," "a guide to us all." Still another was impressed that Darlene Nicgorski, a nun and one of the defendants in the Arizona trial, had a "good story" herself: she had been forced to seek sanctuary when her life was threatened in Guatemala.[1]

These women's dissatisfaction with male leaders reflected their growing resentment over men's domination and their own marginalization in the movement. Women shared many gendered perceptions of the Tucson movement and trial, generally complaining that women did the work and were also arrested and indicted, yet men got the credit. One who claimed that women "got short shrift" located "the gender gap . . . between the public image of the movement and women's actual role in it." Others criticized the trial for its androcentrism. They noted that the judge deferred to the men (he "would never call Darlene Nicgorski 'sister' but priests were always 'father' "). They called the attorneys "patriarchal," "into very male-identified systems."

The media further fueled women's frustration by stressing white male clerics' leadership role and portraying the movement in terms of "Anglo male heroism."[2] Women responded by redefining the movement in terms of their own participation. For example, Kim cited Nicgorski's "brilliant critique" of Corbett and her feminist account of the roots of sanctuary: "She's tired of hearing him call himself the founder of sanctuary. He claims that Moses is the biblical founder. She argues that it's the midwives who birthed and saved him."

Women's criticisms of Tucson leaders' humanitarian approach were ways of making sense of the same issues in the local movement.

Whether to bring people into the movement on a minimal basis or to press a program and lose members became an important question in the "Chicago/Midwest" group's struggle. Women's discussion of this local conflict suggested their own predominantly political approach. For example, Jackie remarked that "a lot of people thought it was just charity. . . . We've always had to educate people—bring people along—that this is foreign policy work." Megan criticized those who saw sanctuary as a "very patronizing, philanthropic" program of housing, clothing, and feeding refugees—"very safe tenets of Christianity." In her view, the Chicago movement came together "precisely to criticize policies . . . to be a political, public witness."

Only two women expressed disapproval of the political direction the local movement was taking, both focusing their objections on CRTFCA. The first ciritized the agency for emphasizing the national rather than the local movement, its concern with "good" refugees, and the importance it placed on "political analysis." Agency women, she said, thought that "sanctuary as a concept of having refugees in your church" was "very stupid." She saw them "sitting in this office downtown" saying that "local sanctuary is worthless"; to her, their commitment to the movement "came off obnoxious—that political stuff." The second criticized the agency for ignoring and belittling the movement's religious basis, for improperly combining faith and resistance, and for relinquishing the leadership role in the local movement. In her view, the agency women lacked "this coming together of faith and politics, faith and resistance"; some had "that antireligious stance," "acting out . . . in not entirely mature ways."

Others, however, commended the agency women for how well they combined faith, feminism, and politics. One woman linked her own political orientation to her association with them. She claimed that the agency women had "faith, but not church-bound faith": "They're good strong feminists, not just regarding women's experience in the white middle class. . . . they had good race, class, and sex analyses and understand imperialism."

LOCAL MEN AND WOMEN

The pattern associating women with the political and men with the humanitarian approach reappeared in women's rhetoric about men in the local movement, contradicting in two ways the stereotypes that link women to caring and men to power. First, women may be more likely than men to experience American culture as oppressive and to identify their own situations with those of the refugees, particularly the female refugees, many of whom had been raped and beaten during their exodus.[3] Identifying with other oppressed groups may enhance women's sense of empathy, partnership, and "standing with" the refugees. Second, the culture may predispose participants to violate prescribed gender norms by socializing women to prefer empowering others and socializing men to prefer taking power.[4] In this view, women's prescribed affiliation with others accounts for their preference for shared power and a political approach.

Women framed the division between men and women as one of "partnership versus paternalism," often claiming to want partnership with refugees and accusing the men of paternalism in wanting merely to support them. Dina described this conflict over the group's budget at First Street Church. Women who wanted to share their economic concerns with the refugees perceived the men as wanting to share only money. She complained that before committee meetings, the men had already made all the decisions:

> Jim wouldn't tell the refugees that we have a budget. Roy and Jim thought I was being too rough on the refugees. I thought we needed to let the refugees in on our budget. Roy and Jim wanted to just give them money. . . . I wanted a list of their needs, but Jim would just give the family money out of his pocket or our budget. Eva and I favored making the refugees aware of budgets, and Jim and Roy favored paternalistic care. My position was that the family needs a budget.

Donna described a similar conflict at Washington Church, identifying one committeewoman and the church minister as having a "paternalistic . . . humanitarian" style of refugee care. Instead of being "paternalistic and condescending," she favored forging a partnership with the refugees: "Edith and Mitch . . . just want to pick up the tab. Others disagree. We give the refugees a stipend, subsidized rent, and medical care. . . . It's partnership versus paternalism. We all have rights and responsibilities. Edith and Mitch are humanitarian and kind but politically backward."

At Westminster Church, which had two clergywomen and a lesbian community within the congregation, "women basically set the tone." Christine linked the woman-based social action committee with the partnership approach. Yet even though no one took the paternalistic approach, there was "a real difference of opinion. Should we help the refugees find jobs, or should we support them so they can do . . . speaking engagements? It was never really resolved, although we had the sense to include them in the dialogue."

Despite complaints about paternalism, some women praised some men as "special"—ironically, some of the same men whom others accused of dominating the movement. They saw the men as "definitely exceptional," "a different kind of men." For example, they praised Roy as a "good, good man," "patient and tolerant," a "relentless . . . doer" and "good speaker"; one called Roy and the minister a "good combination." Other men were seen as "loving, sensitive, and caring," often employed in the middle-class, care-giving roles of teacher, therapist, and social workers. One called them "professionals," noting that her church doesn't "get a lot of beer-guzzling, TV-watching men." Two women disagreed; Charlotte felt that if the men are more "compassionate and sensitive than the norm . . . then so are the women." Dawn noted that if the men are special, "it's because they allow women to control the agenda. As a white person, the question is not, 'Am I a racist?' but 'How much?' For men, I think it's 'how sexist am I?' "

As members of a historically oppressive group, men in the movement may struggle with the conditioned urge to dominate. For example, Christine called two men on the social action committee at Westminster Church "atypical," suggesting a gap between sanctuary work and prescribed male behavior: "In one man I don't see any desire for fame, to be a star. The other man is working harder than any other human being I know at equality issues across the board."

Women's perceptions of men's untenable position in a care-oriented movement suggest that men may be required to take on identities that conflict with prescribed male values and behavior. Margaret believed that men who have undergone religious conversions more easily violate those norms:

> Men have to go through a transformation. Their models have been to become people with power over others. Men have to shake off a false identity in order to surrender themselves to caring. Most of the men have had some sort of conversion experience—that's not particularly encouraged in men.

Comparing men's and women's roles in the movement, she explained her view of a spiritual division of labor that reconciles role incongruities for both:

> Anyone on a spiritual journey has to confront the feminine in themselves. Domination and control are not part of the life of the spirit. Prayer keeps us working together—being deeply in touch with the inner self. . . . [Prayer] puts [a woman] in touch with a certain strength—what's masculine in her—that fuses with her ability to care . . . [and] puts [men] in touch with a different strength—their source of loving and caring, which is their feminine side.

Margaret noted a link between position in the church hierarchy and attitude toward social action, suggesting that the activism of men and women religious is rooted in their contrasting roles in religious groups: "Nuns have always been locked out of the power structure of the church . . . their very powerlessness has made their lives revolve around having a clear vision of what the world needs instead of going up the hierarchical ladder of the church."

Josie explained that women religious "have much less to lose" by participating in sanctuary than do men in the church hierarchy.

The four men in the Chicago Catholic Sanctuary (CCS) belonged to orders and so were a little more "protected." Whereas diocesan priests could "quickly be out of a job," "order men" had more in common with nuns: "We share common elements in our religious life—vows, community living, a collegiate model . . . consensual decision-making away from hierarchical structure, and greater shared responsibility."

The positional authority in church hierarchies of men participating in the movement seems to be a significant factor in whether rules are bent and institutional free space is used for social action. Women noted that male clergy overlooked irregularities on many occasions. As one put it, the minister "just kind of closed his eyes" to the fact that the refugees were "illegals." Another commented that "there are fronts which pastors put up—what their congregations want. Then they endorse other issues privately and are proud of it." Though women generally believed that they were "the most important element" in the movement, a few stressed the "vital role of the ministers" in formally declaring sanctuary. For example, Eva believed that "women may be influential before and after" but need a push from men to speak up or act: "Initially . . . the men . . . were the sparks. They could be considered the prophetic, telling us, 'Take the leap of faith and do it.' But they've needed us to do the work."

Women's rhetoric about conflicts with men reflected their growing self-consciousness as women and awareness of their own importance in the movement. Socially constructing the movement around these conflicts, they seemed to portray themselves as a rising class that was getting somewhere and men as obstructing their path. The paradox of their praise for and criticism of the men revealed their struggles with gendered conflicts in other areas accentuated by their activism. Unresolved, these conflicts may impede women's cognitive liberation, essential to developing a political identity and an activist career.

LAYWOMEN AND WOMEN RELIGIOUS

Ideological divisions were most pronounced between groups of laywomen and women religious at two local Catholic sanctuaries.

Because the church officially opposes the movement and forbids the use of parish property for its purposes, participants in the Catholic sanctuaries not only had to face the same general obstacles as others in the study but also had to contend with church disapproval. Out of contrasting circumstances, for different purposes, and by alternate routes, the two sites overcame this obstacle by violating the church's line of resistance in contrary ways. Their orientations and activities were related both to the barriers they faced in using church property and to their respective positions in families and religious orders.

Three laywomen at St. John's Church became personally involved with the refugees. Julia and Gloria were on the social action committee; Jennifer was "just a very concerned person in the congregation." Gloria and Jennifer were full-time homemakers, married with children, once but no longer engaged in public activism. As volunteer workers, they were well connected to local resources through informal church and community networks. Their relations with the refugees were based largely on mobilizing these resources for the refugees' care and assimilation. They appeared to understand the larger issues, but their involvement generally lacked political intent and content. Julia was more politically oriented: she did outreach work, served as translator at educational events, and took part in public debates in the community's drive to become a sanctuary city. Although she too was married and had children, she worked outside her home and attended graduate school part time.

Sanctuary at St. John's was spontaneous and unplanned. A social action committee member received a call from a priest and special catalyst in a Hispanic community asking the group to take in and care for a homeless refugee family. The committee had worked with the priest before in "education, demonstrations, and so forth." Now, the priest made a strong challenge, asking, "Are you just a bunch of talk or what? A family needs a place to stay." As Jennifer put it, "We [had] . . . always respected him and sent money . . . for peripheral projects, not questioning his need."

The committee lacked time to obtain official approval. The member contacted by the priest called a meeting at her house on

"Good Friday night" to discuss the matter. The group agreed to take the refugees, and the priest brought them over the same night. Unlike CCS's public, well-attended, politicized declaration ceremony,[5] it was a simple, informal reception at which the refugees were immediately "introduced to the community": "We met them. [The priest] interpreted. There were four in the family and the room was filled—ten or fifteen people—the social action committee and pastoral team. The next day he brought them back. He said, 'Here are your new friends.'"

Jennifer's narrative of how the group went about soliciting clothes for the refugee family the next day illustrates the informal local networks through which middle-class volunteers customarily mobilize community resources. It also reveals the caretakers' unwitting imposition of their own cultural norms on the refugees: "The kids had no clothes. . . . We ran around to people's houses with kids that age and asked for clothes. We'd say, 'Maria needs an Easter dress and shoes and socks.' It's a real easy community to do that in."

The refugees were Quiche Indians from Guatemala. Compared with the Europeanized Salvadoran refugee family at the official Catholic sanctuary, they were more disadvantaged by and vulnerable to North American culture from the start, as Julia noted: "When the first . . . refugees came, we didn't realize they wouldn't speak Spanish. They had long skirts, braids. They were Indians. We were really insensitive that way." Gloria also conveyed a sense of the refugees' vulnerability: "We brought them huge Easter baskets. The kids' eyes were huge. Little Felicite seemed so tiny and diminutive. . . . I was very worried for her, stuck in a community where no one speaks her Guatemalan language."

Presenting the refugees' arrival after the fact, committee members employed a secret strategy which they called "the wedge in the door"—a way to withhold the family's actual legal status from congregation and board members, who were told that the refugees were "in the process of application for documented status." In reality, the father "had been denied and was appealing. His wife and two kids had no legal status, but the congregation didn't know that." Gloria explained the group's rationale: "Our congregation is a mix of very wealthy people to lower class. Politically, we range from extremely conservative to those who got up and cried at the microphone the night Reagan was elected. . . . We knew they'd never buy it."

Believing that the refugees were about to become "legal," the congregation and church board agreed to help them "get their feet on the ground." They never "got the full scoop" about the family's actual legal status; as Julia confided, "People on the social action committee were the only ones who knew and . . . still are." Jennifer elaborated on how "the wedge" helped get the refugees into "the community" until they "became real" to the congregation:

> When people asked about their legality, I'd say, "That's not for us to say—[the father] is known to the immigration department—it's a very technical type of law. We can't determine the legality of these people—it's arguable in court." Three or four of us kind of got together and figured, this is the wedge in the door . . . and it seemed to work very well. . . . As the refugees became real to them, people became relaxed with them around.

Caretakers tended to relate to the refugees in humanitarian terms, expressing more concern about them as individuals than about their plight as members of a historically oppressed group. Jennifer's husband, for example, wanted to help but not to get politically involved: "Their comrades would send us [a Guatemalan organization newsletter], and [my husband] asked them to stop. He didn't trust anyone and just wanted to help these particular people."

Caretakers expressed many dissatisfactions at how slowly the refugees assimilated into American culture. For example, some were upset because they hadn't learned more English, which "annoyed people in the community who were not happy with them." Jennifer explained that "if they were taking classes, people would see they're making progress. They're into Spanish soap operas. The kids watch them too." The refugee family had wanted to name a baby born on the anniversary of Oscar Romero's assassination "Oscar," but care-takers told them, "No, people in the U.S. wouldn't like it and would make fun of it"; it would remind them of "puppets, hotdogs, and penises."

Jennifer became the most involved with the refugees, especially their children. As Julia noted, she "jumped right in": "Jennifer took care of education, getting them into schools, getting them pool passes, clothes, toys, to doctors for shots, getting them acclimated. She also took care of Felicite. She and Paulo both had parasitic infections that needed to be taken care of." She had "kids at her house everyday" and the refugee family over "for supper all the time," frequently taking them to dinner at Mexican restaurants. Again, however, caretaking sometimes took the form of imposing her own culture's customs and expectations on the refugees, which they notably resisted: "Jennifer tried to lay down curfews and ground the kids. They just quietly laughed because [her husband] was silent about this, and in Central America this means disagree-ment."

Jennifer's "sense of limits" was confronted when the refugees' extended family arrived from Los Angeles and began contributing to their prodigious birth rate: "She said, 'While they're here, they shouldn't have kids.' She thought they should use birth control or get abortions." Other caretakers too were frankly upset at the refu-gee family's growing size—two women had five babies in two years—and their apparent failure or unwillingness to use birth con-trol. For example, Gloria exclaimed, "Now Dora is expecting her fifth child! It just aggravated the heck out of us!" Jennifer, who had stood as godmother for one baby, said no when asked again: "The grandma told Paulo, 'How could she refuse? All a godmother has to do is give advice?' I told my husband, 'If they'd followed my advice, they'd never have had the baby!'"

The extended family eventually depleted the caretakers' re-sources and patience. Jennifer related that the arrival of additional members and the erosion of good will took place in stages. First, the mother-in-law and two sons came to attend a birth; the sons remained, enrolling in school with the original refugees' children: "They all stayed in this little apartment—now eight. The landlord had a stroke. We explained that they were just visiting until the baby arrived."

Months later, after having returned to the coast, the mother-in-law wanted another son's child baptized and *Comadre* Jennifer as its godmother, so she flew to Chicago for the baptism with her husband, son, daughter-in-law, and the baby. Gloria's narrative of this event reveals that the refugees exercised power through familial values and language, to which caretakers responded.[6] "Grandma" drew power from her position in a matriarchal family, relying on the family's universality to convey and secure her wishes.

It is unclear why the baptism was not held at the church—whether this was a function of "the wedge," playing down the refugees' growing numbers and needs, or of another kind of separation conceived and imposed by the caretakers:

> The grandma wanted Jennifer to be the godmother because she was the *comadre* for that family, and whatever grandma wants, grandma gets. So they flew in for the baptism. The community doesn't just baptize anyone. There was much discussion about it. Finally it was decided it'd be at Jennifer's house with the priest attending, because they really weren't part of the community.

Caretakers learned some months later that the extended family had experienced a frightening INS raid on their apartment building in Los Angeles and were en route again to Chicago to join the first refugee family in the "land of milk and honey." Word of this emergency arrival required rapidly mobilizing enormous resources. Time constraints and the secrecy of sanctuary at St. John's limited shared decision-making and created conflict among committee members, as Gloria explained:

> We as a committee had to make a real fast decision. We met after mass Sunday and said, 'Are we or aren't we?' . . . We just

decided. We made a phone call to the board that we'd support them—if not from within the [church] community, then from outside. We'd made a commitment to them, and we were going to stay behind them. This caused some problems with the committee. Some weren't at mass that day and had no input. It was getting to be wearing on the committee. The family wasn't a pet project of everybody. This caused some tension . . . people began getting upset. . . . They began muttering about how big the family was. . . . Jennifer couldn't handle it anymore and said that others had to get involved. She said, "My commitment is to these children."

Women described the newly arrived refugees' high level of fear and the horror they had experienced in Guatemala. Gloria called the seven new people "terrified." Jennifer related their strategy for avoiding detection at the airport and their lasting fright once they arrived, also noting their "good story":

As it turned out, they didn't come that Sunday. They went to the [L.A.] airport, thought they saw INS officials, and went back home. They regrouped and came in two batches three weeks later, which gave us a little breathing space to find a place for them. But when they arrived, they ended up all staying at that little apartment. And in terror. They couldn't quite see that [this community] would be different. Juan had been a teenager of fifteen or sixteen when a politician arrived in his [Guatemalan] village accompanied by troops. . . . The soldiers wanted to play soccer with the kids, and when the kids won, the soldiers began killing them. Juan escaped alone into the jungle and came back and brought several others out. He went to Compeche, Mexico, where he met Dora. He had gotten Dora and the children up to Los Angeles on his own.

Caretakers faced the problem of quickly locating additional housing for the large and growing family. With "much screaming," they found an apartment but had to reconstitute the extended family into an American-style unit—an example of the kind of cultural repackaging they frequently performed to ease the refugees' adaptation and assimilation. Jennifer indicated how they got around a "standard lease that says children up to age two can sleep in their parents' room":

> With Dora came her cousin Maria, who was sixteen. We had to figure out how to present this to the landlords without their realizing they were illegal. Maria wasn't on the lease at all. . . . We just included Juan, Dora, and their two children. We never told them that Dora was pregnant.

Dora's pregnancy posed an even greater problem. With little time to prepare for the birth, the St. John's women faced enormous red tape because of her undocumented status and medically unattended, "high risk" pregnancy, as Gloria explained:

> She arrived pregnant. We thought, "Oh oh, nobody even told us this." She didn't know how far pregnant she was. . . . Nobody knew. She'd had minimal care. . . . We started hysterically trying to figure out where she'd give birth. . . . I called a woman in the community who speaks Spanish and is a nurse. She made some calls. Everywhere we took her, she was either too high a risk or not in their region. . . . I asked a friend, "What would happen if we just showed up at a hospital?" She said, "We've turned in illegals before."

Time ran out, Gloria continued, and the birth took place at the refugees' apartment, attended by the extended family plus Gloria and Julia and a community midwife they persuaded to help:

> The day after we'd gone through all this, taking her from clinic to clinic, Julia called me about 8:30 that night. 'She's having contractions.' I [said], "Tell her to relax, take a hot bath, and if there's any liquor in the house, give her a drink." A half-hour later she called back: "They're closer together." All my kids were born at home. I said, "Remember that

Spanish-speaking midwife you know? Call her. See how far along she is." So I went over there. I brought everything I could find in the house that could be used for a birth. . . . The whole fifteen in the family were there. [The midwife] had just arrived and examined her before taking her coat off. She was 8.5 centimeters. She said, "We're not going anywhere." This was 9:15, and the baby was born at 10:00. It was an easy delivery.

This event was perhaps the caretakers' and refugees' closest, least conflicted moment together. Gloria's narrative reveals that women's universal experience of giving birth apparently helped at least briefly to overcome their cultural differences:

There were very interesting things going on. In the room were the midwife, Julia, myself, and grandma. Grandma is my age, looks sixty, and is charismatic. She was praying out loud. I spoke no Spanish . . . Grandma spoke her Guatemalan language. When we were trying to get Dora to push, there was this sensation in the room. I felt in touch with women since the beginning of time, delivering a baby. I said that to Julia, who translated it to grandma, who smiled and said she'd just experienced the same thing. It was like I lost track of time, place. I felt this flow of womanness going across centuries of time. It was the strength of women doing what all women can do. It's a bond all women share. They don't need to talk about it—they just experience it.

Yet there were conflicts surrounding the birth. Caretakers were disturbed by what they perceived as the refugees' inadequate bonding with the infant:

In our culture we immediately present the baby to the mother. That didn't occur. At the end she asked Juan to hold her arms and help her push. Grandma wasn't pleased—I could see from her face—it was like an Anglo custom. But he left as soon as the baby was born. . . . Grandma held the baby, then took it

out and presented it to the family. It was wrapped in somebody's shirt, very swaddled. I'd brought baby blankets and everything, but grandma chose a black silk shirt lying there. It
must have been a good twenty or thirty minutes [while the
baby was presented]. I was very concerned about getting the
baby to bond and breastfeed right away. Finally I got mad,
picked up the baby, and brought it to the mother, who finally
took it. Julia explained later how they lose so many babies,
perhaps they don't emphasize early bonding.

The St. John's women were also upset by the refugee women's
apparent lack of interest in breastfeeding and preference for formula. This was an important issue for the caretakers (a local restaurant had been petitioned out of business in a protest against its
parent company's formula products), but they seemed genuinely
unaware of the relativity of their own cultural proclivities surrounding these body rituals.[7] As Gloria put it, "Cultural differences made
a big problem" in the matter breastfeeding:

> We were disgusted. . . . It was the prestige of formula—it's
> Western to them. Dora simply wouldn't breastfeed. We found
> out she'd only breastfed her first child, and it hurt so much
> she wouldn't do it again. Felicite had her third child in Febru-
> ary, nursed for three months, stopped, got pregnant almost
> immediately, and had [the new baby] in March of '87. We
> tried to be real understanding about cultural things. We ex-
> plained, "Breastfeeding is a natural form of birth control." But
> they don't believe in breastfeeding for the first three days—
> they think the cholostrum isn't good. With all its immunities!

Other conflicts surrounded a housecleaning business that caretakers set up for the refugee women at Paulo's request. Gloria explained the group's application of an old American ethic about
immigrants working their way up the ladder: "Our idea was, some
members of the community wanted to help but not just hand them
money. We decided on a better way." Relating how the business

started, she indicated that the refugees achieved economic independence after being shown how to adopt Western housekeeping practices, despite their initial resistance:

> It was just Felicite to start with. It was very difficult—her con-
> cept of cleaning house isn't the American way. They do not
> see things. If they vacuum and move the furniture, they don't
> move it back. You can tell them to do something, but they
> don't realize they have to do it every week, not just once.
> Now they're much better. Floors, dusting, windows. . . . Then
> Maria began. We kept forgetting she's a teenager. She'd come
> up and say, "Finished?" And I'd say, "What about the bath-
> rooms?" And she'd get this look on her face like any other
> teenager would get.

Commenting on the refugee men's lack of chauvinism, Gloria
seemed to overlook her own cultural chauvinism: "The men don't
seem to have the same macho thing that I think of Mexicans as
having because the men will come and clean. When Felicite was near
the end of her pregnancy, Paulo would come with her and clean."

Holidays brought conflicts among the committee members,
who disagreed as to whether Western-style Christmas gifts were
appropriate: some believed that the refugees should get "really nice,
needed gifts," such as "clothes, watches, [and] billfolds, as opposed
to toilet water"; others felt that the children should receive "an Atari
game and ice skates" since they had "no yard or place to play in."
Gloria defended the caretakers' assimilationist position: "Some people were furious at our imposing our Western values. We said, 'Let's
help them fit in a little bit.' "

In the end, they created a traditional, middle-class, American-
style Christmas for the refugees, surprising the children with equally
allotted "piles and piles of stuff." Beyond committee members' initial
arguments, they seemed unconcerned about the cultural intrusive-
ness of introducing the refugee children to these folkways. Gloria's
narrative suggests that they perceived the children as not apprecia-
tive enough:

Jennifer came over, and we lined up all their gifts all through the house and started wrapping. On Christmas eve we brought [the family] over to Jennifer's house for the evening. We had their apartment keys and took all the gifts over to surprise them. The children just went berserk. . . . It was important to us that each child got as much as the others. The kids were saying, "Why did I get this game when I wanted that game?" Jennifer told me she just wanted to wring their necks, then remembered our kids saying the same things.

Eventually, caretakers were unable to maintain housing for the growing family, and the Los Angeles branch moved to another nearby sanctuary. Jennifer recounted how the exhausted committee continued to work toward the refugees' assimilation by planning to sell them an apartment building:

Dora will have [another] baby in November, and their lease can't be renewed because of too many people. We . . . are trying to buy a two-flat . . . which [a church] bought and is putting on the market. We'll either sell it to the Guatemalans or rent it to them with the option to buy.

Though somewhat aware of the unfeasibility of this plan, caretakers blamed the housing problem on the refugees' failure to maintain an American-sized family: "Just by the size of their family they may have to leave. I have to laugh at the idea of [this community] becoming a sanctuary city. What immigrant family can afford the fucking rent?"

The refugees had their own agenda, however: on their own, they rented a large apartment building with an option to buy, partly so they could house more family members coming from Guatemala. Jennifer noted that with several adults in the family working, they had saved a great deal of money. They explained to her that they had always intended to have a large family, and since they could not safely return home, they had felt all along that the United States was the best place to have their children.

These women's narratives reveal deep cultural divisions between themselves and the refugees. Given their underlying belief in the desirability of the refugees' assimilation, they often exacerbated conflicts by being insensitive to the refugees' culture and imposing their own. They helped the refugees get on their feet but made few connections between their circumstances and larger political issues. While the refugees seemed passive and vulnerable to being culturally repackaged, they often successfully resisted inroads on their identity. In the end, they took their assimilation into their own hands, surpassing even the caretakers' expectations for them.

Groups working this closely with immigrants may tend to burn out rather quickly. Whereas participants at other sites maintained their commitment partly through their continued activism in other areas, these sites generally had the strong institutional support that St. John's informal sanctuary lacked. The caretakers most involved with refugees were otherwise inactive, yet notably, they continued interacting with the refugees after they and their resources were exhausted. For example, after more than two years of intense involvement, Jennifer's family entered therapy in an effort to reestablish its own sense of boundaries yet continued to enjoy frequent friendly visits with the refugees, more or less dropping the concept of sanctuary.

CCS, the official Catholic sanctuary, contrasted sharply with the informal one. Its formation was intentional and extremely well organized, created by women religious as a citywide "public" sanctuary in open defiance of government and church policies toward Central America and the refugees. Members interviewed include four nuns—Josie, Kim, Dawn, and Moira, all employed full time, active on prior issues, and three of the four well-traveled in Central America—and two laywomen. Jeannine, a special education teacher, married without children, was a convert to both Catholicism and activism. Megan's lifestyle, orientation, and activities closely resembled those of the nuns; single and devoutly religious, she spent six months each year working in Honduran refugee camps.

Kim claimed that the group chose sanctuary "as a means of facing off with the government." Sanctuary was "concrete and risky" and "exacted something"; it was "a way to truly learn from Central Americans." Josie explained that the organizers had their "first thoughts" about a Catholic sanctuary when they realized that "a lot of women" among their "constituents" were "really concerned about Central America." Many "had lived there or had friends live there," had been personally exposed to the refugees' circumstances, and understood concepts such as "base community" and "liberation theology." Some had also "worked in poor areas in Chicago," where they saw "the same linking issues."

At a "very small one-day conference" in April 1986, the group did "some social analyses of global economics." A national sanctuary leader just back from El Salvador reportedly "made a pitch for women of El Salvador." Others wanted to "talk about sanctuary as a concrete way of facing off with the government." The group met again in May and decided to declare itself a sanctuary. By the time the refugees arrived six months later, they had amassed thousands of dollars, a year's supply of canned goods, and furniture for two apartments.

The refugees included Anna, a Salvadoran single parent, and her three children; her husband was reportedly still in El Salvador, politically "on the other side of the fence." Anna and the women religious were united in their commitment to the same political goals, helping them transcend somewhat their contrasting statuses as "refugee" and "nun." As Josie put it, "Anna doesn't have a lot of regard for nuns. She tells us, 'I don't think of you as nuns but as guerrillas.' "

These caretakers tended to stress partnership and mutuality with the refugees in terms of shared goals within larger political spheres. For example, Kim noted that unlike the case in some other sanctuaries,

> our caring and working with refugees was a means for us. The end . . . was ending U.S. intervention. We didn't begin by talking about helping these poor folks but with the moral obliga-

tion of facing off with the government. . . . We didn't see this as charity but as mutual commitment with the family.

They viewed the refugees as equals in a common political struggle and were open to learning from them. Kim claimed that she had learned from the refugees in ways she "never could from a textbook." Josie stated that the group had "learned a great deal about what's countercultural" about themselves. Megan described her friendship with Anna in egalitarian terms: "I take my friends over to her apartment. We talk a lot about the project, analyze the meetings together. We talk about all different subjects just like I would with another female friend. She loves to give me advice—she's very much the extrovert."

The members of this group, experienced in working in social service organizations and possessing many professional skills, were already busy with work, meetings, civil disobedience, and travel. Unlike the women at St. John's, they did not make caretaking an extension of their everyday activities; for them, caretaking was specialized and less bound to women's traditional caring. For example, Jeannine was tutoring Anna's daughter, who had been diagnosed as emotionally and mentally handicapped. Rather than nurture dependency, they expected the refugees to be adaptive and self-reliant, as Megan explained: "Our family speaks some English so they can adapt more easily to a group of people extremely busy with full-time jobs. It helps to have a family that's extremely independent." Even though she had moved in next door to the refugee family and become somewhat personally involved, she indicated a sensitivity to their need for privacy: "I try to limit it—I don't drop in every day. I don't eat with the family all the time—I won't be there forever. I try to respect their privacy."

Nevertheless, here too conflicts emerged over cultural expectations. Caretakers' customs of social distance and formality contrasted sharply with the refugees' customs of familiarity and intimacy. As Josie indicated, Anna complained that she felt like a "project":

Anna's complaint was, "I never see you." And I spent more
time with her than with my own mother! But her cultural experience is, people drop in and out of the house all day
long. . . . And here privacy is a value. . . . It'd never occur to
us to walk in anytime and throw ourselves on the couch. And
she felt she was just a project to us and not a real person. We
felt we were friends. But because there's always a modicum of
distance in North American culture, she perceived us as business associates.

The refugees were in fact part of a project, its context a citywide
network of women religious who rarely interacted outside of formal
meetings. Although members of the family "received a lot of attention," Kim conceded that they may not have perceived "sending the
children to camp" as "attention":

It's a real weakness of the project in having people live far
apart in the city. Anna's feelings are justified. We're not a
group that sees one another every week . . . we live far away
from each other and meet only for meetings, and it does take
on a little bit of an institutional tone.

Caretakers experienced conflict not over the refugees' assimilation but over their own level of commitment to the refugees' cause.
For example, Josie called Anna's drive to end the war "overwhelming." Anna couldn't understand why the group wasn't spending
every minute working to end the war: "She wants to know why we
can't get 10,000 people out in the street. We think we do well to get
five hundred." Dawn complained that "Anna and her family can be
very difficult . . . she thinks North Americans are all stupid, wealthy,
and indifferent."

Such differences shook the belief of the women religious in
partnership with the refugees, forcing acknowledgment of the disparities between them. "Our realities are so different," Kim explained. "I have rights in this country . . . but Anna has no rights
[anywhere]. I don't know how that feels. I've always benefited from

capitalism. She has not. I'm not saying that this shouldn't change, but I've never gone without. This is her reality."

Conflict also emerged over lifestyle differences. Caretakers were primarily celibate nuns; Anna was a single parent of a family whose supportive functions were badly damaged. Although women religious had built their lives around a patriarchal institution promoting women's reliance on men, they seemed genuinely surprised and offended when Anna took a "live-in lover." As Moira described it, Anna was consorting with the enemy:

> Anna wasn't here very long before Ernesto showed up. . . . She needs that guy. It took a long while for me to realize that she's spent her whole life in a culture where men are terribly important. She feels safer with a man in the house. She relies on him for moral support and to show her how to balance the budget. He's more knowledgeable, and she wants him around.
> Whereas the women she's working with—nuns—say, "Who needs him?"

Anna's "betrayal" made the nuns feel secondary—perhaps like a project in *her* life. This caused a great deal of tension, which some projected on Anna, as Dawn indicated: "I'll go over and she'll be in the bedroom with her lover and it's uncomfortable. I really don't care, but I feel it's a source of tension to her."

Other tensions involved the refugee children's gender-role socialization. A struggle developed over whether Anna's son should be "the man" in a traditional Latin family or learn his place in a modern American one, as Dawn explained:

> Anna's son doesn't have to help with housework or babysitting. His sister, a year younger, has to. He can discipline the youngest, and Anna defers to him as the man in the family. The nuns are tuned into this—they have no appreciation of this. I always make him do the same things as the girls. . . . He wanted to sit in the front seat and me to sit in the back! I told him, "I'm sitting in the front seat."

Despite their contrasting circumstances, the two Catholic groups experienced similar conflicts over different kinds of issues. Anna's parenting style and sex life posed the same kinds of problems for women religious as Felicite's and Dora's refusal to breastfeed, use birth control, and "bond" with newborns posed for St. John's women. In both cases, the caretakers' own biases exacerbated cultural differences, influencing the outcome of their sanctuary projects.

Whereas caretakers at St. John's tended to perceive the refugees' large family as an obstacle to their assimilation, those at CCS tended to perceive Anna's debilitated position as an obstacle to the kind of partnership they had envisioned with her. In the end, they came to see her equality as spurious and her dependency as inevitable. Arriving differently than did their homemaker counterparts at the same dilemma of how to make the refugees self-sufficient, they seemed more aware of how American culture had "corrupted" the refugees' children. Kim summarized these problems:

> There are so many things I never thought of when I entered this. Anna's the victim of rape and torture. . . . From the beginning I presumed mental health, understanding, appreciation. We're somehow responsible for them. . . . We can't simply dump them. But we've got to get them to be able to sustain themselves down the road—learn a trade or something. How to stand in solidarity with someone who's been institutionally victimized, without being manipulated? As a result of Anna's suffering, the only power she's learned is manipulation and dependency. How to wean her from that? As we attempt to, I see more dependency in the process. She thinks our culture has corrupted her kids—they never want to go back. I'd expected it, but it's difficult to watch.

Josie believed that the solution included acknowledging the fundamental inequality between them: "The biggest solution . . . is to be a resource to her without patronizing her and making her dependent—to be with her rather than above her. And tell her she's being unfair or condescending—to be honest is the first sign of mutuality. In reality we'll never be equal."

The gulf between caretakers' and refugees' expectations, compounded by personality conflicts, ultimately outlasted their ability to work cooperatively together. Kim admitted:

I feel my expectations of her are too high and hers are too high for me. Her presumption was that we would fund her for the duration of the war. It's unrealistic. The group's expectation was open communication. She expects us to have a communal sensibility, but . . . she has very little to do with other Salvadorans. She's not a team person. She's very difficult to work with because she likes to call the shots.

Some of the nuns had begun talking to Anna about leaving sanctuary, which raised other issues, as Josie explained: "At least she knows we were never intending to support her for life. At first we said we'd make a one-year commitment, but she claims we never said this. . . . down deep she believes we can get all the money necessary. She doesn't have realistic expectations of what fund raising takes."

Dawn, saying that "lately it's been very difficult," doubted that the group could "afford to take on another refugee. We had to tell Anna that we're running out of money. We may have misled her— we raised so much money initially. Anna is no longer technically in sanctuary because she's applied for political asylum and a work permit. . . . Once she has a job she'll be basically independent."

In sum, for women religious, sanctuary was an intentional, political gesture; for laywomen, it was situational and humanitarian. One group openly violated the church's position on sanctuary; the other discreetly skirted it. One relied on professional associations and networks in place of church property; the other used informal local networks and its members' experience as volunteers in the community. One publicized the refugees' situation, taking a stand on refugee empowerment and collective resistance; the other understated the refugees' presence, emphasizing private caretaking and assimilation. Both groups imposed cultural biases on the refugees, and both faced the problem of making them independent. Both sets of refugees took the initiative, applying for amnesty and jobs and making their own plans to assimilate further into American culture. Already familiar with and active on the issues, women religious continued their sanctuary involvement with other forms of participation. Understanding the issues less directly and in simpler terms, laywomen gradually withdrew from the movement after getting the refugees "on their feet." Undaunted by the inability to use church property, women religious relied on their own considerable resources to construct the movement: their extensive travel and residence in Central America and firsthand knowledge of the issues, experience at organizing and fund raising, and access to a wide network of religious and professional organizations and social justice agencies. Laywomen also relied on their own extensive resources outside the church: their positions in informal, woman-based networks through which they customarily channeled goods and services as full-time volunteers in their communities.

Epitomizing the movement's ideological splits, these two groups provide models for understanding the character of much of women's hidden work in social movements. They illustrate two ways in which women systematically express care, use free space, link issues together, resolve conflicts, and accommodate and resist authority.[8] They also suggest how sanctuary groups will likely respond if confronted by more direct official disapproval—an important consideration, given their illegal activities—either by more publicity to the refugees' situation and openly denouncing official policy, or by manipulating officials' understanding of individual refugees' situations and providing discreet refugee care. Last, they link the outcome of women's activism to their positions in families and religious orders.

IV

PATTERNS AND CONFLICTS IN WOMEN'S ACTIVITIES

Most of the sanctuary movement's "conscience constituents"[1] are white, North American, middle-class women mobilized on behalf of oppressed Third World people of color; conflicts surrounding issues of class, race, gender, and culture inevitably characterize all sanctuary activities. For example, women described dissension between North American men and women over leadership and caretaking styles, between North and Central American women over gender issues and other contrasting cultural values, and between Guatemalans and Salvadorans over differences of class, race, and culture.

Such disagreements take on recognizable patterns in women's narratives. Reaction to the issues generally indicates their orientation within the movement: those who focus on the humanitarian approach tend to ignore them, whereas those whose concerns are political emphasize and seek meaningful links between them. Some sort of analysis whereby women identify others like themselves as part of the problem seems to be a prerequisite for developing political consciousness. Those who are unaware of the issues and others' viewpoints unwittingly tend to perpetuate their own class and cultural hegemony; those who perceive and link issues, recognizing their own part in creating conflicts, tend to broaden their viewpoint and sphere of challenge. Women's accounts of their experiences in all movement activities—leadership, outreach, translating, civil disobedience, travel to Central America, and caretaking—reveal how their level of awareness represents costs and contributions to the movement and their activist careers.

LEADERSHIP

Understanding women's leadership style in sanctuary requires making "the invisible visible"; studies of other grassroots movements show leadership as a collective dynamic process in which consistent efforts are made to flatten decision-making and status hierarchies. Power and authority tend to be somewhat limited in all opposition movements, a fact that women often accentuate by acting in ways not commonly perceived as leadership. As "invisible administrators," they have responsibility without authority. Socialized to empower others, they avoid the traditional uses of power that they identify with male domination and control.[2]

This helps explain sanctuary women's preference for "shared power" and "group care" and their professed aversion to unshared power. For example, one stressed the importance of "parameters in this kind of work," indicating that her group was "very conscious" of "caring for itself." Others emphasized the desirability of "cochairs," "democratically shared power and authority," and "intentionally shared decisions and work." Calling power a "dirty word," Christine was opposed to "power over others"; she believed it should be "on behalf of or with" others, "power to empower others." She called shared power "women's way . . . a collaborative thing permissible because of the position we're placed in." Donna linked unshared power to her "real male role" as coalition staff person in which she lacked "enough partners": "I'm more comfortable with a group, figuring things out together. Now I'm expected to make all the decisions, do all the organizing. . . . I'm closer to the women . . . I feel more like we're working together."

Notably, these two also claimed to oppose the expression of a wide range of views, a practice that they linked with the status quo. Whether they perceived it as a male or a female trait, both attributed to sex differences the "undemocratic tendency" of allowing other opinions. For example, Christine denounced the position that "we must hear all points of view" as "a particularly female phenomenon." She was "not willing to allow right-wing viewpoints"; as she put it, "they can read the paper." Donna complained about her group's new "ultrademocratic male chair"; she called shared decision-making with "uninformed people" "undemocratic."

A psychological theory links women's conflicts over unshared power to their trained helplessness and difficulty in "speaking up." According to this theory, women are socialized to accept a morality of responsibility for others before asserting their own rights or even including themselves within their own circle of care.[3] Yet women's lifelong conditioning to be self-sacrificing and their sense of responsibility for others might arguably more likely lead to speaking up in a movement dedicated to helping the oppressed.

A sociological theory of women's unease with unshared power is more explanatory. A recurrent theme in women's narratives is the issue of secrecy versus democracy: women have learned from personal experience that unshared power and secrecy exclude them from decision-making, whereas shared power and democracy include them. Their vocabularies of motive link this issue to their growing consciousness and sense of importance as women in the movement. Aware that they often do the work for which men get the credit, they tend to be galvanized by the issue of men's patriarchal tendencies, portraying men as obstacles in their struggles with power. Many women expressed somewhat essentialist notions of sex differences in the rhetoric of a self-righteous "rising class." Appearing early on in the movement, this theme recurs often in the case material.

Julia's narrative about her struggle with power traced the difficult course of her upward mobility from a "child's role" to that of an "entitled" woman in the movement:

> Because I was going out debating, people said, "Great." I began to take myself seriously. It's harder to take the child's role. When I taught all those years, I never saw myself as being in-

dependent because I never saw *myself*—only as part of relationships. I still struggle with that. I'm learning how to have
control and not abuse it. Sanctuary gives us a feeling of
power, but women aren't entitling themselves to it. Our self-
esteem improves with our involvement, but it doesn't follow
that we become empowered. Instead, we identify with the oppressed.

She identified with the refugees as both an oppressed group and
an assimilating rising class, revealing uncertainties about her own
ascent and empowerment in the movement:

At first I felt like a Latina battered woman, like it's my fault, I
shouldn't do it. You're fighting power as it's used, so why
identify with it? I'm now getting the sense that people should
be paid for their services. . . . I have a scariness about becoming what we do—becoming like a white male . . . a colonizer.
Yet the refugees are very capable of imitating immigrant patterns of self-help. They don't have trouble empowering themselves.

In a "mourning model now" and "going through the grieving
stages of becoming a person," she used "familistic language"[4] to
trace her ascent in her family, church, and community:

I'm angry and sad that I was so self-effacing, had so little esteem or control. My kids were mindless responsibilities. I had
no idea how to enable them. I'm still angry at myself as well
as patriarchal institutions. I'm bargaining now. How much
power should I have? What should my role be? Can I deal
with having control? What guilt, what punishment will come
to me? I look at it through the church model in terms of good
and bad women. Does not doing as much for my family make
me a bad person?

Studies of grassroots movements generally concur that men tend
to be spokespersons while women do the less visible work of organ-

izing, the importance of which is often minimized or disregarded. Women in mixed-sex organizations are consistently unlikely to be seen as leaders, even by other women and self-described feminists. Women in same-sex organizations may express interests different from or conflicting with men's, whose presence may influence their goals and activism.[5]

Women described many conflicts with men over leadership, conveying their sense of men as obstacles in their path. Lori echoed women's historical lament about doing the work while men make decisions and get the credit. She had "helped" a man in her group organize some workshops—the "mailing, calling, the shitwork of getting it ready"; though asked for assistance, "he kept his hands off and didn't help at all." On a cross-country caravan, "he just started making decisions," after she had done "all the work." She was "mad" but "didn't confront him." A man in the group told her, "That's the way he is"; a woman said, "You should confront him. He's done this to a lot of people and needs to be confronted."

Dina described "a self-appointed chairperson" in her group "who gets on everyone's nerves" yet no one tells him off because they're too polite. He cuts people off when they're speaking, doesn't listen." Women in the group perceived and resented men's domination, which men denied. Then a newcomer to the social action committee confronted the men and made the others aware that the situation was "undemocratic":

Jim defers to Roy's ideas versus Geselle's and mine. A woman recently joined the group and picked up on the lack of democracy at the meetings. A struggle broke out. Her first impressions were how undemocratic the meetings are. Jim has a way of dealing with women as less important. Women's comments didn't get picked up on and she got very upset. Before, Jim would call on people. Now we use orderly ways. We decided to rotate leadership at each meeting, but it lasted only three meetings, then went back to Roy. The same thing occurred over the [refugee] family. When [the first refugee's] mom and two sisters [unexpectedly] arrived . . . the mom locked herself in the bedroom and wouldn't come out. Roy and Jim decided somehow that these three could join the family of five at [the church]. Again it was undemocratic.

Roy was "worried that outsiders" would "take control." He "never allocated very well," was "very protective of the committee," and "worried about being undermined." The newcomer saw "openness" as an important issue and began "taking the reins very quickly," pushing Dina to "speak up." The men resisted: Jim called the new woman a "possible infiltrator," and Roy was "kind of shaken at the idea" that the group was "undemocratic."

Still, not all women noted conflicts with men. For example, Belinda, a married woman with children and a home business, called her group "not male-dominated at all": "Women of the congregation have confronted the minister over the years, told him to shut up and sit down." Claiming that the group had "grown beyond women needing to fight for leadership," she denied the need to "fight for rights anywhere," in her "family, business, or church."

Generally, however, women reported a serious gap between their work in the movement and their visibility as leaders. Although they were aware and disapproving of this gap, their woman-based groups nonetheless supported it. For example, Donna complained that her group's rotating chairship was a "facade," since she did everything. In her view, "if 80 percent of the members are women, then women should be leaders"—yet her group chose a male chair. Dawn complained that CCS had abandoned its original name—Catholic Women's Sanctuary Project—because of the presence of one priest who did "virtually no work." Again, other women both suggested and approved of the name change. The priest reportedly offered to be called "sister," which she found "gross" and "patronizing."

These examples demonstrate that members of a strongly woman-based group, including many self-described feminists, may not necessarily adopt a feminist agenda. They may relegate gender issues to a subcommittee in deference to the presence of traditional women, as Kim indicated:

> I like the men and can work with them, but we never take up the feminist agenda. . . . A lot of women are there because it's a feminist project, but there are a lot of traditional women there also. If we introduced feminism, it'd be a horse of a different color. I think there could probably be a subgroup to deal with it.

Conflicts over leadership, the secrecy-versus-democracy issue, and women's growing awareness of their importance in the movement converged dramatically at a three-day national sanctuary conference organized by CCS nuns in 1987. Its purpose was to forge new alliances between North and Central Americans. Tremendous tension built up, culminating in a bitter confrontation on the last day. The nuns' narratives strongly convey the rhetoric of women as a rising class—in this case, women religious struggling to create a national organizing committee in which women have "gender parity." They recounted how women finally "spoke up," going toe to toe with the refugees in a tense, angry bargaining session over women's place in the movement. Their reports reveal sharp disparities in how North and Central American women prioritize the issues and conceptualize their place in the movement.

"Attitudes were different" from the start, the nuns reported. Central Americans reportedly came with the agenda of wanting North Americans to do more "accompaniment,"[6] support labor movements and women's co-ops, and generally develop "a greater risk campaign" in confronting the U.S. government. North Americans came "to find out who we are and what we can do together." By mid-conference, North American women were complaining that men were dominating the meeting. One calculated that men spoke thirteen times more often in a small discussion group; others objected to sexist Biblical language. Some said "under their breath" that all men should leave, but "nobody left." Finally, about a dozen women went to the microphone and "spoke up," complaining about the lack of gender parity on committees; this produced a cleavage between North and Central Americans for the rest of the conference.

Women indicated that North American women felt dominated by men at the meeting and "all along" because women had done the work while the men remained spokespersons. When they collectively spoke up, proposing half Central and North Americans and half men and women on the national steering committee, Central American women reportedly responded, "No, we won't do it, no gender parity"; "the only thing that counts is *el pueblo*"; "we don't care how many women and men—we can work together"; "whoever has resources should be the basis of participation"; "we're not into this—this is your struggle." Their hostility was "enormous"; reportedly, most in the audience booed.

Consensus was never reached: "Not one North American got up and challenged" the Central American women's position. Women explained that they didn't want to divert attention from other issues; it would have been "suicidal" if they had "taken on the issue then." That "nobody wanted to deviate from the issues at hand," however, demonstrates the fundamental lack of power of women religious. In the sense that they left important issues and hard feelings unresolved, they lost their struggle. In another sense they won; the group finally "had to" accept gender parity because North and Central American women together outnumbered the men, who lacked a quorum.

Women perceived this division as an issue of gender versus ethnic equality. Josie claimed that North American women's economic autonomy made feminism a "very symbolic" issue, and she considered the refugees' response a "real put-down." Kim found it "frustrating" and "disappointing" to have a "very painful" issue "trivialized." As Rose explained, "We don't want to help restructure a system where women don't have parity."

Central Americans, however, were concerned about parity between themselves and North Americans; some had experienced North Americans as "racist." They didn't see feminism as "part of their survival" and felt that it was being "shoved down their throats." Josie noted that Guatemalans were particularly concerned about parity with Salvadorans, who tend to be more middle-class and "Ladino-ized," or European: "Salvadorans are . . . more assertive culturally than Guatemalans. They're organizers from the womb. Guatemalans retain a lot of passive, gentle Indian characteristics."

Women's level of awareness of Central Americans' positions reveals connections they made between related issues of sex, class, race, and culture. For example, Josie distinguished women's equality from "more basic" issues of survival: "I think when you're fighting for your life, engaged in life/death situations in a revolution, gender differences break down. . . . They'd look at our demands as a lot of white middle-class foolishness."

Rose compared the issue to black women's mistrust of white women's collusion in oppression. She noted that Central American women may find men's behavior "troublesome" but that their attitude doesn't necessarily translate into feminism and the making of gender-based decisions; she termed their position "liberal sexism." Conceding that patriarchy may seem less oppressive in the context of a "larger global struggle," Kim noted an important difference in North and Central American women's relation to the church: "For them, the movers are the priests who started the base-community movement and were killed. Their preoccupation is not to fight the church but to make the revolution, and the church is making it happen."

This confrontation epitomizes women's problems with power. It shows the ways in which their leadership concerns raise issues of class, culture, gender, and race and the degree to which their awareness of these issues is related to their understanding of larger political processes. It suggests that the movement may restrain women's leadership and that women's leadership may help enhance or resolve conflicts over the issues. It also indicates a wide gap between North and Central American women's conceptions of their roles in the movement and as agents of social change.

OUTREACH

Women take part in two kinds of outreach activity in the sanctuary movement: formal speaking, the public work of accompanying the refugees and speaking on their behalf; and informal persuasion, the private work of educating others in everyday life. Some do the former and all do the latter. Outreach activities rely heavily on women's access to informal social networks, closely resembling the other hidden work they do as volunteers in their communities. Using formal and informal settings on the refugees' behalf, they tended to "see [their] role as a bridge" between the refugees' cause and "good local church people" who, if they knew what was going on and how to help, "would do so."

Women stressed that the important issue in "the public work" was "the war in El Salvador and Guatemala." Rather than "offer a harsh critique," the goal was to "talk about suffering and how to stop it." They described their pedagogy as a way of educating the public which, instead of arguing "dogma" and "sterile theoretical issues," "personalized" the refugees' stories and conveyed their viewpoint and meanings to the audience. As Jackie said, "the goal was to personalize the story. 'It's happened to this person; because of your apathy and government's policy, this person has suffered this.'"

In discussing the work of getting the refugees' stories to the public, women related important political acts in which the refugees' testimony became a new source of knowledge. For example, Donna recalled an outreach event in which her group accompanied the refugees to speak in a farming community:

> At first [the listeners] asked questions about the role of Communism in the refugees' fleeing El Salvador and Guatemala. They didn't know the difference between any Central American countries . . . they thought these were Communist-backed countries. We said, "Wait til our speakers get their story out." Afterward they were amazed at the parallels in the refugees' situation and their own lives—their relation to the land and

the forces of agribusiness. . . . They said, "We've got the story straight—we understand now." . . . The refugees got a standing ovation. . . . The people were really with them.

Women described making the refugees visible in the same ways that feminists make women visible by "giving their voices a platform"; as one put it, "we have to speak with them." However, Megan feared that the public responded primarily to their sensational stories; that making them "show all their scars and tell all these terrible things that have happened" was "exploitative."

Some women indicated that they would continue outreach work even in the refugees' absence. For example, one noted that while people "do more resistance" once they've been "touched" by the refugees' stories, many had been "outraged" during the Vietnam War when no refugees were present. Another remarked that even if the refugees received amnesty, their efforts were "not going to stop."

While the more politically oriented engaged in formal outreach, all women described using opportunities in everyday life to educate others informally about the movement's issues. As Jane explained: "I don't assume I can tell by looking at someone whether or not I can talk to them about sanctuary. I don't believe in writing people off." And Jackie described how in the cloak of being a "nice person," she can "gently bring people along. . . . My tactic is rather devious. I attempt to relate to people as just a regular human being so maybe they can understand the things I do. It's manipulative, but it . . . seems to work."

Revealing her plan of "very informally" educating some women friends by "opening their eyes" to the refugees' situation, Jeannine indicated the importance of intimate relationships in solidarity work[7] and her somewhat biased view of gender:

I have these friends who are very apolitical and uninvolved. I want to open their eyes through conversation. . . . My women friends are very humanitarian, very connected to people. If moved by someone else's story, they'd be more apt to write a letter or vote. They're easier to influence than their husbands.

It's the relationship. If I were to go to them and say, "Here's the scoop," they'd believe me. The men would be much more skeptical. They'd say, "What's your source?" The women would believe me because they know me.

Ginny recalled "gently" exposing her "skeptical" and "patriotic" family to the refugees' situation. Although only a few were receptive, some "very conservative people at least came and saw some refugees." They asked "a lot of questions" but weren't "sympathetic" because of what the refugees said: " 'If your country didn't keep sending arms and money, this wouldn't happen.' They didn't want to hear this."

Women's access to a wide range of middle-class settings helps them reach those who may be unaware of the issues. For example, illustrating how "conversations get started," Dina related how a dinner party became a "forum" for educating others: "We were invited to a symphony orchestra dinner. . . . The host introduced me to people as the woman whose picture was in the paper who was 'arrested tangling with the police.' People were shocked. I said, 'But let me explain!' There are forums that arise out of getting arrested."

Expressing some modesty about their part in the movement, several women indicated the importance of "planting a seed" for others. For example, Jane, highly placed in a large medical organization, had made a point of exposing her co-workers to the refugees' cause, enduring their curiosity and labeling until the seed took root. Her insistence that "we shouldn't write people off" represents another convergence of democracy and feminism:

The day we made the sanctuary decision, I was on TV. The support staff at the office all saw me. One said, "I saw someone on TV giving an illegal alien a loaf of bread who looked just like you." They think I'm crazy. But this woman recently told me she saw a program about El Salvador and said, "I feel really sorry for these people." Another guy accidentally checked out the film *El Norte* and said, "I never realized that's what was going on." . . . They saw me come back from El Salvador. I talked about that, and about the refugees at [the church]. Not pushing it but sort of putting it out there. I wear a weaving from Guatemala over a black turtleneck in winter, and people ask me, "Where did you get this?" And I tell them. I'm like this. And I don't write people off. I may never be a leader, but I'm always going to be planting these little seeds, even if I never know what happens to [them]. I have faith that people's hearts can be turned from hard to soft and their ears opened.

Women's outreach activities take place in a culture notably open to grassroots collaborative networking. Eva, a French-born woman, stressed American culture's conduciveness to emergent community-based movements. She called the French left's more theoretical approach "very macho" and "incredibly cynical" about "seeking support and community"; because it "starts at the top without the input of little people and women and other groups," it unintentionally keeps people out. Noting how "little people in the U.S." work together toward "political goals regardless of political fences," she raised and brought together the issues of secrecy versus democracy and women as a rising class. Including women among the "little people," she perceived the openness of American culture as a window of opportunity for their ascent.

TRANSLATING

Women play a special role in the movement as translators at both informal and formal events. Women's bilingualism, like spare time or organizing skill, is a resource that shapes the character of their participation, as Eva indicated: "Roy was more or less the head of the sanctuary committee. But during my year of intense involvement, I did much of the work. Roy has a day job, whereas I'm free in the day, have a car, and speak Spanish."

More women than men in the Chicago movement speak Spanish, and those who do are closest to the refugees. Some learn Spanish through interacting with the refugees, as Donna had done: "I knew the most Spanish so I've been the translator. I learned my Spanish there. I don't read or write it; I just speak it."

Bilingualism enhances women's tendency to interact informally and develop close, familial bonds with the refugees. In contrast, men's lack of bilingualism accentuates their more formal "task-oriented" approach. Margaret noted the importance of "presence and friendship" in working with refugees:

> My way of doing sanctuary work is very different from the men's. I'll go over to the refugees' home just to be there, to be part of their family. They tease me, that I'm their oldest daughter. The men are very task-oriented. They won't go for no reason. One fellow relates to them as a doctor, but he doesn't just wander into their house to chat. Bob goes over to plan and organize. It's partly because I speak Spanish and am around all day.

Women also predominate as translators at the formal outreach events where refugees tell their stories to the public. Some observed that women interpret more perceptively than men, especially for women refugees. For example, Andrea sensed that male interpreters "don't get into the feeling level of what's being said." Donna concurred, although she believed that the problem was partly that audiences pay greater attention to white males:

> The way men interpret really bothers me. Something gets lost of a woman refugees' story. I've seen men sit there crossing their arms, looking up at the ceiling or sideways at a refugee woman while she was speaking, then interpret like "She said this, but I don't necessarily agree." At the same time, I think people just respond more to male speakers. So the refugee woman's experience gets lost when people hear it come out of a white male—they focus on him.

Political orientation helps determine who translates for the refugees in public. Interpreters are screened for their fluency and understanding of the issues. Translating is a political act that unscreened translators can sabotage by failing to convey the refugees' meaning, as Christine illustrated: "We had a speaking engagement at [a hospital that] provided a translator. [The refugee] said later it was a lousy job; they weren't in the same political bag. [The refugee] suspected it but couldn't follow the English. Finally a man in the audience stood up and complained."

At one site, a woman's comment that "the refugees are very particular about who translates for them" reflected the importance of their voice in the matter. At another site, Donna and a volunteer consulted the group before selecting the interpreters. "Assessing" translators' skills, they channeled those with "social skills" toward informal caretaking activities and those with "good critiques" toward outreach: "We assess people's skills and ask . . . for what we need. Some have social skills and are good at picnics, with kids, or translating. I try to channel those without good critiques toward these activities. I'm responsible to the refugees."

Women's bilingualism, then, is a vital component of their outreach activities. It links them closely with all movement activities, contributing to their work as invisible facilitators in the movement. Translating raises sensitive issues about giving the refugees a voice and conveying their point of view, bringing together women's concerns about feminism and democracy.

CIVIL DISOBEDIENCE

Most women reported having participated in civil disobedience, or "CD", as part of their sanctuary activism.[8] As noted earlier, twenty-four of those interviewed had taken part in demonstrations, and eight had been arrested. Examining their activism helps understand women's part in protest movements in general. This is important because until quite recently, stereotypic images of activists have relied almost exclusively on male models. Women have invariably been cast as passive or emotional; their activism is often attributed to their attachment to activist men. Ignored as both deviants and political actors, women have been assumed less deviant and more conventional than men. Such an assumption overlooks women's noncriminal protest behavior and fails to recognize their influence on changing norms.[9] Sanctuary women's activism challenges these images and suggests new ways of perceiving women's deviance.

Women's predominantly white middle-class backgrounds are both assets and liabilities to CD. Their status protects them somewhat from police violence and legal reprisals yet keeps them from being arrested when they intend to be. Reactions to women's CD represent the extreme of officials looking the other way, informally condoning or denying women's openly deviant and illegal acts.

Women generally attend planned "actions," which create public forums and sometimes include arrest. Actions range from handfuls of participants at local demonstrations to tens of thousands at mass rallies. Women told of taking part in picket lines at local libraries and post offices, walkathons, sit-ins and "die-ins" (playing dead) at the INS office, and mass marches in Washington. Protest actions took place at annual military parades downtown and at a fund raiser for a visiting contra leader. A licensed rally at a suburban park preceded an unlicensed march on a nearby military base. The most common illegal act was "protesting without a license." Others were lying down in front of tanks at military parades, digging graves and planting crosses in front of military bases and the White House, and "jumping the fence" at a military base. Nothing more intrusive or violent was reported.

Actions are clearly forms of outreach. Women attending actions described talking to hecklers on the sidelines and engaging passersby in streets, courts, and jails in conversation about the refugees' cause. Belinda distinguished sanctuary activists from other kinds by their "concerned" style: "Sometimes you go to these rallies and there are people who must have been beaten by their parents. These people are angry. But in the case of sanctuary, it's concerned people." Dina related her strategy of selling the issues to bystanders as a way of "being on their side": "People say, 'We don't need more refugees here.' I say, 'That's my point!' Then I explain why they're here and agree that we have to change that." Kim described talking to "lots of people along the way": "There are a lot of women of the streets in jail. One asked us, 'What did you do?' I said, 'We put our bodies in the wrong place.' She said, 'so did I.' "

Participants risk arrest by taking part in any unlicensed action, and most women clearly viewed getting arrested as a desirable outcome. Most reported trying but failing to be arrested; only one described being arrested without trying. Some refrained from CD, however, for a variety of reasons. For example, Moira, a college professor, indicated that such activities could interfere with her career: "It's hard to keep a job and go to jail." Others expressed personal fears about being deviant in public or being part of an activist group. Ginny claimed that she couldn't "go to the armory to protest" and had "never gone out and marched on the street." Pam feared demonstrations and didn't like "what happens in a crowd." Those avoiding CD often implied that they were more valuable "behind the scenes," engaged in women's "normal" political ac- tions. As Ginny remarked, "I'm not being immodest, but taking care of the refugees is what I do well." Pam considered herself "very much a behind-the-scenes person" who enjoyed "pulling strings."

Some of those more reticent women did participate in peaceful, licensed actions. Ginny claimed that she had fasted and stood out- side the post office but "not being a very aggressive person," she found it difficult, for example, to "pass out literature to hostile people." She belonged to no antiintervention groups; although she described people who did as "wonderful," she preferred to do "sup- portive things" instead. She had gone to three "prayer vigils" down- town where "they sing, break bread, and give speeches." When the group was asked to leave and some sat down, she left: "that's how brave" she was.

Most women described being introduced to CD by friends or family members who invited them to demonstrations. The personal dimension of their involvement seems quite important. For example, Charlotte related attending her first action with her husband and brothers. Others were initiated through local "affinity groups," small support groups that teach passive resistance skills, help coor- dinate actions, arrange carpools, and raise bail for those arrested.

Jeannine remarked that she and her husband would probably not be arrested together "because somebody'd have to bail you out"—"a nice thing about being in an affinity group."

Women are often deeply moved by their first action, which can create a well of energy fueling their subsequent involvement. For example, Jeannine vividly recalled her first demonstration, which she attended with her husband and in-laws. She wore no bra "for the first time," and a heckler called her a "flat-chested . . . Commie pinko." She was "pissed," but this "really stood out" as a turning-point in her activist career:

> My first demonstration was actually a walkathon but had all the flavor of a demonstration because we were chanting. We all walked together. We began downtown and walked all over the north side. That was the first time I'd participated in an action. People with megaphones would ask, "What do you want?" The group would yell, "Peace!" They'd yell, "When do you want it?" We'd yell, "Now!" In English and Spanish. Before the Republican headquarters we chanted, "Ronald Reagan, he's no good! Send him back to Hollywood!" And "Stop the bombing, stop the war! U.S. out of El Salvador!" I got called a Communist—I wasn't wearing a bra . . . and he made a remark about how small my breasts are. [Laughs] Don't get me wrong, I was pissed.

Deciding to be arrested can be a turningpoint even if arrest doesn't occur, as Lori indicated: "I listened to this tape of my mother's voice in my head—'This'll be on your record!' But I went ahead and did CD and didn't get arrested." Thereafter, she no longer tried to be arrested, because she planned to work in El Salvador one day. The day she left for Costa Rica, she attended a demonstration and watched a friend "being arrested and dragged away," deciding then to avoid arrest in the future. This indicates that CD and travel to Central America, two important movement activities, may have conflicting requirements and goals.

Most women who had been arrested had been cited more than

once. Dina described one arrest in her senator's office, from which she was "dragged and dumped by the police," and another at a fashionable downtown mall at Christmas. Andrea's account indicates the religious character of her activism and a sense of how she assessed different actions:

> We blocked the street before the State Department. We sang and prayed. . . . When we got to jail there were thirty women in a cell. There was a sense of solidarity. At the [army base] demo, [six of us] buried a coffin in front and planted crosses. If we had been arrested, it would have made more sense to me than jumping the fence or spray-painting.

Women can easily avoid arrest: their actions are generally non-violent, and the rallies they attend are often licensed. Arrest is therefore an intentional choice and political act. "[My husband] and I have been talking about what would move us to make that decision," said Jeannine. "I think we're getting closer because of the contra aid vote. It if passes, we'd both allow ourselves to be arrested—or if any of these yahoos get pardoned."

Women often cited instances when they could have been arrested but weren't, even after having made the difficult decision and plans for legal support. Charlotte, for example, remarked that "it took a lot of guts to do CD," but when she did, the police would not arrest her:

> It was a demonstration downtown at the post office. We wore tags with names of the dead in Central America. We poured ketchup on ourselves. . . . We had flowers which we tried to give the police, but they wouldn't take them. Finally they asked us to leave or be dragged out.

Some women reportedly found it "very difficult" to get arrested even at unlicensed actions—another case of officials looking the other way. Jackie "couldn't believe" how far her group was able to go at an INS office "kneel-in":

> We went in at closing, draped the INS desk like an altar, and had communion services. I was committed to staying until I

got arrested, but they wouldn't arrest anybody that day. We had speakers and communion bread from all over the world to symbolize the peoples of the world, consecrating the INS desk as an altar with candles. I couldn't believe they let us do this stuff.

Relating a scene from a different action at the INS office, Dina confirmed the unlikelihood of women's arrest:

We circled the Federal Building chanting against the contras, then had a sit-down candlelit vigil at the INS office of fifty to sixty people. We were intimidated by the huge space of the lobby. A guard said, "You can't light candles in here." He said, "I'm afraid you can't have this here—you don't have a permit. Why not get a permit and come back tomorrow?" The group just kept singing. At that point some . . . went outside to avoid arrest. About thirty . . . stayed in a circle sit-in. About eight to ten police arrived with wheelchairs. They put the people who resisted in them and pushed them outside. We were last. The officer said, "Stay close to me and you'll be okay," so we knew we were being arrested, but when we went outside, everyone was let go.

Kim's experience on Armed Forces Day when her group was locked up and about to be released illustrates the "patronizing" reluctance of the police to arrest women: "A man with real long hair forgot his driver's license. The commander said, 'You can all go except this man.' I said, 'I don't have mine either.' They were going to overlook this—a patronizing thing. As a result they put all of us in for about five hours."

Only Christine recalled being "unintentionally" arrested: "We were at [a mall] . . . singing alternative Christmas songs. I wasn't one of those lying on the floor doing novenas. I thought I was merely being escorted out by the police."

The fact that making a decision to be arrested appears to be harder for women than for men, even though the consequences are generally less serious, reflects the conditioned fear of being deviant in public.[10] Women expressed many fears about CD, particularly fear of police brutality. One remarked that the police are "always rough at the annual military parade." Another described avoiding CD at some demonstrations after seeing a friend "roughed up." Kim recalled Josie's and her treatment by plainclothesmen at a military parade: "Josie and I put our hands in front of the tanks and these plainclothesmen . . . ripped us away and said, 'You little bitch.'" Others indicated that the process of deciding to be arrested raised fears about their standing in the community, the possibility of being hurt, and future consequences at work. For example, Christine feared pain and ridicule: "It's a tough decision. It's not the illegality, but being roughed up—the fear of pain . . . and . . . scorn." Jeannine feared the police and getting a record, adding that "children bring in other considerations":

> I'm very afraid of being arrested. My dad instilled in me a very healthy fear of authority figures. . . . And knowing peaceful protest can turn into violent acts, violent response by police is very scary to me. And it's scary to have a record. Will I lose a job because of this? And if we had children, we probably couldn't afford to get arrested.

Not all the women shared these concerns, however. For example, Jackie described using nonviolent passive resistance to avoid a hostile exchange with the police: "The police weren't rough. We were thirty-five bodies piled against a door. They just dragged us away." Some women take comfort in numbers, using the group to shield them from unpleasant exchanges with police. Dina related taking her children to a demonstration partly to keep the police from being so rough: "We weren't doing anything violent. I thought, what an experience for the kids to see. And I thought it may keep the police from being so rough." And Donna claimed that she was never afraid at demonstrations; she found them "really energizing": "I love to go to demonstrations with my husband—they're fun! We have the best sex afterwards!"

Not all women arrested go to trial. Kim, arrested with six hundred others, was cited for "protesting without a permit"—a felony. Her "little strategy" was to refuse to pay the fine but to send a check for the homeless instead:

> You get arrested and they give you a ticket. I wasn't going to pay the fine. I wrote them a letter explaining that the government was guilty, not I, and sent them a check for $25, the minimum court fee, for Mitch Snyder, who's doing a lot for the homeless. In two weeks they sent my check back and said they were dismissing my case.

Josie got a judge and state's attorney who backed the group's constitutional right to commit CD, another case of officials supporting what they might be expected to condemn:

> We happened to get a very just judge. He gave a wonderful statement to the state prosecutor that the court should not be taking up these cases, and to us, that we were within our constitutional rights to do this, and the court cannot take a position but that we represent a growing number of people and that he hoped these arrests wouldn't deter us from our work. The state's attorney said afterward, "I'm really supportive of your efforts." She had really worked to get them to drop the case. For another arrest on Armed Forces Day, again the judge, a black man, was really just. The prosecutor and police really wanted to get us. The judge had seen this group before. He knew we wanted to be our own spokespeople, so he was going to drop the case. The prosecutor raised a ruckus.

At another trial, however, she received a lecture: "The judge said, 'You could have hurt people by having the police force put in so much manpower. There are murderers and robbers going free!' "

Sometimes the sheer volume of arrests makes prosecution unlikely, as Kim indicated: "I was locked up with six hundred others in Washington and they kept us on a bus, all handcuffed. If you have small hands, though, you can get them off." Overall, repercussions for women's CD are light. For example, Dina told of wanting a hearing but choosing to pay a fine instead so that she could leave the country. Andrea complained about the low personal risk of CD for those like herself, indicating a recognition of and contempt for her class privilege:

> It was very staged—more of a performance. We sang and they gave warnings and arrested us for not dispersing. They held us a couple of hours and released us on I-bonds. It was like a game for a wealthy person to take this out and get national press for the issue. The second time we could pay a $50 fine or stay in jail for three days. I paid the fine—again, a wealthy person's way of making a statement and not following through.

Jane doubted the effectiveness of demonstrating in the 1980s and about the motives of those doing so: "Are we doing it to vent frustration or to help get people to see things differently? Are demonstrations effective in the 1980s? I used to go to all of them, and now I don't have any answers to what works." A turningpoint was realizing the limits of her work: "It wasn't until we had a workshop on civil disobedience that I realized, wait a minute, all my sanctuary work is CD."

Arrested more than the others—seven times in three years— Geselle discussed the highlights of her arrests. She was concerned about arrests coming too close together as a result of a new policy in which two or more offenses may be tried together. She seemed to be at a further stage of commitment, one that may generally divide women religious from others. She no longer feared arrest, and had somewhat overcome the fear of being deviant:

> It used to bother me when we were plastering stickers all over the Federal Building, after all those years as a teacher lecturing against graffiti. But what the U.S. is doing to Nicaragua really goes against my stomach too. . . . The support group said they'd pay the fine, but I'm not going to pay it. After all, look at what the CIA does.

Women religious were especially active in CD. All had been active on prior issues and merely continued such activity in the sanctuary movement, indicating their decidedly political orientation and commitment to social action. For example, Kim linked her extensive activism to having "done CD, had trials, and gone to jail" over other issues—"foreign policy and the nuclear issue." Lori noted feeling "cheated" during seminary if she wasn't "in a demonstration at least once a week." Leslie recalled having gone to "tons of demonstrations" by the time she left seminary.

TRAVEL TO CENTRAL AMERICA

Of the seventeen women who reported having traveled to Central America—primarily El Salvador, Guatemala, Honduras, and Nicaragua—most had gone as part of an effort to "turn the railroad around," an allusion to slaves' passage north in the nineteenth-century underground railroad. Such efforts involve two kinds of "mission": "personal witness"—observing conditions in these countries and reporting them in outreach efforts at home; and "accompaniment and repopulation"—going back with refugees displaced by warfare to help them repopulate their villages. While overlapping somewhat, these missions are marked by increasing levels of travel, risk, and commitment, representing developmental stages in women's activist careers. Laywomen tend to predominate in the first stage, women religious in the second. Participants face two kinds of difficulties: high levels of personal fear and risk, and a variety of conflicts surrounding issues of sex, class, race, and culture. The women's narratives reveal how they coped with their fear and to what extent they defined and resolved the conflict, indicating their humanitarian and political orientations in the movement.

Jackie's trip to Nicaragua with her minister husband and teenage son was typical of missions of personal witness involving low-level risk. The family "did a lot of soaking up of what's going on"; their purpose was to come back and "have an influence" because they had "been there." Before leaving, they conducted a twelve-week class on Nicaragua for their Sunday School, "so they'd understand." The family planned its own trip, staying "only on the West coast, not near contra fights." They went to churches and met with the Minister of Culture—"a very famous liberation theologian." They also met with "community and rural people, trade unions, family and school co-ops, and humanitarian agencies." Back at home, they gave talks and slide shows in the church and community for about four months, until "things kind of petered out." Although "nobody became an activist," the presentations were apparently well received.

On a mission of personal witness with a friend in El Salvador, Lori faced unexpected fear and risk when she nearly caused an "international skirmish."

> The fear was so pervasive, I didn't want to leave the apartment. I'd wanted to go out, see the base communities, meet pastors. But I was too afraid. On Sunday we went to a church that has three ministers in exile. A woman was going to take us to a liberated zone the next day. When she saw me, she said, "I don't know if I want to take an American there. I'd be putting them in danger." If the guerrillas were to kill me, there'd be an international skirmish. She said, "If she goes, we can't spend the night." As it turned out, I got deathly ill and couldn't go.

She had allayed her fear and absolved her sense of responsibility by developing a "sick role."[11]

In a case involving both personal witness and accompaniment and repopulation, Jane traveled to El Salvador with her church group. Either extremely brave or else unaware of the dangers she faced, she reportedly went largely because her minister, a special catalyst, told her, "You ought to go down there." They met human rights groups and the "mothers of the disappeared," visited refugee camps, and spoke with groups whose leaders had been "disappeared." They visited a village where some refugees had attempted to return; bombed out by the army, it was the site of ongoing warfare. Within twenty minutes they were approached by three warring groups—army, civil defense, and guerrillas. Forced to choose sides, at some personal risk, they chose the guerrillas:

> All wanted to know who we were and why we wanted to visit this village. Civil defense and the army said that guerrillas had put land mines on the road. The guerrillas said, "No we haven't. Go on up." So we did. [No landmines but] there was a lot of evidence of bombing—about ten had died. A church was totally gutted out.

Having gone to Guatemala the next year, Jane recalled her surprise at what her life had come to, traveling in war-torn, dangerous countries that she never imagined visiting. This realization represented a turningpoint in her awareness and activism: "I never thought I'd be going to El Salvador—a place of civil war—wanting to be in these environments."

Andrea, who went to Nicaragua on a fact-finding mission with a national peace and justice agency, described a new stage in commitment and risk. Members of her group faced immediate danger when they were fired on and allegedly kidnapped by contras. Her narrative reveals the "excellent job" the agency did in preparing the group for "what to expect and how to respond," how the group handled these dangers, and why the mission required special training:

> We were kidnapped on a boat trip. . . . Eden Pastora . . . put out a statement that we were wolves in sheep's clothing and he'd ordered his men to shoot. . . . I knew we were going into a war zone. The second morning we were fired upon and taken to Costa Rica and held one and a half days. . . . For many of us experiencing gunfire for the first time, we heard the first shot and hit the deck.

Though overcome by sickness and fear on her previous trip, Lori achieved a greater level of commitment and risk the next time she traveled to El Salvador. Rather than nearly causing one, this time she helped investigate an "international skirmish" between a group of "disappeared" North Americans and the Salvadoran army and government. A Chicago antiintervention agency and a church had "commissioned" her as their "delegate," which was a "big part" of her "lessened fear."[12] At a "closing worship," the group

> laid hands on me and sang, "Be not afraid, I go before you always—come follow me and I will give you peace." That was very powerful . . . I felt real protected by it. They said, "You go to El Salvador as our representative, to stand with the people, protecting them from the army." . . . It was an honor to be their representative—they were really standing behind what I was doing. I was their delegate.

The group sent four telegrams announcing her arrival. Along with two nuns and priests, her mission was to investigate the kidnapping and deportation to Guatemala of twenty-four North Americans who had attempted to accompany a refugee group to their village. The attempt had angered the Salvadoran government, which had its own repopulation agenda:

> The North Americans were separated from the Salvadorans and helicoptered to a military garrison and kept one day, then deported to Guatemala. Once deported, there was tons of media attention, but no one knew what would happen to them. There was the fear they'd been gunned down. It took the whole week to learn the reason for their deportations.

The army allegedly wanted to repopulate the area itself, and North Americans accompanying the villagers had "jumped the gun and pissed the government off."

Lori reconstructed the situation from the viewpoint of "the people": "The army is insisting on protecting the villagers, and the people know that's who's killing their numbers." Her group, she said, met with the archbishop, who called the head of the Salvadoran military for permission for them to visit the village. That he could do so illustrates the close ties between the upper levels of church hierarchy, the government, and the military in El Salvador and the tension surrounding the presence and involvement of North Americans, who must be specially handled. Although somewhat frustrated by the patriarchal church, Lori indicated her growing sense of legitimacy and sanction on the mission:

> We met three hours with the archbishop the first day. He called General Blandone, the head of the whole armed forces, to get permission. Otherwise, we couldn't go. We were getting stopped all the time—about twelve times. Once the North Americans got deported, they really cracked down. We arrived three days [later]. We got permission. The permit left my name off, and two nuns just asked the secretary to add it. It had "fathers" in capitals, "sisters" in small [letters], and my name was a P.S. over to one side.

The women who had traveled to Central America reported experiencing a great deal of culture conflict, particularly over gender issues. Acutely aware of sexism, their own assessments clashed sharply with the Latin culture's views of women. For example, Lori recalled walking down a Costa Rican street and hearing, "Hello baby, let me take you home with me." She went to the movies twice with men she "thought were friends" who made passes at her; the fact that they were seminarians "really pissed [her] off."

There was culture conflict with Latin American women as well. Dawn's narrative of how her group "almost got into a fight over feminism" with Nicaraguan "revolutionary" women demonstrates vividly the gap between North and Central American women. Their arguments over birth control and washing machines reflect how differently they see the issues and their roles in larger political processes. What they perceived as the Nicaraguan women's "hostile reaction" placed the nuns in "the imperialist position," a novel and difficult role for them. Echoing the "gender blowout" in Chicago, the two groups struggled over issues of sexism and imperialism. The nuns' questions reveal their extreme gender consciousness. For example, one asked, "What's your reality outside of being a mother?":

She was told, "Our reality is related to motherhood—you can't separate us from our role of being a mother."

Dawn explained her view of the problem:

Nicaraguan women saw the essence of their liberation as integral to the institution of motherhood and the rebuilding of a new Nicaragua. They're saying, "We support motherhood," and liberation will occur historically. They think they're leading the men into a state of raised consciousness. These were very young women. As the result of the revolution, the youth are formulating their own position.

When a nun asked, "Do you see birth control as a means of liberation?" there was a "hostile reaction, as if we'd taken the imperialist position. And a half of their population was lost in the war."

Observing that "all the clothes-washing was done by hand and took days," another suggested using washing machines: "Their response was, 'You're such an imperialist—don't you realize all the parts are made in the U.S.?' There was no appreciation—there was hostility."

Dawn had "no strong impression about feminism" in El Salvador but noted that women were highly active in various organizations working to end the war. She contrasted their predominance in these organizations with the male-based government and military: "The women students headed the organizations and risked their lives to come and speak to us. They appeared the most dedicated and directive in confronting the Duarte regime. By and large it is the women who do the work and were the most committed."

Lori described culture conflicts that emerged among twelve seminarians—half men and women—traveling to Central America. What began in Mexico as differences between four or five "Latin men" and "Anglo women" developed into a split between the "fantasy group" and the "reality group" in Nicaragua as they attempted to adapt to life in a war-torn country.

Early on, they argued about birth control and bilingualism. Lori revealed how Anglo women's gender consciousness desensitized them to Latin women's issues, and how they made conflicts revolve around issues with men: "It started in Mexico with some arguments over birth control. We'd gone to a base community and were asking priests why they insisted on not encouraging birth control in an area where so many babies die because of poverty." The priest's position was, "We can't advocate it," and the group leader,—a Latin male— added: "We can't just take North American culture and throw it at these people. You women can't take your culture and be insensitive to their traditions." Lori felt that "he had no right to say that, because he is a man. The women were talking about quality of life. He's not against birth control but argued that way. It was a typical Latin male argument."

The other "big gender issue" was bilingualism. None of the women in the group spoke Spanish (in sharp contrast with the situation in sanctuary, where few men are bilingual and women predominate as translators), and having to depend on men to trans-late heightened the tension. Women felt "powerless." This illustrates bilingualism's importance in making an international movement: "The men needed to be more sensitive. We were dependent on them to translate. I felt how powerless I was without language skills."

Women also complained about the men's insensitivity to pov-erty and their "paternalism and overprotectiveness" to women. Lori indicated that women claimed for themselves the emotional work of identifying with the poor: "Each day when we'd debrief what we learned, the women bitched that the men talked intellectually, and the women talked emotionally. They'd say, 'It really hurt me to go to that city dump.' As I look back, I see this as a true criticism of the men." Confronted, the men denied their insensitivity. Women spoke up again when they tried to "go off . . . by themselves" and a man "tagged along to protect them": "We felt he was being paternalistic. We would have been fine by ourselves. [When we confronted him,] he didn't take it well. He just didn't think we should go off by ourselves. He kept calling us 'Gals', and we'd say, 'We're women.'"

The group had "kind of patched things up" by the time they

arrived in Nicaragua, where an ideological debate surrounding "reality versus romance" diminished the gender issues. The "reality group" wanted to adapt to and learn from the prevailing war-torn conditions; the "fantasy group" wanted to buffer itself by moving into a hotel. Members of the fantasy contingent were put off by cockroaches, overcrowding, no running water, and not getting their "five basic food groups." They focused their concerns on the health of a pregnant woman in the group, even though she had brought her own food, played down her condition, and allied with the reality side. Conditions in Managua tested the group's level of commitment and threshold for cultural discomfort in a way that separated true believers from those who wanted either to escape or to transcend conflicts. Lori's narrative reveals a new level of consciousness and commitment:

> We stayed at a youth hostel of the Sandinista movement in Managua. It was a nice house. One woman was pregnant. She'd brought dried milk and cheese from Mexico for calcium. She was taking care of herself. The first day, three women said, "We just can't live in conditions like these . . . there's roaches, overcrowding, not enough water—we need our five basic food groups." Just bullshit. We had meat once or twice a week, and tables of food, eggs, people cooking for us. What started as a gender split became an ideological split surrounding reality versus romance. You romanticize "blessed are the poor, blessed are the hungry," but you get there and it's fucking hard to be poor and hungry and listen to stories of killing. The fantasy group wanted to move into a hotel on the second day. The guide said, "You can eat tonight in a restaurant."

Lori went on to tell how she had undergone a sort of conversion experience leading to a new perspective. Facing firsthand the carnage of a war reputedly caused by her country's policies, she was learning to identify the fantasy group as "ugly Americans," whose insensitivity, intolerance, and wastefulness repulsed her. Unable to shield herself from or avoid identifying with them, she at least controlled her "sick role" on this trip:

> I was sick to my stomach—I didn't eat. It was the tension—hearing about how our government is financing this war. A church minister's wife had been raped, and him killed, by the contras. You hear all these things—how difficult everything is—and our guide is apologizing to us because we're not getting our vegetables and sleep. He's apologizing, and I was a part of it, whether I wanted to be or not. That night we had a meeting, and I tried to explain why I was upset. So then this little fantasy group says, "We can do without but we have to think of [the pregnant woman]." She says, "Hey, I'm all right." I was saying, "I really don't want to move into a hotel. I think we're being rude." The big thing was, when we got home from the restaurant, the cook had laid out our whole meal on the table. They hadn't told the cook. It was so rude and typical and American.

A turningpoint came when another group member helped her to reinterpret the situation:

> I tried to talk to [one of the men]. I wept. I said, "I'm a part of this. I came here to learn about Nicaragua. I'm not learning about Nicaragua." He said, "You're learning about North Americans. Maybe that's God's purpose for your being here, to learn about your own culture." . . . That was a turning-point . . . for me. I spent a lot of time [by] myself thinking about what I was learning.

The most estranged moment came at a dinner where broken air conditioning spoiled the fantasy group's prospects for denial and escape, and the group began "congealing into two separate camps":

> It was an interesting experience for the fantasy people to be somewhere and not get what they wanted. Half of us wanted to live in a hostel, and half in a hotel. Then a rich woman had

a big buffet dinner for the group at [a hotel]. The air conditioning broke that day so it was a funny thing.

The split became pronounced in Costa Rica, with no attempt to mend it. The reality group "disassociated" itself from the fantasy group, whose member went shopping. Lori concluded: "The whole trip was very painful. . . . Learning about how Americans act—being part of a group that didn't jell—it was a real learning experience."

CARETAKING

Caretaking is an important activity in the movement but not a major one for many participants. Most are involved in a combination of activities, the least of which is caretaking. Only one woman limited her involvement exclusively to caretaking, exhibiting a purely humanitarian approach. Ginny, who attended a nearby Catholic church, became involved when the Protestant church where she worked as a secretary became a sanctuary. Moved by the refugees' circumstances and their perceived humility and childlike qualities, she overcame her fear of legal reprisals and began inviting them to her home. She described her daily contact with the refugees, and how they won over her family:

> The first time I brought them to my house I didn't do it nobly. I was scared—I didn't want to go to jail. . . . [But] there seemed to be a higher thing—the humbleness of these people. They could have been my own children. My sons had told me, "Don't get involved; you could go to jail." But you see, I saw these people every day. It started to rain as we pulled up. [My son] ran out and carried both babies into the house. So I say it's a matter of being with them.

The sharp class differences she sensed deepened her feelings for the refugees:

> I invited them to see the [Christmas] tree. It was also that I felt how fortunate I was to have this nice house. We had a tree, a fire, a ham in the oven. I was acutely aware of our differences.

My home, where I live, the freedom I have . . . the physical niceties.

At Easter, she took the refugees to a church where a Salvadoran priest celebrated mass. They were "thrilled" to meet him; she had to "pull them away" for a special breakfast she had prepared. An egg hunt organized for the children, however, "went over like a lead balloon. . . . [the] kids didn't know what to do." Having thought of these get-togethers as a "treat" for the refugees, she discovered the irony—the "doubled-edged sword"—that they were only re-minded of their "poverty and circumstances."

That Ginny was deeply moved by their eagerness to communi-cate, their religiosity, respect, generosity, and hospitality, illustrates that "even before behavior occurs, people perform emotional work on their feelings."[13] Her rhetoric was that of a "sentient actor," her emotional vocabulary based on "feeling rules" that defined what she should experience in these circumstances. Viewing herself as the refugees' social better helped mobilize her commitment and actions on their behalf. For example, she wept openly as she recalled how the refugees had prayed for her family: "My three sons and daughter were here. We opened the table and sat around it and prayed. [The refugee mother] said, 'Esta familia,' our family—she prayed for us! I played a tape in Spanish—'The Insurrection'—and we played it over and over."

Invited to dinner at the refugees' apartment, she was deeply touched by their ability to rise above their "grim circumstances" to extend this hospitality:

> She'd made loads of tamales. They had one room with a small kitchen. I thought we'd eat in shifts, but they carried that little table out to the main room. It was beautifully set for four. They gave me the best they had. I asked for a glass of water, and [she] brought it out with a little slice of lemon in it. They were so respectful—they shared every small thing they had. They had a very tiny fan, and it was directed at me. I was treated as beau-tifully as I could be in these grim circumstances.

Ginny's approach to caretaking was humanitarian, her relations with the refugees personal and informal. The "highlights" were their frequent visits to her home for "coffee, music, and company." Her vocabulary of motives reveals that these experiences inspired strong feelings of pity and condescension, which mobilized her commitment. Notably devoid of political meaning, her involvement seemed an assurance of her own good heart and secure circumstances.

THE IMPACT OF BACKGROUND ON ACTIVISM

Women's narratives indicate that in all these areas of their sanctuary participation, they derive enormous power, protection, and resources from their status as white middle-class women. As conventional Americans, they are relatively secure from police harassment and government reprisals. For example, Dina, a married suburbanite with children, considered herself the "perfect person" to be followed "by the CIA or whoever": "I'm completely open. I hide nothing. I have nothing to lose. If anything happened, my neighbors would rally to my defense."

While it protects and empowers, the women's background also isolates them from those on whose behalf they are mobilized and those whom they wish to recruit: "the working class and people of color." Describing this barrier in her outreach work, Donna perpetuated a stereotype about "little people": "We've got to connect with the working class and people of color. . . . Basically we're not trusted. We're a white middle-class movement. If the movement is going to grow it lies there. . . . I liked the farm communities. I'm really interested in these little people."

Women's class-conscious approach may determine whether they "work for" or "stand with" the refugees—a critical distinction between the two orientations. To avoid patronizing those they hope to help, they must give up their own cultural models of organizing and become receptive to the refugees' models. Josie posed this dilemma in terms of "white women's way of doing things" versus "developing a community of resistance":

We're a group of white, middle-class, highly educated women. We keep saying, "If we could just send two hundred nuns to Nicaragua, we could clean it up." We're so highly organized. The hardest thing was the ongoing breaking down of our own cultural models of organizing. But we've made a commitment to learn from the refugees and work with them. The temptation is to think that we know how to do it better. It helped in getting started but was a hindrance in working with the refugees.

Becoming receptive to new ways of organizing takes place slowly and with some resistance even for women religious, who are generally more politically aware, as Christine indicated:

The refugees . . . want more say. Ideas . . . out of places like [a refugee organization] have seemed to me unworkable or unwise, so it's hard for me to support them. I've moved somewhat from this. I don't necessarily know what works. I have more and more respect for ideas which come from the affected community and less need to say "yeah, but." Before, it felt condescending. Now, I don't know what in the hell to do. They know best. I have tremendous respect for their political astuteness.

"Constantly caught" being "white, condescendingly middle-class," she indicated a growing awareness of the refugees' approach to making a movement and a recognition of its legitimacy. She related an experience at a conference in El Salvador in which the refugees had enlarged her awareness beyond her own view: "I said how impressed I was with their global political analysis. The translator looked pained. The answer came—'Only North Americans can afford to be so naive. We have to be more astute . . . to stay out of your way.'" Despite a somewhat self-effacing analysis, she recognized her importance as a "channel" between those like herself and the refugees' cause. Admitting the shortcomings of her role—the "manipulation" and "condescension" that resulted from her being a "white middle-class woman"—she nevertheless viewed it as a resource to be tapped:

> The only power . . . I have is as a white middle-class woman,
> so I want to addresss these issues from that position. . . . I've
> got an entry into the church. . . . There is a power in the
> church to be tapped . . . a white middle class to be chan-
> neled. . . . Basically, my identification is a white middle-class
> woman, but my affinity is with . . . the oppressed. . . . I want
> to claim my right to this position.

The costs and benefits of their background are clearest in these women's high-risk activities of CD and travel in Central America. Women break the law with some impunity, committing deviant public acts to bring attention to the refugees' cause. Yet their background obstructs arrest, as officials almost invariably look the other way. Overcoming fear of police brutality and guilt over public deviance marks development in women's activist careers. So does facing increasing levels of fear, danger, commitment, training, and travel. Resolving culture conflicts and defining their own part in them represents another kind of growth.

Clearly, the movement relies on women in all its activities, since sanctuary is literally produced in the small informal groups in which women predominate. A study of women's role in a hospital union drive confirms the importance of their invisible networks to "making things happen" in movement organizations: even though the official spokespersons were men, certain "centerwomen" became "key actors in network formation and consciousness shaping" by mobilizing already existing "network centers."[14] This closely parallels the influence of women's invisible yet central networks in making things happen in all areas of the sanctuary movement.

The way they resolve the status incongruities of being white, middle-class women involved in a protest movement ultimately determines whether women work "for" or "with" the refugees. Awareness of their own biases and openness to new ways of organizing are important criteria for developing political consciousness—a shift

difficult to make even for women religious. How women successfully exploit the resources of their positions while overcoming the
limitations is reflected in their orientations within the movement.

Linking women's aversion to unshared power with their struggle to be included in decision-making, the foregoing accounts show
how the conflicts women experience are related to issues of feminism
and democracy and to their own troubled ascent in the movement.
Women's sense of themselves as a rising class comes from their
increased self-consciousness as women and growing sense of their
importance in the movement. Resolving the conflicts is an essential
step toward cognitive liberation and developing an activist career.

V

STAGES IN ACTIVIST
WOMEN'S LIVES

The women I interviewed indicated undergoing several stages of development prior to their involvement in the sanctuary movement. Reconstructing their careers as volunteers in a movement organization, they explained how previous religious and political activism had shaped their identities. Tracing turningpoints and changes in their identities over time as they moved through institutional statuses, a "moral careers" approach emphasizes women's "motive reports" (retrospective explanations for changing perspectives and behavior) and "vocabularies of motive" and "situated actions" (rhetorics explaining how they developed shared understandings and mobilized collective actions).[1]

Women described three areas of their lives as influencing their entry into the movement: the humanitarian—their early awareness of social inequality and subsequent caring and volunteerism; the religious—the history of changes over time in their beliefs and institutional affiliations; and the political—the onset of their politicized beliefs and activism. These were parallel rather than successive paths.[2] The women's narratives reveal how "conversion" experiences helped integrate the paths prior to or at their initiation to sanctuary.

HUMANITARIAN PATH

The ways in which these women constructed their biographies generally showed a youthful interest in helping others, awareness

119

of social inequality, and desire for social change. Although these were primarily white, well-educated women from lower- to upper-middle-class homes that were relatively free of hardship, some linked their childhood awareness of how others lived to their eventual sanctuary involvement, contradicting current ideas about childhood development.[3] For example, Dawn recalled at age four "seeing poor kids in church—my first recognition of the injustices of the world. I thought it was terrible. I just thought their mothers hadn't washed and dressed them."

Jane described similar early impressions of the "marginalized" in her hometown and the "common knowledge" about them:

> I always had a curiosity about native Americans. There was a statue in town of one but no living Indians—just plaques marking where they'd been killed. Some Seventh Day Adventists have a place up on the hill, and we called them "bean eaters" because they didn't eat meat. There was a Green Giant plant nearby that drew migrants. "Don't talk to them, don't have anything to do with them" was the common knowledge in town. One winter a woman turned on the gas stove for heat and seven died. Every time I walked by that house I wondered why they had to turn on the gas for heat, but I recall no discussion. They were so marginalized.

Christine identified her early awareness of social barriers between those like herself and the migrant workers at her family's orchard as her "first real up-against-it." Learning later that she was part native American helped her accept feeling different:

> I was raised in [a rural area]. There were migrant workers picking cherries. My family owned a cherry orchard. My first real up-against-it was when my sister and I went to a movie and sat in the back with some cherry pickers we knew. Somebody told my mother, who went livid, crazy mad. I was about eleven. I knew the craziness of that, I don't know why. . . . When I was fourteen my father in a drunkenness let on that I

had a native American great-grandmother. It was "no wonder" for me. I'd always carried bugs outside, sat and watched
the clouds. I didn't immediately align myself with native
Americans, but it reinforced that who I am is okay.

Her immigrant family having escaped from Chicago's stock-
yards to its suburbs, Jennifer indicated that her parents' prejudice
had led to her early awareness of racism and poverty:

My parents were Irish immigrants who grew up in the "Back
of the Yards." Pork was their lives. I see now that they were
very prejudiced people. For entertainment my father would
drive us to poor neighborhoods and point out poor black people and say, "Look at who you are and who they are." Now I
see he was trying to reassure himself that his generation had
taken a step. . . . He was a typical sarcastic Irish type. He'd
tell jokes about blacks. I didn't think he was any different
than anyone else's father. It was a standard thing that everybody's parents were prejudiced.

Women related breaking out of the narrowness of their own
backgrounds and learning to consider human suffering from different perspectives. Many spoke of developing a strong sense of
compassion for and identification with the oppressed, gradually
becoming aware of pervasive structured inequality and their place in
it. Jeannine, for example, recalled: "I always felt compassion for
underdogs. In high school I felt very uncomfortable knowing there
were in groups and out groups. I was usually in-group, which made
me more uncomfortable. I don't know why. . . . It was partly a
religious thing and partly my family."

Jackie reiterated the theme of compassion for underdogs. Crossing race, class, and ideological lines that she sensed were "wrong,"
"unfair," and "baloney," she identified with the "left out," despite
her parents' negative messages about them:

I've always felt for underdogs. I don't know why. When my
mother would say, "Don't drink at that fountain because nig-

gers used it," I knew something was wrong. . . . My father was a landlord, and I always felt sorry for the tenants. . . . I was living in a nice ranch house and was always aware of disparities between how people lived. . . . I remember as a little child always thinking about the person left out—the marginalized. . . . My father. . . . felt those at the low end deserved it and could do something if they tried. . . . I was real affected by the civil rights movement but too young to participate in high school. I remember my father bringing home documents proving Martin Luther King, Jr., was a Communist, showing him sitting with Communists. I remember thinking that it was baloney. I just knew that black people needed a chance—that people had been unfair to black people. I remember not caring that much if King was with Communists. I remember the McCarthy era—watching it on television. But I've just never been afraid of Communism. I'm more afraid of capitalism.

Charlotte, growing up in a "changing neighborhood," noted important "eye-openers" that led to her awareness of prejudice and sense of the gap between others and those like herself:

I grew up on the West side in a changing neighborhood. . . . I went to a Catholic school. The nuns were making efforts to reduce black-white conflicts. They had an exchange program for kids to talk. It was a real eye-opener for me. . . . Many kids I went to school with were very prejudiced. . . . In high school I worked with a group who tutored Puerto Rican kids. It was an eye-opener about education in the public schools. We just knew these kids weren't getting a good education.

Leslie described childhood reading, traveling, and tutoring in inner-city schools as her introduction to others' oppression. And although raised in the South, she believed that her parents had avoided instilling "southern prejudices" in her:

I was exposed to others' oppression through books. I tutored in the inner city in ninth grade. I knew from reading and traveling that not everyone had the same standard of living. I knew there was poverty in the cities. I'd at least been through inner cities. I knew about racism as a child by reading books about black children and by how few blacks were in my schools. Both parents had black servants. . . . I knew the stories of those people. I was raised to think that they were equal but that the social situation was not equal. I was brought up in a way not to share the southern prejudices. I think my parents certainly had an influence not to bring us up with southern values. The tutoring experience was important.

Out of early exposures to and identification with the "marginalized," women indicated developing strong, lasting impressions and feelings of connection and responsibility that became meaningfully intertwined later on. Several unrelated "formative experiences" in childhood gave Margaret a sense of connection with the oppressed and came together in a powerful "conversion" experience in her young adulthood. Her narrative illustrates the women's characteristic eagerness to "do something" about social inequality and the difficulty of overcoming an insular, middle-class life:

When I was growing up I used to go downtown with my dad on the train. Looking at the back porches, I'd be fascinated. I knew how the poor were living was connected to how we were living, but I couldn't put it together. In my childhood we watched TV a lot. One program was a documentary of life in China. There was a long shot of a Chinese woman in a factory putting heads on Barbie dolls. I was nine. I was fascinated. I knew deep inside that was sick and I didn't need to play with Barbie dolls if it meant that woman had to live that way. I cried. The program wasn't about inequality. I connected affluent society and my Barbie dolls with oppression of people in the Third World. My dad tried to comfort me—he said, "That lady has a job; you should be happy." I didn't believe it. . . . I had one other experience as a teenager. I worked in a restaurant where most of the [help] were illegal aliens. It was the first time I'd ever been in contact with the poor. I almost couldn't believe the things they told me, and they weren't even trying to raise my consciousness! Like having thirteen brothers and sisters at home. They lived packed into little apartments together. They worked two full-time jobs and sent home the little money they made. I felt invaded with guilt. I wanted to take them home for dinner. I did once. I took this guy home for Thanksgiving. It amazed me that they wouldn't be eating turkey on Thanksgiving. My mom was nice, but my dad said later they smelled. That whole experience of getting to know these Mexicans . . . I was guilt-ridden about going off to college. I thought, okay, I'll go to college, but I'll study law or something and come back and help these people.

In college, her "social consciousness evaporated" until she "accidentally" toured Belfast, the site of her "conversion." Hiking alone through "profoundly beautiful" Irish countryside, she had "mystical experiences" that "prepared" her for "the Belfast experience." Short of money, she took "the cheaper way" back through Belfast. Meeting some British soldiers on a ferry was her first exposure to the "real" world of "armed conflict." Sharing a truck ride into Belfast with the soldiers, she recalled a "penetrating" sense of its immediacy:

I'd never seen army men. . . . It was a shock. I was fascinated. I sat close and started up a conversation. I asked, "What's it like to be a soldier? What are you doing?" Armed conflict became real for me. The world was becoming real. These guys could be my friends and brothers. I felt pain for them and for those they would injure.

The station was closed and there was a curfew. She accompanied a policewoman who "gave a mini-tour" of "where bombs went off and people fled":

I wasn't shocked by it. It was like someone had torn off a curtain. It exposed . . . the bare bones of oppression. I felt like kissing the ground there. I felt more at home there than here. I felt real. . . . I met my real self and the real world. I had an overwhelming sense of peace in this violent place. It was a powerful experience. My conversion.

Others who had enjoyed relatively comfortable middle-class lives also reported that their initial awareness of oppression had come from outside. They had witnessed unrelated instances of suffering which they later connected. As Charlotte put it, "Once you become aware of oppression in one part of the world, you can make connections in your own back yard. You start seeing it all over. You just become a more critical person."

For members of historically oppressed groups, however, awareness began at home. For example, Hannah, a black woman who had grown up in the South, recalled knowing early that it was "us and them":

My early awareness of what the government was doing was related to blacks. I had to sit in the back of the bus and go to separate schools all my life. This didn't change until I was married with children. We were always in a position to be antigovernment, and we were always labeled Communist. I was never taken in by the government. Even if I never paid attention to international affairs, I was aware of what went on at home. I was never able to put my foot in the city parks of [my hometown] while I lived there. My father was a government employee and mail collector, so he registered to vote in uniform, and they never stopped him. But my mother, they did. We had to pay a poll tax. That was the kind of thing they met, so we were aware it was "us and them."

Two Jewish women recalled their painful childhood awakening to persecution as Nazi atrocities became felt even in their own assimilated lives. Alicia related that upon first learning of this persecution at age four, she lost her belief in God, whose existence she could not reconcile with the immensity of human suffering. Nevertheless, she developed a strong sense of compassion and protectiveness for the "defenseless":

> At some point—I was four, it was 1944—I remember this meeting at my parents' house on how to smuggle this family of relatives out of Hungary. . . . I remember overhearing the fact that the parents were caught and killed at the border. The seven children escaped. Arrangements were being made to smuggle them into the U.S. Later I learned that the children were also caught and killed. . . . All of a sudden I realized that no matter what I'd been told about God, it wasn't true. He did not take good care of us. I just decided if there was a God, that he was a mockery of everything religion makes of God. At that point I became an atheist. . . . I cried myself to sleep for a fairly long time. . . . I was always very protective of anyone who was defenseless or an underdog. I was always bringing home stray animals.

Lena also recalled her first awareness of the persecution of Jews. The connections she made between her assimilated upper-middle-class life and the plight of Jews in Europe repulsed her. Rejecting both the prize and price for her "kittenization," she became a "rebel" and a "maverick." Her early exposure to refugees with "tough stories" set up her "own complex," creating "a certain conflict" in her life which became the mainspring for her tendency to "give a great deal" to social causes, including her "incredibly intense career" as a volunteer:

> My mother's and her mother's goal was to be more American than the Americans. They were somewhat anti-Semitic. I was raised in a home with a Christmas tree. My mother wanted desperately to assimilate. My grandmother, the matriarch of the world, told me, "if you're going to get married, it wouldn't hurt to marry someone with money." When Hitler invaded, my mother said, "Oh oh, Jews are being killed—we must take the tree down and make a statement." . . . [As a result,] I became a

rebel. It was an alienating experience but my maverick experience came from my mother's absolute need to assimilate. I started learning early that there was something else I wanted but I didn't know what. There was a large cedar closet where we kept a family album. I'd go over the pictures and ask about them. I became aware of the fact of some of them being killed . . . [when] my father's relatives were arriving and telling stories. About five or ten came over under my dad's auspices. These refugees were very exciting to me. Dad would bring these people home for dinner. I was fascinated, hero-worshiping these people who'd survived these things. They told some tough stories. Some horror stories were coming through. The ethical issues were real powerful for me. The war didn't physically affect me, because we were a bountiful family. But I'd keep going back to that closet and looking at our relatives I imagined dead. I was still a Jewish-American princess and the recipient of tremendous bounty. I was aware that I was being kittenized. That set up my own complex. At what point do I want to be nothing but? This also set up a certain conflict. That's why I give a great deal to causes I believe in.

These women's emphasis on "doing something" for the "marginalized" notably exceeds their culture's typical care patterns. Feminist scholars maintain that women are socialized to feel personally responsible for others, which predisposes them to characteristically feminine care patterns and to personal ethics based on caring. In this view, women tend to approach moral problems "by placing themselves as near as possible to concrete situations and assuming personal responsibility for the choices to be made." Studies in the sociology of emotion confirm women's cultural predisposition to do the emotional work of caring and relationship management.[4]

This helps explain my respondents' strong orientation toward caring and empathy with others' pain. For example, Jackie saw herself as a "very soft-hearted person" whom things affect "very strongly":

> I have a hard time separating fantasy from reality. When I see
> things on TV . . . I do cry at commercials for long distance
> telephone. My emotions are right to the surface. My empathy
> is strong. This has to do with my feelings for the marginalized.
> And I feel all pain. I get involved . . . when I see a mother
> abusing a child . . . I want to rescue the child.

Jeannine linked her empathy with her mother's death: "I had a deep
compassion for others' pain, but I didn't know where it came from. I
think my mom's death deepened that."

Four women cast their fathers as role models who were important to the development of their own compassion and activism, but
only Andrea specifically mentioned her mother's activism as an
influence. This pattern contradicts studies documenting women's
traditional involvement in charitable work and the likely assumption that they were influenced by socially active mothers.[5] Women in
sanctuary work may identify more with their fathers' activism because of the unconventional, political, or illegal nature of the movement, or because their fathers represented more interesting figures or
had more resources with which to be charitable. Pam's doctor father
"had a great social conscience and was always giving money and
time to charity and things." Belinda's architect father was "very
involved in the community"—"big-hearted but conservative . . . a
role model": "He spoke to the community a lot. I remember him
saying, 'When people come together in a community, we must give
something back.' So I was very active in high school and community
social service clubs." Jeannine linked her father with her "sense of
compassion": "My dad's . . . aligned more with laborers than management even though he moved from a blue- to white-collar job. . . .
He'd joke about being a peon. It helped develop a sense of compassion for me." Charlotte's father introduced her to new people and
ideas: "My father was a great influence on me—always very open to
people. He worked for the post office with a lot of blacks, and many
were friends whom he'd bring home for dinner. Also he had a second
job as a barber in a black barber shop."

Hannah identified with both parents' activism, remembering them as "always involved together" in community activities: "Father was a charter member of the NAACP. He was a pharmacist for fifty years but couldn't become a member of [the state] pharmacological society until the end of his life. My parents were quite active in school and church. Mother had been a teacher till she married and had six kids. She was at meetings every night. I realize now I'm just like this."

Eight women described channeling their feelings for others into volunteer work in early adulthood. For example, Julia found the world of service in high school activities: "In high school we had service clubs. We went to 19th and Loomis and worked in a settlement house on Saturday mornings. The people were Puerto Rican, black, white. I decided then that I wanted to learn Spanish and teach Hispanics." Jeannine also embarked on a volunteer career in high school and recognized that special education would become her profession:

> In high school and college I always seemed to direct my social consciousness toward social service, going to old folks' homes. In college I did volunteer work . . . with a hard-of-hearing class. Most of my compassion was directed toward social services. My special education work is a result of this. I knew I would go into special education in high school. . . . When I got to college I did the volunteer work to get some experience.

Alicia described taking up volunteer work on her own: "When I was about nineteen I decided I was so self-centered, I only worried about myself and I should do something. So I . . . volunteered doing occupational therapy at [the hospital]."

For many, this orientation toward volunteer work had persisted into the present. Lena described the transition: "At [college] I volunteered at hospitals . . . I was a wonderful athlete and it made sense to help kids with cerebral palsy. Even today [my husband] and I are host once a year to social workers from all over the world. I've done this for twenty-five years." Others described their volunteer work as having taken on the character of a career that began when their children were young and kept them close to home. For example, Belinda recalled treating her early volunteer work "like a full-time job": "When I chaired the outreach committee . . . I wasn't working. . . . I was ready for a career but wanted to be home with the kids."

As Dina indicated, however, these unpaid careers were made possible by working husbands:

> [My husband's] getting [his job] changed the whole family system. I didn't have to make the money. This was a deciding factor in getting active. I thought, why work now? My kids were one and three years old. I was a workaholic. A career and a sense of importance through work were important to me. Without the need to make money, I could examine this need.

Pam too linked her long service career as a volunteer to her religion, community networking, and not needing to work:

> When my kids started school I got involved in the PTA. . . . At first I did community service and from there have blossomed into other things. I've been fortunate in that I don't have to work and I have tremendous energy. You can only complain so long, and then you have to do something. My background, being a Jew, aware of humanity and problems, and the fact that I don't work may be part of it. When you get through with this world, you want to know you've left a mark here. . . . I'm a very positive person. I like people. I'm an active person. It's intriguing to do social action and to see things change. I like committee work best. I organize all the soup kitchen work for the synagogue. I've always been very involved in the homeless coalition. . . . And if a woman doesn't work, there's lots of opportunities to do volunteer work. . . . One thing leads to another.

For three of the women, volunteer work was eventually transformed into paid positions after they had demonstrated their capabilities as volunteers over time. Christine compared the merits of volunteering with doing paid work:

> I was asked to become administrative assistant, a position the church never had. My reservations were [that] I didn't need the money. My faith was grounded here in the '60s. I was willing to do it for nothing. But the staff/parish committee said, "If we're to take the women's movement seriously, we must acknowledge women's need to be paid." As a volunteer I could pick and choose what I'd do. "Nobody's gonna tell me what to do" . . . was my illusion.

Lena claimed that a "Ph.D. in volunteering" led to her first paid work: "I had such an incredibly intense career in volunteering until I decided it wasn't enough and created a gifted program at [school]. I didn't get paid for the first two years until I applied for a grant. This was my first formal work." Julia viewed her volunteer work in sanctuary as "entitling" her to paid, socially recognized work: "Sanctuary is not a paying job. I'm not entitling myself to be recognized and rewarded for my work. A professor with a consulting firm realized my experience with refugees and offered me the assistantship in Guatemala. So this has enabled me to get work."

These middle-class women were culturally predisposed to volunteer work. Yet some admitted that middle-class standards of personal cleanliness had caused them culture shock in the course of caring for the oppressed. Pam was at first repulsed by the poor at a soup kitchen:

> I'm not so sure I want to get involved in a hands-on way. I'm more interested in getting involved in an institutional way. At the soup kitchen I do everything—planning, cooking, cleanup—and I'm somewhat compulsive about cleaning anyway. But I don't want to talk to [the poor]. They're so crazy. They run the gamut. It's so pathetic. The first time [I was there], I couldn't eat for hours. [It was] their clothes, how they eat . . . talk . . . smell, all of these things.

Eva found that her empathy helped overcome her revulsion: "In the sanctuary movement there are a lot of shocks and offenses, circumstances of the Third World. Empathy with the oppressed helps overcome these."

Resolving these culture conflicts may influence the character of women's contact with the refugees and the longevity of their activist careers. Overcoming culturally induced feelings of revulsion may affect whether they do traditional volunteer work or more direct "hands-on" social action, an important distinction that affects their developing a humanitarian or political orientation.

RELIGIOUS PATH

Although it overlaps with a larger political movement opposed to U.S. policies in Central America, sanctuary is clearly a religious movement. Founded and led by religious figures, it has been endorsed and sustained by religious institutions and their membership. All the women I interviewed were members of social action churches and synagogues in which they were or had been involved in sanctuary; all indicated entering the movement through affiliations with religious institutions.[6] This study shows them retrospectively situating their changing religious beliefs and affiliations along socially constructed paths culminating in their entry into the movement.

Four women spoke of having lost a faith that they later reclaimed. All left a traditional church early on because of its perceived avoidance of social issues. Becoming politically active outside the church and generally abandoning organized religion as a "barrier" to social change, they rekindled their faith and affiliation later, prior to becoming involved in sanctuary. For example, Jackie left the traditional church as soon as she got to college, finding it irrelevant to life; she returned only when her minister husband was appointed to his first church:

> As soon as I got to college I stopped going to church. . . . It was totally meaningless, steeped in old culture. It had nothing to say about life. . . . When Kennedy was shot, we went to a

[church] memorial service and I took [my husband]. We went back another time, and they wouldn't let him take communion. I was so angry and embarrassed. We were married and went to the seminary. When we graduated, he was appointed to a church, but I don't think we went to church once in three years until we had to.

Donna, a self-described "generic Protestant," recalled her early experience as a fundamentalist "real alienating." Frustrated over trying to make her faith "real," she withdrew:

In high school I got involved with [an organization that] was all fundamentalist theology. That was the first time I had studied the Bible. I got good at faking it, using my experience but their language. I came to call it "navel gazing." I had a lot of trouble at that point. These were my best friends. They'd say, "Do you believe or not? Why these other issues?" [But] the book of James says you need to make your faith concrete in actions in the world. You have to make it real.

She "either quit or was kicked out" and took a degree in religious studies "as a sort of reaction against [the] church." This was "not altogether satisfying," since she "lacked a community of people," so she entered seminary. On learning that the school supported investments in South Africa, she was "so offended" that she left both the seminary and church: "This was the catalyst for my leaving. It was also [a fundamentalist group, with] house churches, et cetera. I said, 'I'm never going into a church again!' I was sick to death."

Jennifer described the sense of stability and comfort the church had provided during her adolescence, helping her cope with parental alcoholism and death. Under the tutelage of school nuns, she began her career as a volunteer caring for the oppressed—a pattern she sustained long after a "life-threatening illness" caused her to see the church as "a lot of nonsense":

My parents were both alcoholic so [the Catholic] school was a stabilizing thing in my life. My dad had his first heart attack at thirty-seven and was sick five years before he died when I was fifteen. So I always had a base of comparison with others' problems. In the Catholic church they always stress our responsibility to the poor. We'd have food and clothes drives at Christmas. In seventh grade I was sent to deliver the goods in a black and Puerto Rican neighborhood. I saw how desolate it was. In high school we got talks about "You have a responsibility to the poor—you can make a difference." My dad died, my brother was in the army, and I could drive. A nun recognized that I had a lot of freedom and decided she'd channel my energies into some positive form. She had me stay after school every day. She would just have me do errands with her. It was a real positive influence on me, going to different places, seeing different sections of the city. I was struck by the poverty of it all and the Christian response, that God loves these people too.

For a time after a cancer operation in college, however, she felt "very different from everyone else." Out of the "natural rebellion" of youth combined with "wondering why God gave [her] this illness," she withdrew from both theological studies and church.

Jane described a fundamentalist upbringing in which "going along with the program" was expected. Becoming aware of "race issues" in college "brought forward a whole different reality," and she began to see the traditional church as "a real barrier" to change. As a summer intern in Chicago, exposure to "being poor and black" turned her "off to organized religion," which she identified as "contributing to people's oppression":

I was a star helper as a child—Sunday school, choir, church helper. We were expected to buy it hook, line, and sinker. There was no environment in which to discuss "do we believe in God?" I never was exposed to issues of peace, justice, that kind of stuff. I went off to [a denominational] college. We had to take basic Bible. I'd been taught that the Bible was the word written by God, literally—that to play around with it is to play with fire. At Christmas I'd tell my mom, "What you think is crazy—we can trace this stuff to four different sources." She'd say, "Here we send you to this college and you come home and say the Bible was written by men, not God." I didn't talk much to my mom about it, but I took some courses. The guy who taught religion and society had us look at race issues. He'd say that Sunday at church is the most segregated day of the week. I became very critical of the traditional church because I saw how very hypocritical it was. I saw you could be a good person without going to church, that there were other ways to work with the poor—advocate for the poor and create a better system. I didn't see at all how traditional religion would facilitate this. I saw it as a real barrier. I spent one whole summer in the inner city interning at a church that had an all black congregation with a white old minister. We got critical of him. I decided this approach was contributing to people's oppression rather than helping.

Two women described developing faith they had previously lacked. Though their early religious experience had been devoid of personal meaning, they were later "captivated" by a faith fraught with "mystery" and symbolism. Brought up Catholic, Margaret's "consciousness had grown past it"; in college, exposure to contemporary religious thought "softened" her toward the church and interested her in the idea of women's communities. Then through a book about nuns she discovered that "there was somebody or something on the other side" pulling her; she wasn't "abandoned in this universe without meaning." Her prior "social experience" "just connected inside":

> In my last semester of college I took a course on feminism and religion. I was interested in feminism, not spirituality. It softened me. I was very bitter toward the Catholic church. My family was a good churchgoing family, but we had serious troubles, and the church seemed unconcerned. I was very aware of the Vietnam War and other vital things, but they

weren't talking about these in church. I was having some gen-
uine insights into meaningless church life but not enough insights to know not to throw the baby out with the bath water.
From the course, I became interested in the idea of women's
community. That summer I picked up a novel about a group
of nuns, still with a chip on my shoulder. I wanted to see how
the patriarchal church was oppressing them and making them
serve out its own ends. Ten pages into the book I realized
there was something more. When I read that this woman
could see beyond things and feel a loving pull, that was my
experience all my life. It was the first time I deeply realized
that I wasn't alone. I recognized my own calling through this.
I discovered all these social experiences were completely intertwined on their own.

Jeannine also indicated her early alienation from the traditional
church and a small-town congregation of farmers who "took the
mysticism out of religion." Her college friends were Catholic, and
she found it "much more fun to go to Newman Center" than to a
Protestant church by herself. She formally joined the church when
she decided that it was "time to stop being a closet Catholic." She
described a sense of "mystery and ritual" surrounding her new
faith—"something very distant but known"—which she found
"captivating." This renewed her "very literal interpretation of the
gospel," with an added politicized dimension: "This is where I value
my early religious fundamental upbringing. . . . Christ was very
clear about what we're called to do as part of a family of believers.
That's what a lot of people in church are saying. He said a lot of
things about politics and government."

Three women explored other denominations than their own by
attending different churches. All identified their parents with the
church, making conscious choices between their parents' and other
denominations before ultimately choosing one compatible with
their parents'. For example, Gina, born in China to fundamentalist
missionary parents, described "breaking away" in young adulthood

from her parents' "theological conservatism" and her "very closed and restrictive upbringing." She saw this not as "a rejection of the church but a fresh look at faith," which had "always been an important part" of her life:

> Breaking away from this . . . upbringing and going to a secular university was a real growth. A late bloomer, I had very much adhered unquestioningly to my parents' religious background until then. That break was a sense of my really taking my life into my own hands and making a decision. Their religious platitudes were unrelated to reality. I'd begun to taste who God was in new ways. . . . It hasn't been a rejection and a jumping off into nothingness, but evolving to alternatives.

Andrea also described changing affiliation without losing faith or leaving the church. Although she "grew up in" and "never broke with the church," she just "joined [it] this year." Church was "very important" to her mother, who was "so excited" that she had formally joined: "I grew up in a white suburb but went to the church downtown. It was my mother wanting us to know everyone wasn't white with green lawns. She coordinated a center downtown that ran shelters for the homeless and soup kitchens. I remember thinking, why can't we just go to the neighborhood church like everyone else?" Going "rarely to church during college," she attended Quaker meetings because Quakers were "more active," but she "didn't know what to do" with the lack of structure. She has since moved "to the left of both parents" while maintaining "their support, so there's been no break with either parents or the church."

Lori recalled her "double life" growing up in a poor neighborhood and attending an elite religious school. Her father taught her nondiscrimination; her mother, to be of a better class. This set up her early sense of "doing class analysis," helping to foster a hatred for elitism and a desire to stand up for others. Torn between her neighborhood's "unhealthy path" and her "prissy and proper" school role, she "broke away" from the school at about the time she decided to become a minister:

My parents wanted the best for me. I went to a private Christian school. Starting in seventh grade I started not liking it. I analyzed it many years later. My parents couldn't afford to send me to this school, so my mom drove the school bus, and we lived in a relatively poor neighborhood. These kids were real rich. I'd felt since seventh grade that I had this double life. I lived in a poor neighborhood and went to this rich school. We'd go out with neighborhood kids and smoke and drink. Then at school I had to be prissy and proper. If I'd stayed at school I'd have gotten into cocaine. I'd have seen that the rich kids weren't what they were cracked up to be. I began noticing differences around seventh grade. I made a clear intention to break away from the neighborhood group. I felt the path I was on wasn't healthy. Older kids were being arrested, getting pregnant. So I broke away . . . I had arguments with my mother because I wanted to leave the private school. I felt I was leading two lives. I reached a point where I just hated it. Looking back, I was doing class analysis. I saw these rich kids stood for things I didn't want to be a part of. They had black maids. I felt my mom wanted me to go there to be of a different class than [she was]. We had a big fight. I said I wouldn't go back. She was afraid I'd become scum of the earth, but I didn't. I stayed in church from ninth grade on. I never really left it.

Six women indicated that they had neither lost, lacked, nor changed faith; despite their criticism and frustration, they made smooth transitions to activism within traditional religious institutions. This pattern particularly characterizes nuns, devout Catholics, clergy, and Jewish women. Nuns tended to have entered the convent as young women without a break in faith or affiliation. Dawn entered the convent "too young," as she put it, "right after college at age twenty-three." Though critical of the church, she never left it: " I never really considered myself not a Roman Catholic. I felt the leaders were misguided. I don't know what constitutes staying. I never did the required things but never considered myself a fallen-away Catholic. I feel there's something salvageable in the church."

Megan too remained in the church. She had always felt that she "had to look for what [she] wanted," and the church's institutional limitations never deterred her. She may not have followed all its rules but considered herself "as much a Catholic" as she was "American, middle class, and white." The Catholic Worker and Latin American base-community movements had provided "good models" for "living [her] faith through action." She "didn't reject anyone along the way—parents, family, church":

> The church introduced me to social issues early on. The content of the Scriptures is full of the need for action. I didn't expect a priest to give me the answer. I assume he has his limitations and interests, but I don't have to follow these. I think the church is just like any other institution. And I've worked with an educational system and not felt satisfied, but I still wanted to be a teacher. But the church is part of my past and culture.

Leslie also described a smooth transition in faith and affiliation. As a child she was impressed with a woman choir director, had been "fascinated" by nuns, and often pretended to be a minister. At her college the acting chaplain was a woman. She took her first Bible course and decided at the end of her junior year to enter the ministry. As a senior she worked in the college chapel and "the next year went to theological seminary," the lifelong thread of her faith unbroken.

The Jewish women I interviewed were not particularly religious yet had never lost their affiliation with synagogues. Their cultural and ethnic identity, rooted in their membership in a historically oppressed group, tended to transcend their religious faith. For example, Lena claimed to be "totally bored" by her religious training but had retained a sense of the importance of "fairness"; specifically, she wondered why Jews were being persecuted. Although synagogue seemed like "watered-down Sunday school," she never left. Alicia, a self-described atheist at age six, recalled "hating" synagogue. Yet even though her assimilated family never celebrated Jewish holidays, she never left the synagogue:

> I hated [synagogue because] it was cliquish. I felt it wasn't practicing what it preached. My parents were very, very assimilated. We had a Christmas tree and colored Easter eggs. We were trying to deny being Jewish. . . . [But] Jews can't really leave. If they do, they're still Jews whether they have synagogue ties or not.

Jewish women indicated that their ethnic identity and religious orientation predisposed them to charitable giving. They noted that Jews have been historically required to provide for their own by creating long-standing traditions of "righteous giving." While this may prepare them for religious activism, it may also limit their concern to Jewish causes—an obstacle to sanctuary at traditional synagogues, as Lena explained:

> The concept . . . *Tzedakah,* willingness to take care of others, [is] one of the most primary mandates in Jewish culture. We give *Tzedakah* for everything. It started out as justice or righteousness, then became a type of charity. It means "righteous giving." The *Mitzvah* is the blessing to give. In the country the Jewish community lived in *shtetl*—ghettos. No Jews were allowed to use the services of the larger community. Jewish people . . . were forced to use their own services for others in the same community who were less fortunate—self-contained charitable organizations to take care of their own. No Jewish child is allowed to grow up without the notion of *Tzedakah.* Jews who see justice only in terms of Jewish issues will only give their *Tzedakah* toward Jewish hospitals and institutions. . . . They by definition still have a ghetto mentality.

Two Catholic women indicated that they had maintained their affiliation in spite of another kind of obstacle—sexism. Dawn noted that although she had "observed sexism from the fourth grade on" and "thought confession was sinful," she never left:

What the priests got by with—the hypocrisy! I quit going to confession because I thought it was sinful. We were emotionally abused. One priest has now been shown to be a pedophile, another an embezzler. I'd lie for anything to get out of going. [But I never left because] at that point I felt I could fight forever. Now I find I'm at odds with so many institutions. I can't fight them all. I have to be reconciled somewhere because it becomes too violent. Too much energy has to go into the fight.

Julie recalled how long it took to "shake the church" and the "child's position" it instilled in her, yet she never left it either:

It took me a long time to shake the church, [which] is the ultimate colonizer, especially for women. . . . It took me a long time to think for myself because of the church. The parallel with the church and the female role is that they both tell us, "Someone will take care of you, tell you the rules, and you'll be in this child's position." The thing about sanctuary is, it's nice to be in an effective position.

Whether faith was lost, found, changed, or constant, respondents indicated that their religious experience generally melded with their humanitarian sense of compassion for and identification with the oppressed, contributing to a moral readiness to take social action once a concrete situation presented itself. For example, Dina's religious upbringing prompted an early sense of "social consciousness"; for her, the link between faith and "concrete action" came early "but not how to do it." Learning about the Holocaust, she concluded that to know people are being oppressed and not to act makes one an accomplice:

I had a Catholic background. I was impressed as a child by the nuns' emphasis on helping the poor. Bringing pennies to put in the box was the beginning of my sense of social consciousness. The main thing about being religious is to alleviate suffering. [Religion] means concrete action. That link came early but not how to do it. I was always looking for a way to act. . . . From 1973 to 1975 I lived in Germany. I'd no previous idea of the Holocaust. I grew up in a small all-white community. I'd never heard of it before, never knew it had happened. I went to the American library in Germany and read *Rise and Fall of the Third Reich.* I kept wondering about all the Germans over fifty I saw, wondering, what were you doing? Did you know? I asked some people. I sensed they put a real distance between themselves and the Holocaust. They said they didn't know. The conclusion I reached is that if I were ever in a position where I know something like this is happening, then I'll act, because if I don't, it makes me responsible. But I never felt I had a knowledge base about anything. When I was a student in the 1960s, I was totally inactive. I didn't know how to decide what was right.

"Not a Bible-thumper," Belinda also indicated that her religious training had predisposed her to take social action. She called U.S. policies in Central America "very wrong." As a citizen and member of the church, convinced that "you either believe in truth and justice or you don't," she had to "take a stand":

I have certain feelings and beliefs regarding how God fits into the world and how I fit. I don't know that I have a strong religious faith. I'm more inclusive. That's why I feel comfortable at [my church]. I see God moving through events and people's lives. Faith is alive. I see it through people. I really feel our government is very wrong. I don't feel angry about that, I'm aware of it. As a citizen of the U.S., I must take a stand. I have the right to conscientiously object. As a member of the church we had to take a stand. It was a no-win situation. We had to support sanctuary. Otherwise, why are we together? That's what makes the sanctuary so special in our church.

These accounts constitute motive reports that justify women's changing religious beliefs and situate past affiliations within a developmental framework. They show that women constructed their activist careers on the basis of caring, and that religious development shaped their identities.

POLITICAL PATH

All women reported being active on other issues prior to their involvement in the sanctuary movement. Whether of age or coming of age in the 1960s, many remembered being significantly affected by events of that era. The civil rights and antiwar and women's movements, political assassinations, Vietnam, Nixon, and Watergate were all meaningful influences on their subsequent awareness and activism. Recent studies of the "sixties generation's" continuing commitment to social issues help explain this pattern,[7] as do the women's ages: their average age was forty-four, and 80 percent were between thirty and sixty. Their narratives reveal their perceptions of how events of the 1960s intersected and shaped their lives. For example, Megan associated those years with race riots, the overthrow of Salvador Allende in Chile, and high school boys dying in Vietnam. Seeing "the same questions come up" through reading and travel, she developed her own view early on:

> I was twelve in 1968, the year of race riots . . . boys in high school were dying in Vietnam. . . . Later on I realized that our own government's hands were not so clean. . . . Living through the '60s was part of it, and the experience of Watergate and overthrow of Allende in Chile when I was seventeen. . . . I wanted to go to see for myself. . . . My political interest came from reading more than any other source.

Charlotte recalled exposure to such "eye-openers" as "Vietnam, Richard Nixon, and Watergate" and her parents and teachers as influencing her awareness that "people are being lied to":

> My parents were very anti–Mayor Daley, so it wasn't so difficult to make the jump between Chicago and the national government. So obviously people are being lied to. In high school

my American history teacher brought in draft resisters for current events. . . . In college I was involved with a community breakfast program for the poor. The group was also anti–Cambodian bombing. It was my first contact with progressive people. I was very influenced by a sociology teacher who taught social movements.

Gloria, an ex-nun, described her exposure to social justice issues during the 1960s civil rights movement: "The religious community I was a part of was very much involved in the 1960s . . . when Martin Luther King, Jr., marched from Selma to Montgomery, a nun [of my order] walked with him. So that was very much a philosophy I was getting [then]."

A self-described "real child of the sixties," Belinda linked exposure to justice issues in college with overcoming her middle-class background and with her continued activism as a mother:

I was very interested in Vietnam and civil rights issues. . . . [In college] I was very with it socially and politically. . . . I took government and history courses and a course on black power. A black woman in my dorm was in the class too. It was so helpful coming out of a white middle-class suburb. My friends and I were all politically aware. I continued to expose myself to justice issues. I was very concerned about the Vietnam War. . . . Later when I had babies, I kept active. I'd take them in the stroller to the grape and lettuce boycott at [the grocery store]. I wasn't angry; I had no axe to grind, but I felt people needed to be aware of injustices.

Jackie recalled the activities which she and her seminarian husband had engaged in as "what white people did then": "In the seminary we were active on anti-Vietnam issues. . . . We both worked in community centers in black parts of towns. . . . I worked on grape and lettuce and infant formula boycotts. I got interested in the women's movement in 1970."

Political awareness generally came early for younger respondents. For example, Andrea remembered growing up "thinking that college was a time for activism. . . . My brother . . . would come home from college and talk about the grape boycotts. There was a feeling for my family that it was important to be active in and care about politics."

Some recalled learning demonstrating and civil disobedience skills as young adults by taking part in community actions. For example, when Donna was fourteen, her best friend's father was an activist minister practicing Saul Alinsky's organizing techniques in the community: "My first demonstration was a sit-in at the police station of about forty people, white and Hispanic. We took over the police station. Nothing happened. The cops already knew the minister and didn't react. We were the church across the street. I was real impressed with that kind of empowerment." She considered her friend's father an "important early role model" for her subsequent awareness and activism: "He had McGovern posters all over the house. He'd go around saying, 'Nixon is a crook!' pace the house, rant and rave. I came from an apolitical but Republican family and all this was totally alien to me. I was fascinated that someone could call our president a crook."

Leslie also learned her demonstrating techniques at an early age. She "wasn't radical" in college in the 1970s because "there was little activism at that time." She took two years off during seminary to work for a large national housing rights agency, which exposed her to "direct action tactics" and taught her "how to appreciate activism":

> Working two years for [the agency], I was well primed. To work for them was important. [They] exposed me to how people in the U.S. lived in different kinds of areas, and I was exposed to the idea of direct action tactics. It was the first time I participated in any kind of direct action. . . . Not civil disobedience. [The agency] gets away with a lot of things— their intent is not to be arrested. We always had a specific demand. When we blocked an intersection on a freezing day with thirty parents, mostly black women, to get a school

crossing guard, we'd refuse to leave until we got the word from city hall that we'd get it. And it worked. A more dramatic thing was when [the Department of Housing and Urban Development] had a conference one year and Coretta Scott King was a speaker, but no [agency] people were invited. It was HUD people in suits. They didn't intend to include grassroots organizations. About two hundred [agency] people went up on the stage to present their demands to HUD. It got attention. They wanted some kind of participation in the process. We'd invade the offices of public service agents to make demands, like utility battles. We'd take over offices and show up at hearings. In a number of cases we'd have a public demonstration, then march to a boarded-up house, open it up, and help a family squat. These were people who lived in the projects and wanted a decent place to live. These were abandoned houses on the city's tax rolls.

Margaret recalled that a religious conversion at age twenty-two inspired her to "do something" about "nuclear issues and world peace." "Looking for answers," she met two women about to embark on a "two-year pilgrimage to Jerusalem for peace":

> Something in me welled up. I said, "I want to do that!" I finished college, went back home and made some money working for a couple of months. Then I joined the group. On Good Friday of 1982 we started walking outside of a Trident nuclear submarine base and walked across the U.S. That took seven and a half months. . . . We flew across the ocean and began walking. . . . We walked through the occupied West Bank to Jerusalem. . . . We finished Christmas Day, 1983. . . . We held a prayer service on the fields where shepherds heard angels singing at the birth of Christ. We prayed, danced, sang, and cried.

On the march, she learned how to manage political activism within a religious framework, a skill essential to her later sanctuary work.

Group members called themselves "pilgrims" rather than marchers; "conversations would get political or religious" depending on "what kind of people" they were talking to. This "theology of peace-making" was apparently well received:

> It was a serious religious quest acting out on faith about a God of peace, not war. We were aware of political implications, but that wasn't our agenda. But we talked about Reagan's policies and everything. We informed ourselves as much as possible about the technology of war. We were saying, "God defends and sustains us through love, and we can't create instruments of war and expect it to work." . . . This was 1982—more people were beginning to ask questions about the arms race. . . . It was timely. Pastors were looking for a way to bring questions before congregations.

For some older women, coming to political awareness and activism occurred more slowly, out of many experiences and across many decades. As Ginny noted, "It wasn't like a lightning bolt." In the 1950s an influential priest had guided her toward working at an interracial center, where she gradually began to change. By the time she arrived at a sanctuary church, "it was like a chicken coming home to roost":

> It was a slow process . . . I was a new bride, not satisfied, unsettled. Something was missing. I went to a priest, a good friend of mine. . . . He opened doors for me. . . . I'm different because of my experience with him. He sent me to [work at an interracial center]. I went to a black person's house, and he had house plants. This is how stupid I was. I said to myself, "Oh, black people have plants too!" I didn't know any black people. I came to [the center] like the great white mother and saïd, "[The priest] sent me, what can I do?" They'd just had lunch and were washing dishes. Someone threw a towel at me! I started out at the bottom of the heap and learned. . . . Little by little I began to change. . . . My Central American involve-

ment began then—my social consciousness. . . . That priest was the head of the Catholic labor movement in Chicago in the early 1950s. [The center] opened more doors for me. I began learning . . . more and more.

Geselle recalled that her slow development of political awareness began with her anger at "the bomb," which prompted her activism in the 1950s, then her involvement in the civil rights movement in the 1960s, and the peace movement in the 1970s:

> I'm so slow at coming to life, but I was so mad about the bomb. In the early '50s I saw some army films on atomic power. . . . It was the Atoms for Peace program . . . a big cover for keeping the weapons. I began writing senators. In the '60s I wrote letters to editors about civil rights issues and got a lot of hate mail. It said things like, "We shall overcome is a Communist phrase." . . . I was gradually getting a political awareness of the nuclear issue. . . . In 1975 [an anti-hunger agency] began. I joined and helped with the first symposium. I went to its meetings for the first few years . . . and to Springfield to lobby. I did a lot of picketing in Chicago.

Two women described suspending their activist careers to attend to child rearing and divorce. Lena recalled her 1960s involvement in local politics—"civic stuff"—and her more "global" 1980s perspective. She was "not involved in Vietnam" in the 1970s because of the strain of divorce on her family:

> I was politically active in [community] politics. . . . My first husband was very good about civic stuff, so we'd push doorbells together in the '60s. . . . I was not involved in Vietnam. It was the only place where I literally took a back seat. My marriage was breaking up, and I was psychically drained. I got divorced during Vietnam. I was torn up. The kids were in great pain and so was I. . . . In 1965 I was very aware of integration issues. By 1975 I was aware of a broader political world. . . . Toward the 1980s I became more aware of the global picture.

Alicia too recalled limiting her activism because of "going through a horrendous divorce" and having young children:

> After my first son was born I got involved in the civil rights movement . . . [and] in pro-abortion. I'd pass out pamphlets door to door. [I didn't march] . . . because I had two babies at home, I couldn't leave. That's why I'm willing to do the things I do now—no one is dependent on me.

Donna indicated that similar family-related interruptions occurred frequently at her church: "All the women activists had babies at the same time one year. They and their husbands took a sabbatical. Some came back. One didn't, one did, and a third came back halfway. They'll participate if the meeting is held at their house. These families were real active."

Women considered their prior political awareness and activism important precedents for their sanctuary involvement. Their narratives reveal how they situated past political views and behavior within the framework of a socially constructed career leading to their participation in the movement. Many had already learned the skills of managing political activism within a religious framework. Integrating caring, faith, and activism and finding a socially active church or synagogue were generally the last steps before their initiation to sanctuary.

INTEGRATION OF PATHS

Many women described "conversion" experiences that had helped redefine their social and political identities and launch or relaunch their activist careers. For two young clergywomen, these occurred during college and led them to the ministry. Leslie related how college experiences and working for a national housing rights agency had taught her that "standing up for justice" can be a "faithful activity":

> I was primed by my experience in college. A religion teacher talked about there being a need for radical voices that move

us forward . . . prophetic voices. Also in college, reading Paulo Freire linked for me the scriptures with standing with the oppressed. . . . The [agency] experience I saw as a faithful activity. [Agency] people knew that was my basic commitment. . . . But there was something missing—God was not central enough for me. . . . I felt called to the church. . . . In seminary I tried to integrate the practical experiences in [the agency] and the academic and theological experiences in seminary.

Lori also spoke of college experiences that had helped "focus" her faith and taught her gradually that "politics isn't all that bad." In "standing up for the oppressed," she found that her "confidence just grew" until she decided to enter the ministry:

My first two years of college were real eye-openers. I was learning sociology and economics. This helped me focus my faith. It taught me that everything can all come together. I did a program called, "Must We Choose Sides?" When I look back to my conversion point . . . I look back to that [program]. . . . That's where everything made sense to me. . . . It all congealed for me. . . . It broadened my faith but it was also more focused on liberation, hope, justice, and peace. . . . My first year [a friend] kept bugging me to go to protests. I said, "I don't protest—I'm not that kind of person" . . . deviant, radical, extreme. . . . That book really showed me that politics isn't all that bad. Being faithful means you have to deal with politics, because if you don't, you're on the side of the oppressor. I didn't get involved right away. By the end of the year I hadn't gone to any protests. The second year I was asking myself, "If I really believe these things, then why aren't I getting involved?" My third year I began getting involved. . . . I first learned about kinds of oppression, then began putting them together. . . . I gained confidence because I was standing up for the oppressed. . . . I really felt what I was doing was right. I felt my faith was leading me there. I then decided to become a minister.

As with political awareness, integration of faith and activism came later for some older women. For example, Lena described the recent activities that had led to a new awakening; reminded of her "violated" early religious sense, she felt compelled to act:

Three years ago . . . [I] started to work for [a Holocaust foundation]. In three months I learned more about refugees than I ever learned at home. I wrote speeches for women on the speakers' bureau. I'd put their experiences in speech form. I looked upon these survivors as extraordinary beings. . . . It was a combination of things, hearing John Stockwell, Reagan lies, and lies in the press about Agent Orange. I began a book on Agent Orange in '81. . . . The EPA, VA, and every government official is involved in the conspiracy. . . . The media has totally suppressed the data implicating the war contractors. . . . So you're still talking about "lady naive," because I didn't know they had the power to buy off the press. . . . I'm a johnny-come-lately to true cynicism. . . . I finally lost the last vestiges of the idea that America was a good place. It was my Agent Orange book. I got every underground newspaper in town and started reading pieces here and there. I became passionately aware that the Central American story was not being told. Here was another story of people's lives being violated. The word "violated" comes up in my vocabulary a lot these days. The people living innocently in Times Beach were violated. The people living innocently in a Nicaraguan village are violated. That early "milk-and-honey nirvana" doesn't exist anymore, and that pisses me off. It's just not right.

Christine recalled her similarly delayed awakening, which occurred during a trip to Central America, where she discovered a new sense of empowerment and activism. Transformed by the "courage and spirit" of those in struggle, she returned "knowing" she was "different now" and began infusing her environment with this new sense:

> Going to El Salvador, I realized I didn't have the answers. Seeing this country's policies, including the church's, and how they affect Central America, grounded me. It affected my gut. It opened me up to the possibilities of something else being right. Other solutions. I had a sense of my "we-ness" getting much larger. . . . It includes all these folks I never knew existed. . . . These people are far more than I ever imagined. The power of that—we're not alone! The passion of these people, how life is lived. . . . Something is calling them forth when they have nothing to lose. This is what I want! That force which calls us to life, to full being. Where can I find that? . . . I was sick and utterly terrified but afraid to come home to business as usual in the U.S. . . . It was a wonderful feeling to be there, but I was afraid all the time. Yet I saw how courage and spirit cut through even the fear of death. It heightened everything. I gave a sermon on it when I got back, giving witness to what I'd seen. Coming back knowing, "You are different now." . . . Everything is different. . . . "Gentle" is a term that's become very meaningful to me. Gentleness is very present in the face of terror and horror. It's a new learning experience.

Most of the women had found social action churches and synagogues prior to their sanctuary involvement, and some were converted to activism by the refugees' compelling stories. Their narratives reveal how these transformations, grounded in personal knowledge and experience, led to shifts in identity and mobilization into the movement. For example, Christine, who left her traditional church early on, recalled finding a church that "established" her "development":

> Discovering this church in 1962 . . . began my social consciousness. . . . The pastor invited me to an open housing

march. . . . That struck home and hearth. . . . When I left the church it was out of apathy, part of getting out of the home. I went back when the kids were old enough for Sunday school. I was fortunate to come here. My involvement here absolutely established the course of my development, and who I am has affected this church.

Gloria told of joining a special church that was making a political statement about U.S. involvement in Central America:

What made me join this parish was a priest who went down and lived with guerrillas in El Salvador. [The parish] community was doing a lot of educational things—demonstrating—in the early 1980s. Just on a political basis of being very involved with our government doing this again, another Vietnam thing, getting involved again in some place we shouldn't be involved, and being part of a group where . . . they were making a real political statement about that. That's what made me get involved there.

Some indicated that finding a special church or synagogue—after a prolonged period of alienation from religious institutions and the onset of secular activist careers—helped integrate unresolved faith issues with activism. For example, Jennifer had left a traditional church and become politically active in the 1960s, seeking "God somewhere among these activities." When she married a man with "no religion," they attended church for lack of "anything else to do." When her husband decided to become Catholic, they were drawn to a social action church:

My husband was taught that religion was for the psychologically weak. He was just back from Vietnam. I told him, "It's a good thing I didn't know you before, because I was out protesting Vietnam." . . . At [college] . . . I went to all the marches, wore a black armband—anti-Vietnam and civil rights marches. I was dating black people. I didn't go to Washington to march, but I contributed money. . . . I told myself, I

think I'll find my God somewhere among these activities because these are such terrible injustices. . . . So I'm marrying
somebody who doesn't have any religion. . . . Culturally, it
was real important to have a marriage in the church, because
my whole extended family would have been offended. . . . I
felt [the church] was a hollow institution, and I was fulfilling
my minimum duties so I could have a happy wedding day. . . .
It was more of a cultural thing. . . . Then we never did anything after that, never went to church, never had any discus-
sions about God. . . . Later we went to a cathedral because we
didn't have anything else to do. . . . [My husband] came home
one day and said, "I want to be Catholic." I was appalled and
shocked. I really didn't want him to do this. I wasn't supportive at all. . . . We moved to [another community], and that's
when we came to [this church] through a friend who was a
member. . . . What drew me the most was hearing people's
stories about how their lives had been changed . . . the way
people could take their faith . . . and experience it every day.

Jane also recounted leaving the traditional church, becoming
politically active in the 1960s, then returning to a special church
where she could integrate faith and action. During the "Kent State–
Jackson State year" she had concluded that "the system is the oppressor," "cashing in" the desire to be "part of any church." After
marrying, she decided to "check out" a progressive church where
she could explore her faith again. She "kind of stumbled into it" and
"just kept coming back":

During the height of [the 1960s], there were lots of opportunities to get involved. I was never a leader, but I did participate. . . . Big marches and demonstrations in Chicago I went
to. . . . After Kent State, we boycotted the whole spring semes-
ter and graduated without going to classes. . . . Regarding the
church and religion, I didn't need it in my life. I felt organized
religion was part of the problem, not a solution. None of my
peers were involved. It never occurred to me to relook at orga-

nized religion. I still felt it was a waste of time. . . . [My hus-
band] and I met in 1978 and married in 1980 at a friend's
house in a nonreligious ceremony. It was a seven-minute wedding with a big party. . . . I felt I'd missed community. [A
friend] suggested [a church that] was a pretty progressive
place, a good place. One Sunday we just decided to go. . . .
The minister knocked our socks off. . . . We just kept coming
back. It was 1981. Reagan had just been elected. We needed
to stand up and make a statement about it. I liked that. It was
a small congregation. . . . I felt I could say, "I'm really struggling with this stuff." We could talk about it. They see faith as
on ongoing struggle. It seemed like a good place. At first we
thought we'd just go on Sunday, not get involved. . . . We've
been at [that church] for over six years.

For some women, faith and action were integrated with their
introduction to sanctuary, a powerful learning experience that immediately converted them to new perspectives. Alicia told of becoming involved upon merely learning about sanctuary. Before even
meeting the refugees or hearing their stories, she had stepped forward and offered her services:

I first heard of sanctuary in October of 1986. At the Friday
night service the rabbi talked about it. It struck some kind of
chord in me. I asked afterwards, "What can I do?" He said,
"Come to the next social action meeting." At the meeting I
said, "If you need someone to do the legwork, I can speak
Spanish. If someone must take the rap, I can." I felt it would
be better to be me because I'm committed . . . and have no
children at home.

Lori recalled that learning about sanctuary had "percolated all these
things together," which she viewed as God's plan: "I see this is how
God works in my life. I've been led. There have been these little
flickers or sparks that led me, but I don't necessarily know what's
going on. But I have faith that someday it'll be clear."

For others, conversion to sanctuary took place in stages. For example, Jane remembered her early resistance. She first learned about the movement when a local antiintervention agency asked her church to issue a letter endorsing the first sanctuary in Tucson and then to declare itself a sanctuary. Her first reaction was, "Absolutely not":

> In '82 I was chairing the property and finance committee when a woman from [the agency] came to a meeting and told us about a Tucson church declaring sanctuary and asked us for a letter of endorsement. . . . I thought, well sure, let's. The next question was, "How about [the church] doing this?" At the same meeting! I thought, what's she talking about, sanctuary? I thought, sanctuary is a safe place for endangered species. I said, "Where would we put these people?" Initially, my response was . . . legally, what are we getting into? . . . I got in touch with my personal fear. Will I get fired from my job? Will I sit in prison? [My husband] and I were talking about children. How would they figure in? Then I realized that . . . I was nervous about . . . a sense of security as society defines it—respectability. I got scared by the whole thing. Here I was in a leadership position. I thought of the big rich church on [another street]—I thought, let them do it. I wanted the whole thing to go away. . . . I wanted to go along with it, but in my core I was hoping it wouldn't happen. I didn't want to take that responsibility.

Converted by the decisionmaking process and the politicized religious interpretation of sanctuary, she felt "called" by an "old tradition." Once the vote was taken, she "jumped in":

> What happened was, the minister reflected on biblical tradition and the faith perspective. . . . Old Testament stuff—Israelites' cities of sanctuary, and old English law, and tracing it here to the old underground slave railroad, which I really connected to from my community work. I realized, this is an

old tradition with roots. I was seeing it in historical context. I began to see myself as one of God's people and [our church] as being called. How can we turn away folks needing help? At the same time I learned more about what was going on in Central America—the persecution of catechists, who were doing the same thing as people at [the church]. And I learned about INS laws, our deporting people back to an uncertain future. And . . . that the 1980 amnesty law allows for these people to be here. I was moved by the experience of decision-making the biblical reflection and discussion of our government's role. I felt, I can't sit in the middle anymore. I felt, how can we not do this? The vote was taken. We had two weeks to prepare before the family arrived. At that point I jumped in. Once I made the decision I felt so alive.

Jeannine's initiation and early stage of conversion to sanctuary occurred at a mass for "the martyrs of El Salvador," where her exposure to the refugees' moving stories and handkerchief-covered faces "blew everything" she believed in:

In 1985 there was a mass for Oscar Romero. . . . Some refugees . . . spoke there. I'd been vaguely aware of and generally become disturbed about American policy. . . . What the refugees had to say really bothered me. Here we were in America and someone had to . . . cover their face. That blows everything I believed in about living in . . . a free and democratic society. I thought, why are they in danger here? . . . That was the first time I remember being personally confronted with the idea of sanctuary . . . when it took on some flesh for me. . . . Something was different about sanctuary—it was these refugees standing in front of me telling me my government's foreign policy made them refugees, and that they're not even safe here. That was too much.

Jeannine's narrative indicates how quickly informal networks within religious settings constitute micro-mobilization contexts for the movement: "I was really upset and moved by what they said. I was saying, 'I feel really helpless. I need to be with other people who are doing something, because I can't make an impact on my own.' . . . [My husband] was saying, "We've got to get an affinity group." "Nervous" because of her "upbringing about Communism," she joined a prayer group that was going to "do something." This is when "it finally all started to make sense":

> [My sister-in-law] asked us to be part of [the prayer group]. We said, "Yeah, we want to do that." That was what I was looking for, a group of concerned people who are going to do something. And I felt I needed a source of information. They were also a group interested in liberation theology. A Christian orientation was a big attraction . . . having a paradigm to attach to what's kind of been fermenting all along.

The women's accounts indicate that all were motivated to some degree by humanitarian concerns. As Julia put it, "When you look at people's personal motives for doing sanctuary work and ask what's in it for them, there's no question [that there's] a humanitarian focus." Jewish women tended to see their sanctuary involvement predominantly in humanitarian terms, indicating low levels of religious and political concern. For example, Pam remarked that

> it's more humanitarian than religious. I don't think I have a belief in one being. I believe in the values that religion teaches and the roots and having a place to go, but I don't think there's one guy up there. I'm not a real religious person, and I may be getting nicer as I get older. I'm more tolerant [in a humanitarian sense]. . . . I think this issue is political, but I don't know how to express it.

Alicia described a "totally humanitarian," existentialist orientation in which being Jewish made her "keep trying":

> I have almost as much contempt for politics as I do for religion. I feel political man sinks to a lowest common denomina-

tor. I think both institutions end up serving their own ends. If religiously I'm an atheist, then politically I'm an anarchist. So long as we must have government, it should be socialist, but I don't want any part of it. . . . I don't believe in the better nature of man. . . . I think we're like Sysiphus. We push the stone up and it rolls back down. The Jewish part of me says, "But you've got to keep trying." [Why?] Because we've survived against such enormous odds.

Some women indicated the relative significance of the three paths over time: early on, the humanitarian and religious were more important to them; later, the political became more important, often after they had found a way to act. For example, Andrea called herself "more spiritual" in high school and "more political, actually antichurch," in college; once she "made the connection between the political and spiritual," she "went back to it." Dina similarly connected early religious convictions with later political activism:

This began more as a deep-rooted religious and moral conviction about people. I didn't know much. I was politically naive. It was a gradual awareness. The nuns were always talking about helping people and alleviating suffering. Once I found a way of expressing my convictions, then I felt compelled. Once I saw the route. Just talking and not doing has never appealed to me.

Ginny referred to this pattern in her development as "evolving" to a higher stage of "growth": "My orientation was mostly spiritual when I was young. . . . I did evolve, but it was spiritual at first. . . . Later it was humanitarian, now more political. [It was] growth—reading, listening, and learning."

The women tended to describe their political awareness as developing in the context of intimate relations, small groups, and personal learning experiences. As Jeannine recalled:

Politically I was pretty naive. I was afraid of getting involved. I didn't really know what was going on. I wasn't buying my dad's line of "America, love it or leave it," but I was starting to wonder if what we were doing was right. I still had the idea that people involved in protest were deviant. For a while my whole idea about protest was controlled by the media. . . . Change came through relationships with friends. . . . I'll have some things percolating inside and may process them individually, then some kind of relationship brings me to a group or transformation. That's what happened regarding this political transformation. [My husband] and some other people really helped me transform some of my earlier religious and humanitarian ideas into a political framework. I don't necessarily believe [my husband] is "the" person. If not him, it would have been somebody else. I was ripe. The time was ripe.

Relating that once politically aware, she felt "compelled to do something," she indicated the responsibility that comes with "having your eyes opened":

As long as people are comfortable . . . they'll keep their eyes closed. . . . people don't want to make political decisions. I was one of those people. Having your eyes opened doesn't make life any easier. . . . The scales fall away, and you can never put them back on . . . people like not asking too many questions. They can let somebody else carry on the business of government because it's work to become politically informed and active. A lot of people feel comfortable trusting government officials to have hired good people to do good work. Therefore that alleviates responsibility on my part to do anything.

Acknowledging the importance of political activism in bringing about change, women invariably expressed their newly integrated values in religious terms and justifications. For example, Margaret described her basically "spiritual" view:

The world is one, and we can't be authentically religious without a sense of political significance. But my basic orientation was and is more and more spiritual. An essential part of my faith is concern for the poor. [It] would be empty without it. It's my faith and religious convictions that keep bringing me back to political and social arenas.

Gina recalled that once her "politics and religion" became "intertwined," her activism became a "faith-based enterprise":

I can remember in Guatemala saying to a friend that I long for the day when my politics and religion come together better. . . . I find my faith to be stronger. At one point it was meaningless routines, and now it's become a very meaningful discipline. [Thanks to] my experience in Guatemala, my friends, and my reading, my politics and faith are very intertwined. I don't separate them out. . . . So for me, sanctuary is a very . . . faith-based enterprise.

Only one woman indicated that her political awareness had preceded her religious development. A student in France during the 1960s, Eva was already active in the peace movement when she found a social action church. Her sanctuary involvement brought her "back" to the church, fulfilling her "religious quest" by adding the religious component she sought. However, her development was similar to others' in that she used personal connections and interactions to move in a chosen direction:

After my early motherhood I wanted more involvement outside my family. I began leaning to the left. I wanted to meet people concerned with world issues. . . . When I was in the peace movement, I met some [church] people. . . . I grew into this church because of this congregation's emphasis on faith and responsibility toward self and society—on commitment. . . . The sanctuary movement is how I came back to the church.

She stressed the spuriousness of boundaries between these values, which "depend on where and when . . . people enter the move-

ment. . . . There's no boundary between the humanitarian and political and spiritual. These are highly interchangeable. . . . For me the
sanctuary movement made me more spiritually involved. I was already politically oriented. For others, the opposite."

All the others indicated entering the movement with a particular
religious viewpoint, which they maintained even as it was transformed and politicized through activism. Situating the political dimension last and minimizing its importance, they emphasized the
religious basis of their activism. Women religious exhibited this
pattern most strongly. For example, Moira claimed that although
many groups were active for "good humanitarian and political reasons," this wasn't enough for her because it didn't "enliven [her]
spirit." Similarly, Lori remarked, "I really don't like politics. I'm
involved only because of my faith. . . . My faith compels me to stand
against injustice and for justice."

Although most women religious were active in politically oriented antiintervention groups, they still expressed a strong preference for religious-based involvement.[8] As Megan declared, "I'm not
opposing political solidarity groups, but for me personally, I want to
keep my faith perspective on this." Christine hoped for "more inter-
linkages with broader antiintervention groups" but called her activism "very much faith-based." And although sanctuary and other
"solidarity" groups overlap in membership and goals, as Moira
indicated, maintaining their distinction helps alleviate the stigma of
being political:

> You could change the sanctuary movement's name to "soli-
> darity committee" and you'd pretty accurately describe it. But
> it'd be very foolish to do so because that would reduce us to
> another Central America solidarity committee. Because our
> whole identity and sense of protection comes out of our re-
> ligious roots. . . . It's a religious movement we're into.

Hannah noted the frequent reluctance of congregations to be "political," which also accounts for women's preferred identification as
religious rather than political activists: "Many church people won't

get involved because it's political. But it's not partisan politics. It's the will of the people to act."

Women named several politicized religious concepts that had mobilized their activism. Catholic and Protestant women referred to liberation theology and creating a "new covenant" and "kingdom on earth"; Jewish women pointed out the historical parallel of the Jews' exodus out of Egypt and the importance of "righteous giving" and "saving lives"—both illustrating how participants legitimate and shape the movement by claiming religious precedents for harboring refugees. Their activism is political but in a nontraditional sense: neither partisan nor national, it is both grassroots and global. Women's efforts to mobilize local communities to awareness and action in order to affect large-scale change in the balance of power are characterized by the New Age maxim "Think globally; act locally."[9]

Because memories often correspond poorly to previously held views, I present these women's explanations for their sanctuary involvement not as objective reports but as "skillful accomplishments of actors" with "the official version of their movement's rationale" at their disposal.[10] Frame alignment theory emphasizes that movement organizations try to synchronize potential recruits' beliefs and attitudes with the movement's ideological frame and that activists seek to construct legitimating accounts to support their own and others' activism; such efforts include fashioning ideological rationales to legitimate the movement's behavioral proscriptions.[11] These are based not on observation or empirical evidence but upon "cuings" among group members, who jointly create the meanings they read into current and anticipated events.[12]

This analysis helps explain women's recollections of their entry into the movement, their adoption of politicized biblical rhetoric to account for the refugees' presence, and their citation of religious precedents to legitimate the movement. It also explains the importance of the small informal groups at churches and synagogues, whose micro-dynamics transform women's consciousness. These groups are the "repositories for the existing frames that are . . . the

raw materials for alignment processes," established churches providing "a rich and detailed 'worldview' or frame that can be used to
encourage activism." Their significance derives from the "established organizational and interpersonal settings they afford insur-
gents."[13]

The women's narratives show their faith development as "inter-
active and social," requiring "community, language, ritual, and nurture," its dynamics as located in "the ways [they] go about making
and maintaining meaning" throughout the life cycle. Like the socially constructed self shielding a vulnerable inner being in a dangerous social world, faith development is "a coat against . . . naked-
ness" forming a dependable "life space."[14]

Women's accounts also show them as calculating actors who
judge the potential costs and benefits of various lines of action.
Those who see participation costs as high may choose a more
humanitarian-oriented line of action and withdraw early from the
movement. If anticipated benefits are high, a political orientation
and lifelong activism are more likely.[15] This suggests that women
chose their lines of action not because they were psychologically
compelled to such choices but because their structural location in the
world made certain choices easier than others: laywomen may avoid
taking political risks because of threatened costs to their families;
women religious are relatively free of such cross-cutting solidarities.
These structural differences affect women's conceptions of themselves as agents of social change and the character and longevity of
their activist careers.

VI

THE EFFECTS OF
LIFE STRUCTURE

Patterned differences in women's styles of activism are related to
structural-organizational conditions in their lives. A "micro-
sociology of knowledge" of the interaction between actors' ideas
and circumstances links women's views of liberation and their behavior as agents of social change with their location in families and
in religious orders.[1] Pronounced differences between the two groups
indicate the conditions that give rise to political consciousness and
incipient feminism and in which female revolt becomes a part of
women's activism.

FAMILY CONFLICT AND SUPPORT

Family attitudes figure prominently in women's "risk-reward
calculus" in the decision to be active in sanctuary; families represent
powerful cross-cutting solidarities affecting the character and longevity of their activism.[2] About half the laywomen in the study
indicated that their families disapproved of their involvement and
that family reactions included shame, frustration, and disappointment. Women's activism may also lose them the support of friends;
for example, Eva noted that Dina lost a good friend who "now shuns
her as a Communist."

Some families disapproved of or denied women's involvement
in a political movement. Dina believed that her husband's family
thought "their son wouldn't be involved" in sanctuary if not for her;

she saw her in-laws as silently opposed to her sanctuary work—"a blank wall, no questions." Margaret also described her family's denial, judgment, and disappointment: "Dad saw some old friends of mine and told them I was a social worker. I said, 'Dad, I'm not a social worker. I work with Central American refugees.' My older brother thought I was crazy. He'd just graduated from college and was looking for a job."

Women often deal with family disapproval by not telling their families about their activism. According to Julia, this is "characteristic of women in the movement—they don't tell their parents." Others use their activism to get back at families for their perceived conservatism. For example, Charlotte recalled inviting her disapproving family to a refugee baby's baptism, and her pleasure in introducing them to an activist nun: "They thought [the nun] was just the sweetest person in the world. I told them about her social activism and arrests. It was an eye-opener for them. They couldn't believe it. They don't respect our opinions, but they respected her." Others made class judgments against disapproving families: Jeannine called her father an "Archie Bunker Democrat," and Dina described her in-laws as "working-class" and "apolitical": "My activities put [my husband] in touch with his anger at his parents— how repressed they are . . . and let him verbalize it."

Some families disapproved because of the political nature of women's activism, but more disapproved because of a perceived loss of caretaking for themselves. Parents and in-laws tended to be judgmental; husbands and children were more resentful of women's absence from home. Julia called this "the case of every woman in sanctuary": "Sometimes I see women in sanctuary who are totally absorbed in the movement. Everyone's family is mad at them for taking time away from the family." In liberal feminist rhetoric, she noted that "women are used to meeting everyone's needs but ours. It's a morality of responsibility, not rights." Recalling her family's anger over her activism and her frustration at their dependency, she justified her rights in terms of making her family more accountable, illustrating the guilt that women may feel as activists:

One day I came home from [picketing] the post office, and the family was mad because dinner wasn't ready. They reflect [my husband's] view. My daughter says, "You only have time for refugees." But I want to make them more accountable for themselves, not do things . . . that they can do for themselves.

Eva described the encompassing nature of her involvement and its disruptive effect on her home life: "My sanctuary work entailed making contacts, phone work, giving people rides, and bringing people to my home by day. Things would get pretty hectic at my house." Commenting on Eva's situation, Dina indicated how women's caretaking of refugees and families may merge, obliterating boundaries and arousing families' confusion and resentment: "Eva had a hard time separating herself and her family from [the refugees], keeping the big picture. She did everything—had them at her house every day, did their laundry. She got so bad, her husband got edgy and her kids complained."

Some women's husbands posed a problem for their activism. Some held opposing political views. For example, when Jennifer asked her lawyer husband's advice about the refugees, he said—in a "funny, sarcastic way"—"Tell them to go back." Julia's activism caused "tremendous strains" with her husband:

He's not active. He thinks there's more to the picture than I'm aware of—like the administration must be right. He's not sure of my position. He was a marine—primary control is the way to do it, like in Vietnam. He sees himself as a colonizer and my position as untenable.

Some husbands were threatened by women's decision to travel to Central America and take personal risks. When Julia told her husband about wanting to go to Guatemala, he said, "Fine, we'll get a divorce"; it was, she reported, "nonnegotiable." Undaunted by his ultimatum, she planned to go the next year as a research assistant for a repatriation program. Christine described her husband's equally unfavorable response to her traveling:

He was . . . snotty and uncommunicative. I thought, okay, it's come, the straw that breaks the camel's back. . . . [His view was], "If you love me, how could you put yourself in this position?" They don't know what it's like to risk a life, so they don't understand. That we keep together is a miracle.

Sometimes the women's children posed the problem. Jennifer, who had integrated the first refugees and then the extended family into her household, related that her son became overwhelmed by competition, disturbed by blurred family lines and double standards of behavior for the refugees and himself. His resentment and guilt as expressed in family therapy reflected the underlying stress borne by the entire family, which then had to "set new limits." He "put it all into words"—"all the frustrations" they had experienced for two years. She indicated a class-based link between guilt and anger and revealed how customs of sharing and fairness, of being lenient and perhaps patronizing toward guests, are learned at home:

> My son totally blends in with the children. The negative side is sometimes he feels I'm more lenient with the Central American kids than him. When all the others came, there was more vying for attention between the children and more competition. He began feeling funny. He just let go about all this stuff about the Guatemalans, that they were really poor and we weren't. He felt guilty. But he was very upset that the little girls could eat apples in the living room, and nobody else could. The little girls would spit out the peels on the floor. One time the grandpa sat on the couch and peeled an apple with his knife. And at school Miguel would take [my son's] food. He'd take a bite and [my son] wouldn't want it back. . . . [My son] never wanted to tell us about it. But we became overwhelmed, thinking, breathing Guatemalans. When he said all this, it was really clear that it was bothering us all. The kids would walk in without knocking. With only four, it was okay, but with so many, they'd be more rowdy. When I wasn't there, they couldn't come in. We gradually set new rules.

Setting limits took time, especially since the caretakers had tended to indulge the refugees' children: "When they first came, they didn't know what gifts were. . . . Now there's all these kids, and we've had to set limits."

Christine described a struggle to integrate her activist and family roles and the risk she took of looking like a "bad person" in order to teach a grandson from a military family about the issues:

I was going to [the military base] to block the arsenal and . . . I explained to my eight-year-old grandson what we were doing—that we might go to jail. He was astonished. He thought only bad people go to jail. On the way there I turned my ankle and couldn't go. My grandson said, "That's a good thing you were going to do—wanta play cards?" What really bothers me is his war toys—it makes me want to weep. I won't play with them. . . . But I don't say anything.

Other women's families were more approving of their activism. Some husbands were cooperative and accommodating, although their attitude may have reflected more appreciation for their wives' volunteer work than for their political activism. Pam described receiving "tremendous support" from her doctor husband, who didn't "seem to mind": "He never tells anybody what to do." Belinda indicated that her family "could always talk." Although her architect husband came from an old-fashioned family that "expected the food to be on the table," he had "let go of that model."[3]

Most women described their children's experience as positive, tending to discuss the children's involvement in terms of educating them to the issues. Dina remarked, "I took my kids to the apartment to see the [refugee] family. I got them in touch with the situation and how to act on it. These are examples of courage and sacrifice." Julia spoke of a family career, of coming to know others and making new rules:

We have a real active houshold, and the kids are real aware of what's going on. I take them with me a lot when there's something going on with the refugees. At first they say, "I don't wanta go—I don't know anyone." But then they have a great time, running around the church, playing with the refugee kids. At first [my son] was hesitant; he said, "I can't talk to them." My daughter was already connecting.

Relating her family's pattern of becoming active, then taking a rest, Belinda stressed the importance of "balancing" family life "so as not to become martyrs to a cause. . . . We always involve our kids. The kids respect and understand. They were very much a part of this and have very strong feelings about this. They know not everyone's life is on a tree-lined street."

Whether or not their families were supportive, women perceived family reaction as significantly affecting their activism. Some described conflicts between their sanctuary activity and being a "good" woman, wife, and mother. For example, Donna saw a conflict between her work as a coalition staff person and her responsibility in marriage. Perceiving "leader" and "wife" as anomalous and leadership as a "male role," she feared being seen as "taking power":

Sometimes because of the role I'm in—it's such a male role—I wonder about my femininity. It's about power and control. If [my husband] did sanctuary, he'd have to deal with his wife in leadership. We're both leaders. If we were in the same organization, he'd be accusing me of taking power.

She also saw a conflict between power and femininity, which surfaced around issues of sex: "Sometimes I wish he'd just do something. I wish he'd initiate at least once in a while. That coupled with my role in the group makes me feel I'm not a good woman but a good man." Given the conflict she perceived about the roles of leader and mother, a miscarriage had made her feel "irresponsible":

When [the group] first got going, I was working fifty to seventy hours a week. I was pregnant and miscarried. I felt [it was] because I was being ambitious, acting like a man. Later I found out how common it is. It's all tied up with conflict about being in . . . leadership . . . and having a baby.

She expressed serious concern that she could not fulfill her dual roles:

I worry that because of my activism, I won't be a good wife and mother. And I really want to. . . . It makes me very sad to think about. One day I was so absorbed [at the church], I forgot to pick up my husband from work four hours earlier. The group was teasing me. A man said, "[your husband] is either headed for sainthood or a divorce!" This really stung.

Her rhetoric illustrates how having children, or even planning to, may cause some women to redefine their expectations of their future activism. She believed that she would eventually "restructure and reprioritize" to accommodate motherhood and activism, although she was unclear about how to do so.

When I have children I'll probably straddle the two. . . . I couldn't be happy just being a mother, although I could be happy just being an activist. . . . my sense is that things will change when we have kids, that my sanctuary work will be cut in half. . . . I've seen my friends go through this. They settle for a smaller part but most stay active.

Also married and without children, Jeannine expressed similar concern and frustration over the perceived conflict between motherhood and activism. She too believed that she would somehow "organically" straddle the two—another case of women's expectation that having children will reshape their activism:

I plan to have kids fairly soon. That brings up a whole other set of questions about how it all fits together. I'd like very much to stay at home when they're little. I don't know if we could afford that. I don't feel conflicted about having kids but about how all this will work out. I feel real boxed in right now. I wouldn't stop [my activism]—I just got started. I think somehow I'm going to organically evolve into these things all fitting together.

For Jane, married with a baby, the outcome of trying to create a balance was to limit her activism, including CD and travel:

> When [the baby] came, I pulled back a bit. I was on the outreach committee until December, but I don't want to spend my Saturdays away from [the baby]. Right now . . . my extra-curricular time is limited. I've got to figure out what my involvement will be. I'll keep working at [the church] and at the [the coalition]. I'd love to return to Guatemala and El Salvador, but with [the baby] that's got to wait.

That as many women's families resented and resisted their involvement in sanctuary as supported and encouraged it illustrates the mixed fit between women's activism and middle-class family life.[4] Studies of women's outside work indicate that families generally do disapprove if that work includes a shift in the division of labor at home.[5] The more families depend on women at home, the more easily women can negotiate their approval and, sometimes, their willingness to do more work at home. Important class differences characterize women's and families' views. Working-class women tend to see their families as a source of support; middle-class women, as restricting their individuality and independence. Middle-class families tend to see women's work as unnecessary because of the husbands' higher incomes; women with less economic need to work have less leverage justifying working to their families and renegotiating the division of labor at home.

Women's volunteer work may enhance their families' social status without altering who does the work at home. A family's commitment to egalitarian principles is actually a relatively weak predictor of household behavior. Whether or not women work, with or without pay or family approval, other family members generally consistently resist doing more work at home. Whether their outside work is viewed as a sacrifice or satisfaction, women generally face neither unqualified support nor unqualified opposition.[6]

Most women in the study were middle-class, married with children, and employed only part time or not at all. Theoretically, then, they had less leverage for negotiating family approval of their sanctuary work and were more likely to view family roles as restrictive. However, family opposition or support may be more closely related to family members' own participation in social action churches and synagogues. About three-fourths of the married women's husbands were active, and these tended to be supportive of their wives' activism, whereas the inactive husbands tended to oppose it.

Family roles imply reciprocity and hierarchy, and women used "familistic language" both to empower the refugees and to express their perceived dependency.[7] For example, Megan likened her work with refugees to the job of "a family that has to feed and clothe its children." Margaret described her "sense of keeping the family together": "The refugees are brothers and sisters in need, and we take them into our family." She saw the direction of "caring energy" away from families and toward social causes as "natural":

> Women's whole orientation is toward growing, changing, caring, and loving. When women are through with their life work . . . raising families, they're ready for more. . . . Men spend their lives achieving and getting ahead. When their life's work is over, there's nothing left for them. Because when you can't achieve things anymore, your life collapses.

Those trained in helping professions tended to combine familistic and therapeutic rhetorics in describing their sanctuary work, thus confirming a theory about the increasing fit between "the therapeutic attitude of self-realization and empathic communication" with the nature of work in the United States.[8] In this view, therapy is work, and much work is a form of therapy. Women's family and therapy rhetorics illustrate this fit in their sanctuary work. For example, Dina, a social worker, related her view of the family as "a unit where all people have input, even kids," to her understanding of "the interpersonal struggles of the movement."

Jeannine, a special education teacher, articulated a view of the refugees as "identified clients" who are part of a "sick family system." Casting them as dependent children, she made a connection between nondemocratic families and oppressive U.S. policies. Since parents are part of the problem, her solution included seeing Americans as "creators of what's happening"; otherwise, sanctuary merely constitutes "Band-Aid treatment":

> In family systems, the identified client seems to have the problem. The refugees are like the identified client—we have to concern ourselves with their safety needs. But sanctuary itself isn't going to work—we're part of a sick family system. We're all invested in keeping it going. Our government is invested in calling the refugees Communists and insisting they go back to their own country. We have to then admit that we're the source of evil. We are the oppressors. It's like a family where a kid is abused and acting out. He's saying, "Somebody do something because this is crazy!" That's what the refugees are saying to us. "We can no longer stay there because it's crazy!" That's why their message is so powerful—not just their suffering, but at our hands. It's our fault. If we don't see ourselves as oppressors, everything we do will be Band-Aid treatment. It's like the parents sending the kid to therapy but not going themselves. And the therapist that allows that is colluding with the parents.

Likening the refugees to "kids leaving for college," she believed that the United States will always create refugees so long as it denies Third World countries their transition to independence:

> In anybody's normal development there comes a time when people become adults. To continue holding power over them is to deny normal development. In a healthy family, transitions are handled well. The system adjusts. Like a kid's leaving

for college—parents don't do fucked-up things to keep the kid at home. We as a nation don't allow other nations to make those transitions. We pretend they can't do it without us. When that kid leaves home and goes to college, you want him to come back and have healthy relationships. It's going to happen—they're going to leave home. It's a presumptuous analogy because this isn't their home. In exerting power over others, we'll always create a situation where we have refugees.

WOMEN'S VIEWS OF LIBERATION

Women predominate in the movement because of their high levels of prior organization, residential and occupational concentration, extensive ties to other groups, and positions in established network centers already distributing resources to outsiders.[9] However, this has neither made sanctuary a feminist movement nor made sanctuary women feminists. As noted, women religious won a fight on the issue of gender parity on a national sanctuary committee only by default—their sheer number at the meeting—and a nun called the idea of introducing feminism at the heavily woman-based Chicago Catholic Sanctuary "a horse of a different color." This clearly indicates that sanctuary is not a feminist movement. Women's ideas about feminism are nonetheless important to it, revealing how they interpret their roles as women, identify with others' struggles, and view the terms of liberation, including their own. Like their forebears in other moral reform movements, sanctuary women have untenable positions; as members of the colonizing class, they struggle to empower the colonized, sometimes developing greater awareness of their own oppression as a class. How they define and act on their own behalf and see themselves as agents of social change affects the outcome of the movement and their own activist careers.

Fifteen of the women discussed their ideas about feminism and liberation theology; some perceived links between them.[10] Liberation theology is a concept useful in explaining the refugees' situation at home and sanctuary members' identification with their cause. This philosophy emerged in the late 1960s out of the base-community movement in Latin America. Beginning with the belief that Christianity offers liberation from human sin, it holds the church responsible for helping people to liberate themselves from poverty and oppression. It is based on the principle that human suffering exists on a massive scale, which is inconsistent with Christian moral principles and contradicts God's vision for human existence; as an expression of faith and conscience, Christians must act to relieve this suffering.[11]

Striking differences appeared in how laywomen and women religious conceived of feminism and its relation to liberation theology. Laywomen generally identified with both ideologies but made few claims on them, whereas all women religious linked them in the language of a "feminist theology" equating women's oppression in male-dominated hierarchies with that of the poor, all placing women prominently in conceptions of human liberation.

According to feminist theology, neither women's oppression nor poverty is the will of God; both are sinful. Scripture and theology are seen as rooted in a "patriarchal-sexist culture" and sharing its biases and prejudices: "Christian theology is not only white-middle-class but white-middle-class-male. . . . The 'maleness' and 'sexism' . . . are much more pervasive than the race and class issue."[12]

Important claims are made for feminist theology:

Feminist theology . . . can integrate the traditionally separated so-called male-female areas, the intellectual-public and the personal-emotional. Insofar as it understands the personal plight of women in a sexist society and church through an analysis of cultural, societal, and ecclesial stereotypes and structures, its scope is personal and political at the same time. . . . because women belong to all races, classes, and cultures, its scope is more radical and universal than that of . . . Liberation Theology.[13]

Feminist theology is related to the transition of women religious "from nuns to sisters," both rooted in historical changes in the church. The gradual acceptance of chastity and poverty vows in the Middle Ages eliminated women's roles as wives and mothers and led to the establishment of cloisters, providing the structural conditions for women's collective action. In keeping with Vatican II's message about creating a church responsive to the needs of the poor, women religious began interpreting the meanings of these pledges to fit with global political and economic developments. Their emphasis on collaborative decision-making, their view of sexism as part of a range of oppressive conditions, and their highly visible integration of faith and action are part of a growing trend among nuns and clergywomen.[14]

That women religious profess feminist theology is no surprise; their greater access to religious ideas and more political orientation fit with their more articulated, goal-oriented behavior. A study of women's political resocialization and predisposition to learn feminist attitudes indicates that adult socialization contexts can significantly enhance women's politicization.[15] This helps explain how contrasting locations in nuclear families and same-sex religious orders constitute important adult learning contexts that contribute to the political development of laywomen and women religious.

As noted, the two groups were also generally divided between those who had lost, found, or changed faith prior to their sanctuary involvement and those who never left the institutional church. Out of their continuous experience in religious institutions and communities, women religious made more connections between women and social change. This is important because both groups' lives are rooted in patriarchal institutions in which women accommodate and resist male power. How women interpret their positions says something about the conditions in which they develop political consciousness and activist careers.

Laywomen displayed more diversity in the ways they identified feminism and liberation theology. Most indicated that liberation theology had politicized their religious beliefs; even the few who had barely heard of it had a favorable idea of the concept. They had mixed use for feminism, and all expressed reservations about linking it to liberation theology. Most spoke of feminism in the rhetoric of a liberal feminism concerned with women's class rights, which they seemed to dismiss along with the middle class.[16] In their struggle for power in the home, church, community, and movement, they generally failed to develop a unifying view of their own place in a larger struggle. Acknowledging the importance of women's "entitlement," they nevertheless tended to reject it along with their backgrounds. Viewing women's rights as class rights while condemning their own class, they rather self-righteously denied a claim to them. None saw a comfortable fit between the two ideologies or considered their experience as women the basis for a unifying principle of social change. For example, Eva recalled first recognizing her "feminist consciousness" during an argument with her mother: "I shouted at her that I wasn't going to go along with something even though that's what was expected of me as a woman. She said, 'Oh, Eva, you sound just like a feminist!' " Identifying feminism as women's "right to speak out, to have our own ideas, values, and priorities," she linked "suffering as women" with "relating to others' oppression." In her view, women are more empathic toward suffering: "We can either victimize or empathize. Suffering helps us empathize." She knew little about liberation theology: "I have an article at home I haven't read yet on that."

Belinda claimed to have no use for feminism; as noted earlier, she was quite certain that she didn't need to "fight for rights anywhere—in [her] family, business, or church." She had no personal meaning for liberation theology but saw it as part of the "desire for justice to prevail":

> I don't know how it fits in, but I suspect it's because of the courage of people like Oscar Romero. Whether we do sanctuary or not, liberation theology will go on. You can't hide the truth. . . . These people are coming across our border. Someone was saying that these injustices are closer to us than Maine.

Ginny related to feminism and liberation theology in the personal terms of her own experience. She linked feminism with feeling

"very disadvantaged" by her divorce, which she "just wanted . . .
over with"; she "didn't get anything." She felt that "more equality"
was important—"not just paychecks." She linked liberation theology to choosing a church, not to political activism:

> I've always been a bit of a maverick with worship. Now that
> Central America is experiencing liberation theology, I agree
> with those people. If the government is suppressing people,
> and the church hierarchy at the top helps, I think it's sinful. If
> I lived in Central America, I'd be doing that too. If not, I'd
> just worship within myself. I couldn't go to cathedrals where
> government officials go.

Charlotte linked liberation theology with the "inspiration," the
"energy and hope," that "the people of Central America" gave her,
acknowledging that she was "not oppressed by the same things": "I
see people in Central America who can still laugh and love as
inspirational, to show that the kingdom of God is in this world. I see
people in the sanctuary movement as trying to build that kingdom in
the U.S." She saw no link between feminism and sanctuary. She
expressed the liberal feminist notion that feminism means "progress
in the business world" and the cultural feminist view that women are
more nurturing than men:

> Feminism depends on how you define it. The kind that says
> women are better than men or should be like men, I don't fol-
> low. Instead of becoming more like men, we should make the
> world more feminine. Nurturing men should be the role mod-
> els and leaders. It's a real mistake to give this up.[17]

Jeannine related her interest in liberation theology to a book her
prayer group had read; its rhetoric had helped develop the group's
political view:

> It's basically saying what Christ said—we can't elevate any-
> thing to be above God. When Caesar asks to be put above
> God, he's asking us to indulge in idolatrous behavior. Our

> government is asking us to put them before God. Sometimes
> we have to say no to our government. We're being asked by
> our government to accept their decisions about foreign policy,
> illegal actions, covert operations, without any sort of chal-
> lenge. They're asking to be put above God.

Her view of liberation theology was personalized, based on a con-
ception of her wedding vows. Her narrative illustrates how the
rhetoric of liberation theology melds with women's religious, political, and humanitarian concerns and how easily women become true
believers in a "community of other people":

> The priest gave a beautiful homily at our wedding about mar-
> riage being liberating. I think that's what liberation theology is
> all about—reclaiming the gospel message that Jesus came to
> liberate us from oppression and fear. People involved in sanc-
> tuary have been very strongly moved by Latin Americans' in-
> terpretation of the gospel, making it come alive in a real, new
> way because we have an example of what Jesus was talking
> about. Sanctuary people are deciding what part they'll play re-
> enacting the gospel. We are compelled to put our money
> where our mouth is. A big part is about having the support of
> our community, which allows us to criticize systems and chal-
> lenge authority the way Jesus did of those who put themselves
> above God.

As for feminism, she believed that sanctuary "moves beyond" it. She
knew "some men" and "some women too" who were "turned off by
it." She claimed that sanctuary moves "past the angry strident feminism" to "relating to people from a compassionate position, not a
power position"; feminism "takes a back seat to being human together." She perceived a conflict between women's compassion and
the image of feminists as angry, power-broking women:

> I don't see sanctuary as a feminist movement. While I consider
> myself a feminist, there's something beyond feminism, like
> going beyond being "politically correct," which is no longer

important. Feminism may have taken us into a power realm by helping us find a place in a hierarchy or having some power in the world, but you move beyond that to relating to people in a compassionate way.

Donna recalled learning about feminism at age eighteen when she was "caught" reading *Our Bodies, Ourselves*.[18] Her father accused her of "reading pornography"; her mother was "too embarrassed to even talk about it." The book became a "rite of passage" imparted to her sister with the warning to "hide it from the folks." Yet her sense of feminism failed to relieve the conflict she perceived in her "real male role" as staff person and the feeling that she was "not a good woman but a good man." To her, liberation theology meant "ideas the oppressed have about liberating us." While it had politicized her viewpoint and rhetoric, she had little faith in North Americans to act. Rejecting the middle class, which she seemed to believe was better left unorganized, she expressed contempt for her own background:

> Liberation theology means liberating ourselves from others' oppression. . . . When you ask people around here, "What are the real issues of concern?" they say, "Dog shit on the lawns." If they adopted liberation theology, they'd be real reactionaries. The idea of bringing liberation theology to the U.S. makes me nervous. It could just make people more entrenched.

Jackie also doubted that liberation theology would transfer to the United States, which she felt had to come up with its own version to liberate people "horribly oppressed by the system." Perceiving the system as unsavable, she called for "some kind of revolution": "I think we're still working on our own liberation theology. We haven't even liberated our own people from our government—Indians, women, minority people here. If enough people could realize that, we'd have some kind of revolution." She believed that an "embracing" theory was necessary to liberate all oppressed groups but expressed doubt about feminism as an organizing principle, rather associating it with "white feminism" and rejecting it along with the "system": "It depends on what feminism we're talking about. I know struggles black women have expressed about white feminism. Liberation for people in this country has to happen for women and minorities—we have to find a way of embracing all oppressed groups so we can liberate all people."

Julia indicated the connections she was learning to make between liberation theology and her own community: "Paulo said something . . . that really struck me. He was talking about base communities, and someone said, 'It's fine for you, in your situation, but it doesn't relate to me.' He said, 'I'm part of your community too, and I'm oppressed.' "She identified feminism as a middle-class women's movement for "entitlement," which she failed to claim for herself. Her sanctuary work was a source of conflict at home, and she worried that doing less for her family made her a "bad person." Working with battered refugee women, she identified with "Latinas", noting that liberation theology hasn't yet "hit" them: "Liberation theology occurred because priests made people aware of their oppression, that they're entitled—but this hasn't yet hit women refugees. They see themselves as contributors, but in the domain of the home."

Jane saw no link between liberation theology and feminism but indicated the connections that liberation theology was helping her to make between her position and that of the oppressed:

> I'm part of the oppressed—the U.S. is causing this oppression. I'm part of the moneyed class. I've read some liberation theology stuff, and it's so exciting. What does it mean for me, an upper-niche white woman working for a conservative health agency? In what ways am I contributing to this oppression, and being oppressed too?

In contrast to the laywomen, the women clergy and the nuns articulated the integration of feminism and liberation theology in terms of a feminist theology equating women's oppression with that of the poor. All placed women prominently in their conceptions of human liberation, expressed as a radical feminism in which sex is the basis of oppression and women are the center of social change.[19] For example, Lori saw feminism as North America's contribution to the Latin and Asian traditions of liberation theology. To her, the appeal of liberation theology to North Americans was that it cut through "all the crap of institutional religion" and brought them back to the "mandate of the gospel," which includes "being political." She was disgusted at "institutional traditional patriarchal oppressive civil religion" in the United States.

> I've been shaped by liberation theology. It makes sense to a lot of North Americans, and that's why we've bought into it. . . . It brings us back to feeding the poor, liberating the oppressed, being political. A lot of people are turned off by the religion we have in this country that's so tied to being an American that it's disgusting—that we have flags in our churches, that criticizing the government is unpatriotic. Liberation theology brings us back to the truth.

She believed that women's exclusion from traditional liberation theology was "more than an oversight"; women's liberation from patriarchy is "what North Americans can add to it": "Women's liberation from patriarchal oppression has to be included in liberation theology. The character of liberation theology has been Latino and Asian—this hasn't been recognized. I think this is what North Americans can add to it from our own experience."

Christine's perceptions of liberation theology revealed how it had politicized her religious beliefs:

> Liberation theology comes out of "God in the midst of," not "God greater than" or "other than." God and justice are equated. It brings with it the power to operate out of that. I believe there's a preferential option for the poor—that Jesus made a radical decision to talk among the oppressed—that therefore the Christian community has explicit guidelines.

Rather than "the poor, they shall always be with you," . . . "you shall always be with the poor."

She "absolutely" perceived a link between liberation theology in Central America and the North American sanctuary movement:

> I see sanctuary as intervention or resistance that says to forces standing in the way of life for Guatemalans and Salvadorans that we stand here too; that you're preventing the life that we're here to enable. It moves the focus to El Salvador by doing accompaniment, by saying, "El Salvador should be a sanctuary." We're saying, "No more!"

As for liberation theology and feminism, she claimed that she "honestly" didn't know the difference between them. She believed that liberation theology was "true" for whoever read it in "exactly the same way" that it was important for Central Americans: "I assume feminism is liberation theology for women."

Dawn identified what she perceived as the significance of liberation theology for North American culture: "How it translates on our soil is, we're vacuous in theology. We don't have a theology, or I'd hate to think what it is." She articulated a feminist theology of women as "the underside of history." That "women are the poor" is the "starting point" for linking feminism and liberation theology. She saw a connection between "women . . . the poor . . . [and] the voiceless"—the same link women make in giving the refugees a "platform":

> Women and the children for whom they care are the most disenfranchised. Most liberation theologies are by men. Knowing of the Divine Person's special care for women as the poor provides a basis for a feminist movement. God has a special love for the poor, and women are the poor . . . the voiceless. Women are full human beings in the eyes of God.

Active for almost four decades, Geselle described her "first awareness of feminism": "When I was teaching in [another state, a nun] wrote that I should read Mary Daly's *The Church and the Second Sex*.[20] It was spring 1969. I read it and thought, yes! I was resonating with what Mary Daly said." Calling feminism "another way of condemning oppression," she offered a critique of patriarchy and a model for shared power as a basis for world leadership: "It's patriarchy. At first, I couldn't articulate it, but now I see. We need people with a whole new kind and style of leadership. It's not who's in power; it's how it's used. So far, we've had only a male-style power system." She perceived a link between feminism and liberation theology and a connection between women, the poor, and women of color in developing countries:

> Feminism and liberation theology recognize oppression and domination and work toward equality. Liberation theology articulates the attempt of the poor to come to equality, to take their rightful place in the world. They have no desire to dominate, just to be treated as human. This is like women, especially women of color in Third World countries.

Kim saw "all kinds of links" between feminism and sanctuary:

> It's women taking responsibility not only for their own lives but for the life of a nation. Feminism is the transformation of a value system. The women's movement wants mutuality, cooperation, collegiality. Sanctuary and the women's movement will do a lot for humanitarianism. The women's movement breaks down old structures.

Josie claimed that for women religious, activism comes out of "a whole idea of women as people who give birth." She linked giving birth with giving the poor "a voice": "The majority of us [in orders] are celibates, and the world hardly understands that. But we think of ourselves and how we live as giving life to a new vision and to the poor—giving them a voice because we have a voice." She took a radical feminist view of sex as the basis of human oppression: "The historical treatment of women is quite possibly the foundation of all kinds of oppression, because if you can own your wife, you can own a country, and other races. Others are less because someone in your home is less. It's not only legitimate but normative." Asked why she believed that this viewpoint was not more widespread among sanctuary women, she articulated a cultural feminist notion of women's special nature: "Because women are sensitive to suffering, they make real issues of hunger, homelessness, and think of themselves last. Relating to other women has always been . . . a value, but we'd never say it out loud that other women are important." In the rhetoric of separatist feminism, she defined women's communities as spaces free from "male dominance.":

> I'm not anti-male but what I find intolerable is a patriarchal system. Many women have to separate themselves from men because they're living out the rage and anger. Because I've lived my adult life in a community of women, I don't, but I feel it's certainly justified for women who feel they need to be free to discover our strengths.[21]

In sum, the roles of activist and woman religious tend to coexist in a seamless web, whereas those of activist, wife, and mother tend to occupy discrete, often conflicting spheres. The reluctance of women to tell families about their activism and their experience of family disapproval and complaint indicate the difficult fit between the latter set of roles. Laywomen's activism was often local, short-lived, and a source of conflict at home; that of women religious was more international, enduring, and unfettered by families. Although both groups' lives are rooted in male-dominated institutions, the day-to-day activities of women religious generally exclude men. Identifying less with "male systems," women in their world are important political actors. That religious communities' collective space may facilitate women's cognitive liberation, which families' private space may inhibit, says a great deal about women in movements and the future of sanctuary.

VII

CONCLUSION

This study locates many common threads between the macro-sphere of the national sanctuary movement and the micro-sphere of women's lives. It shows how the movement's inherent tensions between humanitarian and political impulses shape women's orientations and activities; it also suggests the outcome for the movement and women's activism of the ways women resolve these tensions. It reveals that sanctuary is a free space giving rise to and created by women's activism in woman-based groups that keep local sites going and sustain the national movement. It illustrates the importance of women's hidden work as volunteers in their communities and shows how their status as white, middle-class American women represents costs and contributions to the movement. Linking their styles of activism to the life structures of laywomen and women religious, it suggests two models for understanding women's activism and predicting the emergence of incipient feminism and female revolt.

These models show how women both facilitate and deter collective action. Women religious contributed to collective action by their greater awareness of the issues, their risk-taking, and their alignment of actions and goals with the refugees. They may have deterred it at times by failing to accommodate Central American women's views of women's place in society and the movement: the conflicts they reported over issues of gender parity, birth control, washing machines, and reliance on men suggest their anticipation that Central American women would become like them—middle-class, independent of men and families.

Married homemakers contributed to collective action in their careers as volunteers, using their established networks and their status in their communities to reproduce the refugees' lives. They may have deterred it at times by imposing their own cultural values: the conflicts they reported over issues of family size, birth control, bonding, breastfeeding, and assimilation suggest their anticipation that the refugees would follow their example as upwardly mobile nuclear families. The expectations of both groups created tensions and conflict, revealing their contrasting interpretations of the refugees' success.

Homemakers tended to care for particular sets of refugees, to view themselves as almost full-time volunteers, and to see little or no connection between the refugees' and women's situations. In contrast, women religious tended to focus on changing U.S. policies, to view themselves as almost full-time activists, and to see women as special agents of social change. When women look at local action as isolated from broader issues and fail to connect those issues with their own struggles as women, their activism tends to be relatively short-lived. When they link local action with larger political processes and make a connection with their own struggles, they tend to continue their activist careers.

Both groups experienced conflicts over their assumptions; neither seemed aware that their expectations for Central American women—to bond, breastfeed, use birth control and washing machines, and live apart from men—reinforced their own class and cultural hegemony as middle-class women. An important difference was that homemakers, whose families often opposed their activism, tended to withdraw after the refugees moved on. Women religious, lacking these cross-cutting solidarities, planned to continue their activism. Their background and training provided more opportunities to resolve issues, realign actions and goals, and continue activist careers; the fit between the roles of activist and woman religious helps explain their more enduring commitment. These models bear more generally on women's roles in movements and on the future of sanctuary and women's activism.

WOMEN IN SOCIAL MOVEMENTS

Sanctuary women share much with their forebears in other moral reform movements. Women's predominance in these movements is striking. For example, the abolition movement had substantial female involvement, and women played an important, sometimes dominant role in the underground railroad, after which sanctuary was modeled and actually exceeds in size. In the temperance movement, women probably outnumbered men from its inception.[1]

Women's participation in such movements has served both humanitarian and political ends, from Americanizing immigrants' lives to supporting broad-based reform on diverse issues.[2] A pattern appears in which women act on an ethic of caring, using their status and resources as middle-class women to organize on behalf of oppressed groups. Encountering resistance to their activism in their families, communities, and churches, they have at times developed feminist consciousness and pursued their own empowerment. For example, their exclusion from full participation in the abolition movement provided much of the impetus for the nineteenth-century women's rights movement.[3]

In the temperance movement, women's roles were narrowly restricted to family concerns until the movement began pushing for prohibition at the state level in the 1850s; thereafter, women engaged in more public and militant acts. Linking female suffrage to temperance, they perceived the vote as the most practical means of gaining temperance goals. Men's return from the Civil War and attempt to recontrol the movement coincided with the emergence of the Women's Crusade and women's almost total takeover of the movement. The crusade ended with the formation of the Women's Christian Temperance Union (WCTU), the largest women's organization of its time, which led the movement until the Anti-Saloon League took over around 1900.[4]

Women have also predominated in the peace movement. Though American women were little involved before World War I, by 1915 the Women's Peace Party was supplying much of the leadership and performing most of the "difficult, but unrecognized, behind-the-scenes organizational work." In what was basically an urban, middle-class movement, women's peace efforts were intertwined with suffrage and other reform movements of the era. The peace movement declined during the McCarthy period; women's involvement resurfaced in 1961 when, frustrated by male leaders' reluctance to deal with "mothers' issues" such as radioactively contaminated milk, five members of the Society against Nuclear Energy (SANE) called for a Women's Strike for Peace. An estimated 50,000 women attended, at the time the largest women's peace action in U.S. history. The press defined participants as "unsophisticated wives and mothers," but the House Un-American Activities Committee collected forty-three volumes of material on the movement.[5]

This study shows that women are inclined toward democratic movements and illustrates the fit between women and the democratic process. As a "collective democratic organization" (CDO), sanctuary is characterized by "value-rational authority," belief in values for their own sake, and conviction-mobilizing actions.[6] Authority resides in groups, not individuals; the aim is organization without hierarchy or domination, egalitarianism through low levels of stratification. Sanctuary women's strong preference for shared power accentuates these qualities in the movement. Often casting conflicts over leadership in terms of male domination in the movement, they stressed openness and democratic procedures partly in order to be included in decision-making.

CDOs rely on personal and moral appeals as a primary means of social control. Membership is homogeneous, which increases agreement on issues but constrains efforts to broaden such an organization's base. This closely describes sanctuary, an ethical, religious-based reform movement whose members are predominantly of the same sex, class, race, and culture. While this homogeneity lends cohesiveness, women frequently indicated that their white, middle-class background interfered with recruiting across these lines and including the refugees in decision-making.

Relations in CDOs are based on holistic, affective values. Recruitment is achieved through friendship, personality attributes, and social-political values; incentives to participate have little to do with advancement or material gain. This also describes sanctuary, which is produced in women's friendship circles. Most of the women are experienced volunteers, long accustomed to low status and little or no pay; their reward is related to caring, a value instilled in childhood. Sanctuary is also based on caring, an affect historically attributed to women.

Operations in CDOs are generally conducted in an ad hoc manner with minimal reliance on rules. On this issue, sanctuary women differ; viewing discretionary decision-making as a male prerogative that excluded them, some frequently spoke of confrontation with the men over their informal application of rules. Others adamantly defended the importance of rules—for example, by insisting that "the refugees need a budget" and calling the men "paternalistic" for arbitrarily giving them money. Because of their sensitivity to being excluded by unshared power, sanctuary women may actually surpass most CDOs in their emphasis on democratic procedures.

Because major institutions reinforce ways of thinking that are incompatible with collectivist orientations, all CDOs include some individuals unsuited for participatory democracy, resulting in "culture disjunctures."[7] Women in this study clearly identified some men as unsuited for democratic participation, and patriarchy as the culture disjuncture. Linking openness with their own participation, they found the solution in the democratic method itself. In doing so, they upheld an old tradition: democracy has predominated in middle-class women's rhetoric since liberal feminism first appeared in the seventeenth century.[8]

A study of an abortion collective reveals similarities between sanctuary and other illegal woman-based CDOs.[9] In such movements, law officers often informally support and comply with illegal activities; recruitment through participants' personal networks enhances their sense of security; illegal activities and the salience of an external enemy heighten group commitment, cohesiveness, and efficiency; and solving problems compounded by the law satisfies participants and helps sustain the movement.

Although character traits and predisposing attitudes fail to explain movement participation, the study shows that the impetus to collective action is nonetheless cognitive. Value expectancy theory locates the impetus to act in group settings, where individuals assess the costs and benefits of activism partly by assessing others' actions. Activism is most likely when individuals have high expectations about the number of other participants, their own contribution to the probability of success, and the likelihood of success if many people participate.[10]

The life structures of laywomen and women religious account for their contrasting assessments of the costs and benefits of activism, resulting in distinctive orientations and activities. Their perceptions of the efficacy of their own and others' actions help explain why laywomen tend to work as volunteers in local communities whose participation is humanitarian and short-lived, and why women religious tend to work as activists in a national movement whose participation is politically oriented and ongoing. This says something about the relative influence of private families and same-sex religious groups on the character and longevity of women's activism.

The study shows women geographically dispersed in society, linked to men through a variety of ties that give some more interest in emphasizing the cooperative rather than the conflicting aspects of their relationships with men. Those outside the family system have an advantage in organizing for collective action: "The absence of ties to other groups minimizes the effect that appeals to loyalty might have in the case of better integrated antagonists."[11] Laywomen and women religious both emphasized conflicting aspects of their relationships with men. Despite their greater dependency on them, laywomen tended to view men as obstacles to power yet failed to claim feminism as a liberating ideology or link gendered conflicts with other issues. Women religious also struggled with "male influence" but owed no loyalty to individual men, as did laywomen, the "better integrated antagonists." Their greater autonomy in religious orders enhanced the process of developing a political consciousness and engaging in collective action. Further, although they criticized the patriarchal church, their positions within its hierarchy reduced the chance of reprisals for their activism.

Other studies confirm the primacy of structural-organizational factors in accounting for the contrasting roles in the movement of laywomen and women religious. For example, prior contact with movement members is closely linked with activism. Though both groups were recruited through interpersonal channels—the "single richest source of recruits"—women religious were more closely connected to core movement members. Membership in other organizations is also linked with activism; "joiners" are more likely to be aware of and drawn into movement activities. Both groups were joiners but tended to join somewhat different groups—that is, charity- versus politics-oriented ones—and women religious seemed to join more formal organizations. Prior activism influences the likelihood of future activism. Women religious had previously acquired more knowhow and learned new roles in ways that confirmed their activist identities; they expended more "sunk social costs" in long-standing lines of action.[12]

"Biographical availability"—the biological circumstances of people's lives that encourage or constrain their participation—is also linked to activism. The two groups were available in different ways; laywomen tended to have family duties and part-time jobs; women religious all had full-time jobs and multiple organizational commitments. Movement participants are consistently recruited along established lines of interaction that constitute a communication network whose strength and breadth largely determines the pattern, speed, and extent of movement expansion.[13] Laywomen were more locally involved and organizationally isolated; women religious belonged to a greater variety and number of local and national organizations, making their facilitative contact and recruitment more likely.

Studies indicate that established groups within movements ensure the presence of recognized leaders, who are among the first to join the new movements by virtue of their central position in earlier ones. The groups to which women religious belong are more formal and enduring, making up the movement's invisible leadership. They represent "movement halfway houses": established groups, only partially integrated into the larger society, whose members are actively involved in efforts to bring about social change. These groups serve as repositories of information about past movements, strategies and tactics, and inspiration and leadership—particularly important during lulls in movement activity.[14]

As educated middle-class women in their middle years, both groups of the women interviewed had been affected during their lives by the changing status of women, the emergent women's movement, and women's rise as a "new class." However, laywomen's micro-mobilization contexts had more "infrastructure deficits" in the density and number of informal and formal associations, whereas those of women religious better enabled them to transform the "mini-feminist revolts" they experienced in other settings into a rhetoric of feminist theology.[15] These differences account for women's contrasting orientations and activities, and their effect on the future of the movement and women's activism.

THE FUTURE OF SANCTUARY

The "organizational trajectories" of social movements indicate that their outcomes are never simple. Winning acceptance by authorities is substantially more likely than achieving stated goals. In some cases, collective action may actually stall new public policy innovations. Indirect effects—including changes in public perceptions, the creation of committed activist cohorts, and the emergence of countermovements—are usually more lasting. Retaining old members' energies and loyalties helps sustain others' commitment, contributing to the "bandwagon effect." Some members remain active during long periods of movement decline, initiating others at a later time; some take up other causes, using their skills in other movements.[16]

Though social movements may affect political systems in many ways, they are often co-opted or repressed. The very success of a movement may lead to fragmentation and demise—typically after it has enjoyed a period of success and respectability—and more often by co-optation than repression. Fragmentation occurs when accommodations and co-optations have stripped away the outer ring of supporters who, believing that things have improved, turn to other causes or drop out altogether. Remaining members may fight among themselves over continuing, modifying, or replacing the original goals. Strategy outcomes depend on participants' differing interests, locations in the social structure, and personal commitments. As leadership requirements change and the movement's earlier charisma is routinized, leaders may contend for supremacy, attempting to create their own followings within the movement. Some leaders may be co-opted by society; others may attempt to lead segments of the movement down new paths. Members seldom recognize a movement's demise, viewing it instead as a success or temporary setback. However defined,

> it is simply a "mopping up" phase for . . . society. . . . Co-optation . . . has "bought off" . . . its leaders and most effective members, and has choked off most of its outside support. This leaves only small bands of "true believers" who appear increasingly ridiculous . . . [and] are either driven to complete secession . . . or left to face the onslaught of total repression from a now unrestrained public consensus.[17]

In the case of sanctuary, the movement is down but not out. It flourished between 1984 and 1987, then took new directions. The same U.S. policies exist, similar conditions prevail for the refugees, and only one participant has actually done time—Stacey Merkt of Casa Romero, Texas. While its outcome is unknown, the movement's future course is speculative.

A serious setback for movements is that "localists" and "global-ists" active on the same problems often work in isolation from each other, diminishing the potential impact of both. Because sanctuary includes both focuses, it represents "possible transformative pos-tures": occasions to explore the problems that have led to disjunc-tions between the "local" and the "global":

> There are many people . . . concerned with global issues (e.g., the arms race, communications, ecology, militarization, pov-erty, and war). At the same time, there is considerable grass-roots activity on social issues focused on local commu-nities. . . . Yet with notable exceptions for short periods of time (e.g., the nuclear freeze movement, Sanctuary, anti-apartheid movement, etc.), there appears to be a lack of re-sponse by grass-roots activists to global issues.[18]

Sanctuary's dual focus on local and global issues enhances its chances of survival by providing alternative routes for its develop-ment. The movement is in transition along humanitarian and politi-cal paths, suggesting the lines of action that participants may follow in response to changes in U.S. policies and the refugees' situation. Its goals of educating communities on the issues and changing the balance of international power will make its outcome instructive for understanding other movements' futures.

Whether the Reform Act extends asylum to more refugees or co-opts the movement by diverting attention from their plight, it has created a fork in the movement's development, indicating the routes by which participants may act. Evidence suggests that since it was passed in 1986, there has been less emphasis on transporting and sheltering refugees and more on attempting to assist those already in the U.S. to win legal status, particularly those previously deemed ineligible. Evidence also suggests that there has been more overt opposition to U.S. policies in Central America. As the Reform Act has swept political and economic refugees into the same category, masking their distinction in a one-time-only opportunity for citizen-ship, many participants have shifted their attention to protesting and "turning the railroad around" by accompanying the refugees home to repopulate their villages.[19]

May 4, 1988, was the deadline for applying for amnesty under the Reform Act. About 120,000 of Chicago's estimated 300,000 illegal immigrants applied for legal status, more than 10,000 filing on the last day. The deadline was followed by stepped-up INS raids, the use of children as "bait" to capture their undocumented parents, and continued denial of political asylum to Salvadorans and Guatemalans. Shortly before the deadline, INS agents arrested eighty-five people; a week after it, they raided a factory with 126 employees and arrested 122 suspected of being undocumented. During the month, agents boarded city buses and detained several passengers suspected of being undocumented, many apparently because they had Hispanic features.[20]

Some women anticipated the new wave of government harassment and repression following the Reform Act. For example, Kim believed that its "residual effects"—deportations and family breakups—would make sanctuary more necessary. Dawn expected to see "strategically targeted groups": "Our government [will] say, 'See, we have only Communist subversives entering the country. The decent people who want to join us and be Americans and get real jobs and pay income tax have applied. The others are expendable.'" Others perceived the need for more direct action in the future, naming "repopulation and repatriation," "turning the railroad around and getting the refugees home," "escalation and creativity of activities," and "targeting those more directly complicit—the army, military, and police."

The women were nearly united in the belief that sanctuary was and would continue to be effective in challenging U.S. policies, a belief they tended to express in the rhetoric of winners; as Dina put it, "We're on the right side." Some gauged the movement's effectiveness in terms of the government's repressive sanctions against it, citing "all the FBI infiltration and bugging," "church people targeted by the CIA," "the Tucson trials," and "sanctuary break-ins" as evidence of "just how effective" the movement had been. One noted that "the media picking up on the Tucson trials backfired on the Reagan administration"; another, that "the government lost the trials," giving the movement "publicity," "attention," and "name recognition."

Others gauged the movement's effectiveness by its ability to "educate" and "expose" nonparticipants to the issues. For example, Belinda stated that "people on our own peace and justice committee who knew nothing about Central America found out about it." Megan claimed that sanctuary's educational function—"its concern for the growth of North American people"—was "the whole key" distinguishing it from other "solidarity groups." Lori believed that others' awareness "will eventually have an impact" but that "it takes a long time for that groundswell to manifest itself."

Several women linked the movement's effectiveness to its partnership with other antiintervention groups, for example, describing sanctuary as "one of hundreds of resistance movements," one that has "added legitimacy to antiinterventionist work." One woman stated that "all these causes are interrelated"; another, that because of these organizations, "you can't deny there's a war going on." Still another considered these groups "the reason we're not involved in a war in Central America right now." Three women believed that sanctuary and other solidarity groups "may have staved off an invasion of Nicaragua."

Women generally indicated that they were "in this for the long haul," perhaps "fifteen to twenty years," and that "the war in Central America" would "be around for a long time." Anticipating "radical grouch" (activist burnout), they discussed the problems of "how to sustain work over time," even without the presence of refugees. None expected change immediately, and some commented that they didn't believe they would see change in their lifetime. In sum, they perceived that "the U.S. empire isn't going to give up."

Their rhetoric indicates how the religious character of their involvement helped them maintain their commitment. One called the "inevitable outcome" of sanctuary the "Kingdom on Earth"— the "New Earth, with capitals N and E." Others claimed that "when the time is right, people will be converted ... [by] an unseen power"; that "we have to be converted as a nation"; and that sanctuary was fighting for "the salvation of the soul of America." One declared that she had been "called" to the work.

Women often acknowledged the importance of religious institutions as weapons in their struggle to change U.S. policies. For example, Gina called the church "a formidable opponent" of the State Department. Similarly, Dawn located the church within her political strategy for "getting the truth out": "We don't receive a balanced picture from the press—the print and electronic media are all controlled, and the military is the government. The church is probably one of the main vehicles for getting the truth out."

One woman, a member of the national task force of Ronald Reagan's denomination, reported attending a meeting Reagan (then president) called to chastise the group's "strong stand against his policies." Recalling his accusation that they were "deluded by the propaganda machine of Nicaragua" and his claim that "the U.S. government has access to more information than anybody else in the world," she indicated that the group's response had used "the church" as a weapon: "We said, 'There is no institution outside of the church that more permeates society and has access to more information in Nicaragua.'" Interpreting the meeting as state recognition of "the threat by the people of God in this country," she spoke of "the power of God" and "church people" as weapons: "Secular powers recognize the significance of, in our case, the Christian faith way more than we Christians ever believe—it's the power of God that threatens them. Otherwise, why are church people the first to be killed?"

Women articulated a variety of perceptions of sanctuary's problems and solutions, only a few revealing a naive or simplistic understanding of the issues. Claiming to know only what she "thinks, feels, and sees," Ginny believed that "the government is creating these refugees"; she didn't think sanctuary had been effective or know "what more we can do." Charlotte saw "greed" as the problem and "sharing and greater compassion" as the solution. Pam disbelieved that "our leaders know" how "repressive Central American governments" are: "They're not that smart . . . they don't even speak Spanish"; they may simply be afraid that the refugees will "take all our jobs." She hoped that the refugees would assimilate and "meld into the country" as her maid and the "boat people" had done: "If they have a work ethic, they can survive." Unconcerned that "what's-his-name in Nicaragua" might be a Communist, she saw no viable solution to the refugees' overall problems, though she hoped that sanctuary would play a role in "stopping the whole cycle."

Others cast problems and solutions in more political terms. Some indicated their concern with movement strategy. For example, Josie spoke of preserving plurality by including "legislative acts like letter-writing" with "civil disobedience." Andrea ranked "getting the people back home and bringing peace and justice to their countries" ahead of "making a national movement." Dawn located the solution in being a prophet and community organizer: "People in the Old Testament were prophets [who] could criticize and get out of town. They didn't stay to orchestrate a movement. The challenge is to remain strategically clever."

Some offered somewhat sophisticated political analyses. For example, Megan spoke of the "historical arrogance of the U.S." as evidenced by the Monroe Doctrine and Alliance for Progress. She perceived Nicaragua and Grenada as "real threats" to U.S. policy in that they posed an "alternative model that addresses human needs." Alicia described the "confluence of events" creating the situation in Central America and the U.S. government's role as an "active participant" in maintaining "this system." Lena linked sanctuary problems to "denial in America," the same kinds of problems her Jewish relatives had faced during her childhood: "We're talking about a nation of cowards who choose illusions over reality." Hannah named the "charisma and sensationalism" surrounding President Reagan as what "worried" her "the most": "Once the public raises somebody to the pinnacle they have Reagan, it's hard to realize the emperor has no clothes."

In sum, the women were nearly united in their view that sanctuary had challenged U.S. policies in Central America and in their commitment to changing them. They claimed to be prepared for the "long haul" that such change would require and trusted their religion-based approach to bring change about. Speaking in the rhetoric of winners, they used "God," "the church," and "church people" on their "side" as weapons against U.S. policies. They also tended to talk tough. Although "CD is never convenient," Moira vowed, if the U.S. were to invade Nicaragua, she would "be out there." She believed that for every "frontline resister" there were "fifteen more who . . . when push comes to shove" would resist, and "twenty-five to thirty more" who would "at that point come out of the woodwork." Noting that "everybody in all these solidarity groups has friends," she claimed that "the network is much, much larger than the government thinks." She was quite confident that "if push comes to shove," the American people would "side with a revolutionary movement."

These women were far more optimistic about the movement's future than social movement theory would predict. Their indefatigable optimism was part of their strategy of talking tough, using religious rhetoric as a weapon against state policies. This study predicts, however, that laywomen will continue to have a high turnover in the movement while women religious remain active on related issues. Only time will tell which path the movement as a whole will take and how its woman-based constituency will influence the outcome.

METHODS

This is an ethnographic study of twenty-nine women who participated in the Chicago sanctuary movement between 1982 and 1987, based on in-depth interviews conducted between May and November 1987. I was interested in women's participation in social movements, found the literature fascinating but sketchy, and wanted a closer look at the details of activist women's lives. Reading about the 1985–86 Arizona trial in the newspapers made me realize that seeing sanctuary as a woman-based movement provided an opportunity to examine issues surrounding women's activism, especially given its international concerns and illegal activities.

Initially, I knew no one in the movement and would have relied entirely on cold calls had I not run into a friend who had a friend active in sanctuary; I interviewed her first, and she referred me to others. Using a snowball sample, I was recommended among acquaintances within a citywide network. At its limits, I phoned ministers and rabbis at publicly known sanctuaries, described the study, and asked for referrals; in every case, I received the names of a few active members.[1]

I generally first interviewed the caretakers at local sites who were doing the day-to-day work of sanctuary, then the leadership. I contacted women by phone, introducing myself and my study of how women in social movements contribute to social change. Before requesting an interview, I named other women—usually those I'd already interviewed—who'd recommended them. We then set up a time and place for the interview, as they preferred, anywhere from a week to two months away. I often sensed women's mixed feelings about participating: their interest in the study and desire to talk about the issues were tempered by an understandable caution about discussing their activism with a stranger. I assumed that were any so inclined, they could check on me between the call and the interview or reconsider participating. To the best of my knowledge, no one called my university to confirm the study's legitimacy, and no one canceled, even though three women did mention their concern that I might be a "spy."

The Chicago movement includes a network of about fifteen churches and synagogues or "sites" that make up six neighborhood coalitions, loosely allied with several local and national groups concerned with antiintervention in Central America. My interviewees were active at eight sites, evenly divided between the city and suburbs: two Jewish,[2] two Catholic, and four Protestant. One woman was active at the Overground Railroad (OR), a parallel but unrelated sanctuary operation whose headquarters are nearby.

The sample comprises fifteen Catholic, eleven Protestant, and three Jewish women (see Table 1). Twenty were laywomen, and nine were women religious (six nuns, three clergywomen).[3] Twenty-eight were white, one black.[4] Ages ranged from twenty-six to seventy-three; median age was forty-two, mean age forty-four. Sixteen women were married (two had been divorced and remarried); five were single laywomen; six were nuns; one was divorced and one widowed. Sixteen had children, ranging from age one to adult. Married women had a fairly low divorce rate—three divorces in the sample, or about a third the rate of their national counterparts. All women were from middle-class backgrounds, ranging from lower- to upper-middle class. All had attended college, and only three lacked undergraduate degrees; fifteen had graduate degrees, six of which were professional (law, social work, theology, pharmacology). Fourteen were employed full time and ten part time; four did no paid work; one was retired. Among women religious, eight worked full time and one part time. Among laywomen, six were working full time, nine part time, and five not at all.

I interviewed each woman at least once (four women, twice) for an average of two and two-thirds hours. I met with nineteen at their homes, three at restaurants, and seven at their jobs: three at antiintervention agencies, two at universities, and two at churches. Because of the sensitivity of sanctuary issues, participants' confidentiality was central to the research. I used no tape recorder, instead recording the interviews by hand and transcribing them later on a computer. Except for well-publicized national sanctuary figures (John Fife, Jim Corbett, Renny Golden, Stacey Merkt, Darlene Nicgorski) and one agency (CRTFCA), all activists, sanctuary sites, and support organizations remain anonymous or pseudonymous; denominations appear only as "church" (Protestant), "parish" (Catholic), and "synagogue" (Jewish).

The sensitivity of sanctuary issues shaped the study in other ways as well. I learned early on in the fieldwork that the paradigm of the social research interview according to methodological texts was inappropriate for gaining entry to and information about an illegal movement. This standard paradigm casts the interview as a "mechanical instrument of data-collection" in which one person asks questions and another gives answers.[5]

APPENDIX TABLE I. SUBJECTS BY RELIGION, AGE, CHILDREN, AND MARITAL STATUS

Subject/Religion	Age	Children	Married	Divorced	Single	Widowed
Clergy						
Lori	26				X	
Leslie	31				X	
Christine	51	5	X			
Nuns						
Dawn	34				X	
Rose	50				X	
Kim	53				X	
Josie	57				X	
Moira	62				X	
Geselle	62				X	
Lay Catholic						
Margaret	28				X	
Megan	31				X	
Charlotte	34	1	X			
Dina	38	2	X			
Jennifer	39	1	X			
Julia	40	3	X			
Eva	43	2	X			
Gloria	44	6	X			
Ginny	59	4		X		
Lay Protestant						
Andrea	27				X	
Donna	30		X			
Jeannine	33		X			
Jane	41	1	X			
Jackie	42	1	X			
Belinda	42	2	X			
Gina	53	4	X			
Hannah	73	3				X
Lay Jewish						
Alicia	47	2	X			
Pam	48	2	X			
Lena	55	4	X			

Note: Names are fictitious. $N = 29$. Median age = 42; mean age = 44. Laywomen's religious affiliations are those in which they were brought up.

Such a procedure was clearly wrong for investigating the sanctuary movement because it made the interviewer's role too much like that of a government agent. (One woman noted, "INS always wears a yellow shirt and blue tie.") I gave up attempting a neutral role early on and settled for a strategy of talking over sanctuary-related issues with women before beginning the formal interview. Fortuitously, the televised Iran-contra hearings were ongoing during this time, and women were invariably watching them when I arrived for the interview. These broadcasts provided an excellent backdrop: not only did they touch on many sanctuary issues, but exchanging news and gossip about the hearings helped establish a sense of trust and mutuality. This approach accepted a smaller risk of biasing the views of those already committed to the issues by appearing to concur with them in exchange for the greater risk of learning little by acting like a spy and being too neutral.

My sharing certain traits with these women was both an asset and a liability. I generally resembled them in sex, age, race, education, class, and background, and they seemed to open up and confide as readily as they would with a friend. Yet these same traits made me a more likely suspect as a spy. As my third informant put it, "The government would send somebody like you to infiltrate the movement in the North." At first I was quite concerned to avoid seeming like a spy, but the more I learned about the movement's issues, the more freely participants shared; hence, my role became easier over time.

The interviews were somewhat unstructured and open-ended, depending on women's available time. I asked several questions of all women, followed by more specific, individually tailored queries seeking details and explanations. Patterns in background, orientation, and reasons for participating in sanctuary emerged early. Rhetoric about early caring, special fathers, volunteering, desire to make their faith real and "do something" about social issues, finding a special church or synagogue, and subsequent activist careers strongly suggested the importance of humanitarian, religious, and political paths as central concepts.

I asked questions along these lines: How did you first hear about sanctuary? How did you first get involved? What were your first thoughts and impressions? How did you decide what to do? What was your experience? Are you still active? Describe how sanctuary came to your church or synagogue. What kinds of sanctuary activities do or did you take part in? How has your family responded to your participation? Are there conflicts over it? Do your children or husband participate? Do you see differences in what men and women do in the movement? Are there conflicts between them? What do you make of these? Do you feel that anything in your background helps explain how you became involved in sanctuary? Have you done other volunteer work? How did you start? What was your religious background and development? How did you first become politically active? What course has your activism taken since then? Were your reasons for getting involved humanitarian, religious, political, or other? What does feminism mean to you? liberation theology? Do you see links between these? between these and sanctuary? What do you see as the movement's problems and solutions? Do you feel it has been or will be effective? How do you perceive its future?

Discussion was expanded or narrowed depending on women's time constraints. The interviews with nineteen of twenty laywomen took place at their homes; these were generally longer and more focused on life histories and day-to-day experiences with the refugees. Those with seven of the nine women religious interviewed at their jobs were briefer, more focused on the movement, and more difficult to arrange. Interviews with these two groups also differed qualitatively. Laywomen tended to speak freely and at length about their personal histories; interviews averaged three to five hours, interrupted frequently by children, pets, visitors, phone calls, and meal preparations. On the whole, laywomen were extremely generous with their time. Women religious had much less available time, rarely exceeding two hours, and they tended to stick to the larger issues. These differences create unevenness in the case material; it reveals a great deal about the personal lives of laywomen and little about those of women religious, who seemed reluctant to speak personally. This makes comparing the two groups' early development difficult; for example, laywomen's "cognitive liberation" is more apparent. Other comparisons—their orientations and activities, how they perceive and resolve conflicts and link personal and political issues— were easier, partly because the differences were so striking.

NOTES

CHAPTER I

1. See Ignatius Bau, *This Ground Is Holy: Church Sanctuary and Central American Refugees* (New York: Paulist Press, 1985); Gary MacEoin, ed., *Sanctuary: A Resource Guide for Understanding and Participating in the Central American Refugees' Struggle* (San Francisco: Harper & Row, 1985); Renny Golden and Michael McConnell, *Sanctuary: The New Underground Railroad* (New York: Orbis Books, 1986); Paul Burks, "This Is Sanctuary: A Reformation in Our Time," in *Churches In Struggle: Liberation Theology and Social Change in North America*, ed. William K. Tabb, pp. 291–300 (New York: Monthly Review Press, 1986); Judith McDaniel, *Sanctuary: A Journey* (Ithaca, N.Y.: Firebrand Books, 1987); Ann Crittenden, *Sanctuary: A Story of American Conscience and the Law in Collision* (New York: Weidenfeld & Nicolson, 1988); Robert Tomsho, *The American Sanctuary Movement* (Austin: Texas Monthly Press, 1988); and Miriam Davidson, *Convictions of the Heart: Jim Corbett and the Sanctuary Movement* (Tucson: University of Arizona Press, 1988).

2. John Fife is quoted in "Answering to a Higher Obligation," *San Jose Mercury News,* Jan. 1, 1985, p. 1.

3. See Doug McAdam, John D. McCarthy, and Mayer N. Zald, "Social Movements," in *Handbook of Sociology,* ed. Neil J. Smelser (Newbury Park, Calif.: Sage, 1988), p. 718.

4. See Doug McAdam, *Political Process and the Development of Black Insurgency: 1930–1970* (Chicago: University of Chicago Press, 1982).

5. See George Herbert Mead, *Mind, Self, and Society* (Chicago: University of Chicago Press, 1934).

6. See Crittenden, *Sanctuary,* pp. 222, 234–35.

7. "Ideal types" means hypothetical pure types, which don't actually exist; see Hans H. Gerth and C. Wright Mills, *From Max Weber: Essays in Sociology* (New York: Oxford University Press, 1958), p. 59.

8. See Cynthia H. Enloe, "Bananas, Bases, and Patriarchy," *Radical America* 19, no. 4 (1985): 7–23.

9. See Verta Taylor, "Sisterhood, Solidarity, and Modern Feminism," *Gender and Society* 3, no. 2 (1989): 285.

10. Incipient feminist movements call for a radical restructuring of relationships between men and women; see Janet Saltzman Chafetz and Anthony Gary Dworkin, *Female Revolt: Women's Movements in World and Historical Perspective* (Totowa, N.J.: Rowman & Allanheld, 1986), pp. 20–21.

11. In other words, "if female disadvantage is so pervasive across time and space, what explains the emergence of women's movements in specific places . . . [and] eras?" (ibid., p. 1).

12. See Arlene K. Daniels, "The Hidden Work of Constructing Class and Community," in *Families and Work*, ed. Naomi Gerstel and Harriet Engel Gross, pp. 220–35 (Philadelphia: Temple University Press, 1987); and Daniels; *Invisible Careers: Women Community Leaders in the Volunteer World* (Chicago: University of Chicago Press, 1988).

13. Free spaces are "settings between private lives and large-scale institutions where ordinary citizens can act with dignity, independence, and vision"; see Sara M. Evans and Harry C. Boyte, *Free Spaces: The Sources of Democratic Change in America* (New York: Harper & Row, 1986), p. 17.

14. Chafetz and Dworkin, *Female Revolt*, pp. 21–22.

15. See Robert Bellah, Richard Madsen, William Sullivan, Ann Swidler, and Steven Tipton, *Habits of the Heart: Individualism and Commitment in American Life* (New York: Harper & Row, 1985).

16. See McAdam, McCarthy, and Zald, "Social Movements," p. 704.

17. See Evans and Boyte, *Free Spaces*, pp. 7, 16, 19.

18. See Bau, *This Ground Is Holy;* MacEoin, *Sanctuary;* and Golden and McConnell, *Sanctuary.*

19. See Charles L. Blockson, "The Underground Railroad," *National Geographic* 166, no. 1 (1984): 3–39; Sheila D. Collins, "The New Underground Railroad," *Monthly Review* 38, no. 1 (1986): 1–7; and Shelley Baranowski, *The Confessing Church: Conservative Elites and the Nazi State* (New York: E. Mellen, 1986).

20. See Morris J. Blachman, William K. Leogrande, and Kenneth Sharpe, *Confronting Revolution: Security through Diplomacy in Central America* (New York: Pantheon Books, 1986), pp. 4–9; and Tom Barry and Deb Preusch, *The Central American Fact Book* (New York: Grove Press, 1986), pp. 313–15.

21. See Blachman, Leogrande, and Sharpe, *Confronting Revolution*, pp. 12–14. "Base communities" are the grassroots Christian communities that first emerged in Brazil in the 1960s as small, church-based social action groups; see Leonardo Boff, *Ecclesiogenesis: The Base Communities Reinvent the Church* (Maryknoll, N.Y.: Orbis Books, 1986), pp. 1–3.

The number of people living in poverty in the Central American region increased from 130 to 165 million between 1980 and 1989, while per capita income dropped 20 percent to the level of the early 1970s and unemployment rose from 26 to 41 million; 68 percent of available housing is inadequate, and 40 percent of families do not earn enough to meet their caloric needs; each year 700,000 children die of hunger, and each newborn inherits a debt of $1,052 to banks in the developed world (Mimmo Candito, *World Press Review*, July 1989, p. 22).

22. See Blachman, Leogrande, and Sharpe, *Confronting Revolution*, pp. 12–15, 31; Barry and Preusch, *Fact Book*, p. 313; Phillip Berryman, *Inside Central America* (New York: Pantheon Books, 1985), p. 137; Blase Bonpane, *Guerrillas of Peace: Liberation Theology and the Central American Revolution* (Boston: South End Press, 1985), p. 99; and "Guatemalan Repression," *World Press Review*, July 1989, p. 46.

23. Blachman, Leogrande, and Sharpe, *Confronting Revolution*, p. 16. See also Berryman, *Inside Central America*, p. 137.

24. Barry and Preusch, *Fact Book*, p. 315; Berryman, *Inside Central America*, pp. 39, 82; Jon Reed, "Bringing the War Home: El Salvadoran Resistance Takes the Offensive," *Zeta*, May 1989, p. 45; Janet Shenk, "El Salvador: Central America's Forgotten War," *Mother Jones*, July–August 1986, p. 72.

25. American Friends Service Committee pamphlet, *Invasion: A Guide to the U.S. Military Presence in Central America* (1983), pp. 3, 12.

26. See Barry and Preusch, *Fact Book*, p. 316; Georges Fauriol, "Refuge from Reality: The Sanctuary Movement and Central America," *Humanist*, March–April 1986, p. 13; Harris Meyer, "Immigrant Tide Floods Clinics to Breaking Point," *Chicago Tribune*, May 14, 1989, p. 8; Lois Armstrong, "Trouble: Busted by Federal Agents, a Tucson Pastor Keeps the Sanctuary Lights Aflame for Fleeing Salvadorans," *People*, March 25, 1985, p. 53; James Lemoyne, "Salvadorans Stream into U.S. Fleeing Poverty and Civil War," *New York Times*, April 13, 1987, p. A1; and Jorge Reyes Estrada, "The Journey to the Rio Grande: Crossing Mexico 'Is Worse than Hell,'" *World Press Review*, April 1989, pp. 30–31.

27. Detainees were now required to post bond for status hearings, "a procedure generally waived by pre-Reagan administrations"; see Armstrong, "Trouble," p. 57. See also Seth Miller, "The Immigration Control Act," *Basta!* Dec. 87, pp. 4–5; and Rachel Kreier, "Tending the Psychological Wounds of Central American Conflict," *In These Times*, Sept. 2–8, 1987, pp. 2–3.

28. See Fauriol, "Refuge from Reality," p. 14; Crittenden, *Sanctuary*, pp. 18–20, 22; Eric Jorstad, "No Routine Smugglers: Reverberations from the

'Sanctuary' Trial," *Commonweal*, Oct. 10, 1986, pp. 522–25; John Cummins, "The Sanctuary Tradition," *Humanist*, March–April 1986, p. 9; *Basta!* Dec. 1987, p. 18; "Sanctuary—A Public Debate," *Nuestro*, Sept. 1985, p. 16; and "No Hiding Place Here," *Newsweek*, March 4, 1985, p. 15.

29. See Crittenden, *Sanctuary*, pp. 354–55, 359–63, 367–69; McConnell, *Sanctuary*, p. 33; Americas Watch, *Report on Human Rights in Nicaragua* (July 1985), p. 3.

30. William Sloane Coffin, "The Tasks Ahead," in MacEoin, *Sanctuary*, p. 177.

31. Cummins, "Sanctuary Tradition," p. 9.

32. Crittenden, *Sanctuary*, p. 365.

33. See Miller, "Immigration Control Act," pp. 3–4; "Thousands Skirt Immigration Law," *Chicago Tribune*, Nov. 12, 1989, p. 3; Crittenden, *Sanctuary*, p. 348; "Immigrant Advocates Protest End of Amnesty," *Chicago Sun-Times*, May 6, 1988, p. 35; and Carolyn Patty Blum, "Canadian Immigration Policies Changes," *Basta!* June 1987, pp. 45–47.

34. See Crittenden, *Sanctuary*, pp. xvi, 44, 52, 54, 61.

35. Ibid., pp. 6, 8, 10; Fife quoted in Armstrong, "Trouble," p. 53; Bau, *This Ground Is Holy*, p. 10.

36. Bau, *This Ground Is Holy*, p. 11.

37. Golden and McConnell, *Sanctuary*, pp. 41, 45–57.

38. Gary MacEoin, "A Brief History of the Sanctuary Movement," in MacEoin, *Sanctuary*, p. 22.

39. See *Basta!* Feb. 1986, p. 8; *Newsweek*, "No Hiding Place Here"; and Crittenden, *Sanctuary*, p. xvi.

40. See *Basta!* June 1987, p. 51; and "First 'Sanctuary State,'" *Christian Century*, April 23, 1986, p. 408. Cities declare themselves sanctuaries as a symbolic gesture in support of the refugees, meaning that local agencies including police will not enforce INS laws by checking on refugees' status or handing over suspected refugees (Crittenden, *Sanctuary*, p. 298). See "Arizona 'Sanctuary' Convictions Are Upheld," *Chicago Sun-times*, March 31, 1989, p. 27; *Basta!* Feb. 1986, pp. 42–46; Golden and McConnell, *Sanctuary*, p. 3; and Crittenden, *Sanctuary*, p. 245.

41. See Golden and McConnell, *Sanctuary*, pp. 48–52; and Crittenden, *Sanctuary*, pp. 88–89.

42. See Golden and McConnell, *Sanctuary*, p. 53; *Sanctuary: A Justice Ministry* (Chicago: CRTFCA, 1986); *Public Sanctuary for Salvadoran and Guatemalan Refugees: Organizer's Nuts & Bolts* (Chicago: CRTFCA, n.d.).

43. Crittenden, *Sanctuary*, p. 90.

44. Quoted in Golden and McConnell, *Sanctuary*, p. 56.
45. Crittenden, *Sanctuary*, pp. 91–92.
46. Crittenden, *Sanctuary*, pp. 88–90, 203.
47. See MacEoin, *Sanctuary*, 1985, p. 24. Eleven church workers were prosecuted for helping undocumented refugees enter and remain in the United States; three were acquitted, and eight were convicted and sentenced to five years' probation (see *Chicago Sun-Times*, "Arizona 'Sanctuary' Convictions Are Upheld"). See also Crittenden, *Sanctuary*, pp. 141, 203, 234–35, 252; Alan C. Nelson, "The Sanctuary Movement: Humanitarian Action, Political Opposition or Lawlessness?" *Vital Speeches* 52, no. 16 (1986): 483–84; Claudia Dreifus, "Women of the Sanctuary Movement," *Glamour*, Sept. 1985, p. 418; *Nuestro*, "Sanctuary," pp. 14, 18; and *Basta!* Feb. 1986, p. 3.
48. See Crittenden, *Sanctuary*, pp. 93, 95–96, 204; and "More on the Sanctuary Movement," *Monthly Review*, Sept. 1986, pp. 39–40.
49. Renny Golden, "Sanctuary: Choosing Sides," *Socialist Review* 16, no. 6 (1986): 105.
50. See *Basta!* June 1986, p. 23.
51. Ibid.
52. Ibid.
53. All names used for the study participants are pseudonyms; their comments are quoted from the interviews (see the Appendix).
54. According to congressional hearings, the Central Intelligence Agency, Federal Bureau of Investigation, and National Security Administration have monitored the activities of sanctuary members and other opponents of U.S. policies in Central America; over three hundred incidents of harassment, including one hundred break-ins, were reported between 1984 and 1988. See Brian Glick, *War At Home: Covert Action against U.S. Activists and What We Can Do about It* (Boston: South End Press, 1989), p. 2; and Jane Juffer, "Sanctuary Crackdown Nabs Reporter," *Progressive*, May 1988, p. 14.
55. For examples of political process theory, see Charles Tilly, *From Mobilization to Revolution* (Reading, Mass.: Addison-Wesley, 1978); Theda Skocpol, *States and Social Revolutions* (New York: Cambridge University Press, 1979); and McAdam, *Political Process*.
56. McAdam, McCarthy, and Zald, "Social Movements," pp. 716, 719; and Charles Tilly, "Social Movements and National Politics," in *Statemaking and Social Movements: Essays in History and Theory*, ed. Charles Bright and Susan Harding (Ann Arbor: University of Michigan Press, 1984), pp. 297–317.
57. See Edward Shorter and Charles Tilly, *Strikes in France: 1830–1968*

(London: Cambridge University Press, 1974); McAdam, McCarthy, and Zald, "Social Movements," p. 700; and Skocpol, *States and Social Revolutions*.

58. See McAdam, McCarthy, and Zald, "Social Movements," p. 731 n. 7; and McAdam, *Political Process*.

59. See Frances Fox Piven and Richard A. Cloward, *Poor People's Movements* (New York: Vintage Books, 1979).

60. See Armand L. Mauss, *Social Problems as Social Movements* (Philadelphia: Lippincott, 1975), p. 66.

61. See "The Movement: Anti-Intervention or Anti-Empire," *Basta!* March 1988, pp. 5–7; and Crittenden, *Sanctuary*, p. xvi.

62. See Edward J. Walsh, "Resource Mobilization and Citizen Protest in Communities around Three Mile Island," *Social Problems* 29, (1981): 1–21.

63. See Crittenden, *Sanctuary*, pp. 300–3, 351–52; Ward Churchill and Jim Vander Wall, *Agents of Repression: The FBI's Secret Wars against the Black Panther Party and the American Indian Movement* (Boston: South End Press, 1988), pp. 370–72; Don Edwards, "Sanctuary: The Unsolved Break-ins," *World*, July–Aug. 1987, pp. 8–10; Nat Hentoff, "Who's on First: Snoops in the Pews," *Progressive*, Aug. 1985, pp. 24–26; "I.N.S. on Trial," *Nation*, January 25, 1986, p. 68; Gerald Renner, "Black Bags Are Back," *Christian Century*, March 5, 1986, pp. 229–31; Elissa Dennis, "Are the Plumbers Back?" *Progressive*, Sept. 1986, p. 17; Charles R. Babcock, "FBI Surveillance of Policy Critics Alleged," *Washington Post*, Feb. 13, 1987, p. A34; "FBI Surveillance Continues," *Basta!* March 1987, pp. 28–31; John Manuel Andriste, "Charges of Break-ins and Infiltration," *Christianity Today*, April 17, 1987, p. 44; "INS/FBI Assessment of the Sanctuary Movement," *Basta!*, June 1987, pp. 17–18; Dennis Bernstein and Connie Blitt, "Death Squad–Style Violence Haunts Salvadoran Organizers in the U.S.," *In These Times*, July 22–Aug. 4, 1987, pp. 6, 22; Peter Mantesano, "Death Threats Continue," *Basta!* Dec. 1987, pp. 15–16; "Sanctuary Groups Implicated in FBI Files," *Basta!* March 1988, pp. 8–12; Anthony Schmitz, "The Spy Who Said No," *Mother Jones*, April 1988, pp. 16–19; Michael Briggs, "FBI Disciplines 6 Probers," *Chicago Sun-Times*, Sept. 15, 1988, p. 9; "Stop FBI Political Spying," *Chicago Sun-Times*, Sept. 19, 1988, p. 23; Marylou Gramm, "Stifling Dissent: FBI Spies on Madre," *Madre* 6, no. 1 (1989): 10, 22; and Ed Magnusen, "Double Standard for Refugees? A split over Sanctuary," *Time*, April 28, 1986, p. 34.

64. Crittenden, *Sanctuary*, pp. 219–20.

65. See McAdam, McCarthy, and Zald, "Social Movements," p. 699; and Herbert H. Haines, "Black Radicalization and the Funding of Civil Rights: 1957–1970," *Social Problems* 32 (1984): 31–43.

66. See Chadwick F. Alger and Saul H. Menlovitz, "Grass-roots Initiatives: The Challenge of Linkages," in *Towards a Just World Peace: Perspectives from Social Movements,* ed. S. H. Mendlovitz and R. B. J. Walker, pp. 333–62 (London: Buttersworths, 1987); and Golden, "Sanctuary," p. 109.

CHAPTER II

1. See Doug McAdam, *Political Process and the Development of Black Insurgency: 1930–1970* (Chicago: University of Chicago Press, 1982); and Anthony Oberschall, *Social Conflict and Social Movements* (Englewood Cliffs, N.J.: Prentice-Hall, 1973).

2. On the role of previous organizational experience in woman's political activism, see Sara M. Evans, *Personal Politics: The Roots of Women's Liberation in the Civil Rights Movement and the New Left* (New York: Vintage/Random Books, 1979); and Jo Freeman, "The Origins of the Women's Liberation Movement," *American Journal of Sociology* 78 (Jan. 1973): 792–811.

3. The natural history of a social movement is defined as the process of evolution through which it passes, primarily as a result of interacting with the social environment; see Armand L. Mauss, *Social Problems as Social Movements* (Philadelphia: Lippincott, 1975), pp. 57, 61–67. In the 1970s and 1980s social scientists rejected this approach, seeing movement development as less stagelike and more variable than had previously been thought; however, such an approach clearly portrays the refugees' passages as important markers of institutional and group involvement. See Doug McAdam, John D. McCarthy, and Mayer N. Zald, "Social Movements," in *Handbook of Sociology,* ed. Neil J. Smelser (Newbury Park, Calif.: Sage 1988), p. 729.

4. Names of all sites, coalitions, organizations, and participants in the study have been changed (see the Appendix) except the CRTFCA; its real name is used, mostly in reference to published information about the agency. See *CRTFCA Newsletter,* Spring 1987.

5. See Charlotte Cooper, "Commission Requests Sanctuary Forum," *Oak Park Oak Leaves,* Nov. 26, 1986, p. 8; and "Evanston Declares Sanctuary," *Basta!* March 1988, p. 18.

6. See *Report from the Chicago Religious Task Force on Central America* (Chicago: CRTFCA, 1988–89), p. 2; and "Popular Education and Base Community Organizing," *Basta!*; Summer–Fall 1989 (special issue).

7. See Michael J. Behr, "Area Catholics Establish 'Sanctuary' for Refu-

gees . . . Cardinal Bernadin Warns of Illegality of Movement," *Chicago Catholic,* Dec. 5, 1986, pp. 1, 30.

8. See Charles Feinberg, "Sanctuary: A Jewish Perspective," *Basta!* June 1987, pp. 31–33.

9. See Blase Bonpane, *Guerrillas of Peace: Liberation Theology and the Central American Revolution* (Boston: South End Press, 1985); Leonardo Boff, *Church: Charism & Power: Liberation Theology and the Institutional Church* (New York: Crossroad, 1985); Boff, *Ecclesiogenesis: The Base Communities Reinvent the Church* (New York: Orbis Books, 1986); and William K. Tabb, ed., *Churches in Struggle: Liberation Theology and Social Change in North America* (New York: Monthly Review Press, 1986).

10. The idea for these names came from a nun who compared the "pre-refugee" with the "refugee" stage; "post-refugee stage" seemed a fitting final designation.

11. Mary Douglas describes the culturally universal fear of social pollution in *Natural Symbols: Explorations in Cosmology* (New York: Pantheon Books, 1982).

12. See Howard Becker, "Becoming a Marijuana User," in *Outsiders: Studies in the Sociology of Deviance* (New York: Free Press, 1963), pp. 41–53.

13. "Collective feeling"refers to the participation of many subjects in the same feeling and may include a strong sense of "we-feeling"; see Henry Pratt Fairchild, *Dictionary of Sociology* (Totowa, N.J.: Helix Books, 1984), p. 119.

14. Wearing bandanas began in Tucson at the first sanctuary declaration as a means of protecting the refugees' identities; (see Ann Crittenden, *Sanctuary: A Story of American Conscience and the Law in Collision* (New York: Weidenfeld and Nicolson, 1988), pp. 72–73. A CRTFCA pamphlet recommends that refugees "wear masks or bandanas to conceal their identities and use an alias during any press coverage"; see *Public Sanctuary for Salvadoran and Guatemalan Refugees: Organizer's Nuts and Bolts* (Chicago: CRTFCA, n.d.), p. 6.

15. See McAdam, McCarthy, and Zald, "Social Movements," pp. 709–11.

CHAPTER III

1. Renny Golden, who coauthored with Michael McConnell the important book *Sanctuary: The New Underground Railroad* (New York: Orbis Books, 1986), has played a prominent role in the local movement. Darlene

Nicgorski won a *Ms.* magazine "Woman of the Year" award; see Rusty Brown, "Sister Darlene Nicgorski: For Giving Refugees . . . Sanctuary. . . ," *Ms.*, Jan. 1987, pp. 54, 56, 90–92.

2. See *Basta!* Feb. 1986, p. 10. Extensive media coverage may be due to the "inherent racism which sees acts by whites, however risky, as newsworthy," compared with "the same actions carried out by blacks, Native Americans, or Central Americans"; see Renny Golden, "Sanctuary: Choosing Sides," *Socialist Review* 16, no. 6 (1986): 109.

3. An estimated 90 percent of Guatemalan women have been raped passing through Mexico. See *Sanctuary: A Justice Ministry* (Chicago: CRTFCA, 1986), p. 22; and Jane Juffer, "Abuse at the Border: Women Face a Perilous Crossing," *Progressive,* April 1988, pp. 14–19.

4. See Jean Baker Miller, *Toward a New Psychology of Women* (Boston: Beacon Press, 1976).

5. This was described in Chapter II as part of the "refugee stage."

6. Karen Brodkin Sacks examines women workers' use of familistic language in their struggle to extend their family stature as adults to their diminutive roles in the workplace; see her "Gender and Grassroots Leadership," in *Women and the Politics of Empowerment,* ed. Ann Bookman and Sandra Morgen, pp. 77–93 (Philadelphia: Temple University Press, 1988).

7. See Horace Minor, "Body Ritual among the Nicerima," *American Anthropologist* 58 (1956): 503–7.

8. Eugene Genovese describes the two-step strategy of slaves in the United States accommodating authority when necessary and resisting whenever possible. See his *Roll, Jordan, Roll: The World the Slaves Made* (New York: Vintage Books, 1972).

CHAPTER IV

1. "Conscience constituents" are outsiders who provide resources to aggrieved groups. See John D. McCarthy and Mayer N. Zald, *The Trend of Social Movements in America: Professionalization and Resource Mobilization* (Morristown, N.J.: General Learning Press, 1973).

2. See Karen Brodkin Sacks, "Gender and Grassroots Leadership," in *Women and the Politics of Empowerment,* ed. Ann Bookman and Sandra Morgen, pp. 80, 90, 93, 77 (Philadelphia: Temple University Press, 1988); Pauline B. Bart, "Seizing the Means of Reproduction: An Illegal Feminist Abortion Collective—How and Why it Worked," *Qualitative Sociology* 10, no. 4 (1987): 339–57; and Jean Baker Miller, *Toward a New Psychology of Women* (Boston: Beacon Press, 1976).

3. See Carol Gilligan, *In a Different Voice: Psychological Theory and Women's Development* (Cambridge, Mass.: Harvard University Press, 1982).

4. See the discussion of the "familistic language" of women participants in a union drive in Sacks, "Gender and Grassroots Leadership."

5. These conditions in 1960s political movements help explain the modern women's movement. See Sara Evans, *Personal Politics: The Roots of Women's Liberation in the Civil Rights Movement and the New Left* (New York: Vintage Books, 1980); Jo Freeman, "The Origins of the Women's Liberation Movement," *American Journal of Sociology* 78 (January 1973): 792–811; Natalie Porter, Florence Lindauer Gels, and Joyce Jennings, "Are Women Invisible Leaders?" *Sex Roles* 9, no. 10 (1983): 1035–49; and Joanna Brenner and Nancy Holstrom, "Women's Self-Organization: Theory and Strategy," *Monthly Review* 1, no. 34 (1983): 34–46.

6. In these activities North Americans travel to Central America, witness refugees' displacement from the land, and accompany them in their efforts to return to their war-torn villages.

7. Georg Simmel describes the qualities of intimate relationships that differentiate them from political ones: "As soon as a third element is added . . . party formation is suggested instead of solidarity." See *The Sociology of Georg Simmel*, ed. Kurt H. Wolff (New York: Free Press, 1950), p. 141.

8. "Civil disobedience" refers to "the deliberate and open violation of a norm for the purpose of changing it because it is perceived as being unjust"; see Allan G. Johnson, *Human Arrangements: An Introduction to Sociology* (New York: Harcourt Brace Jovanovich, 1986), p. 692.

9. See Marie Marmo Mullaney, "Women and the Theory of Revolution and Personality," *Social Science Journal* 221, no. 2 (1984): 49–70; Marcia Millman, "She Did It All for Love: A Feminist View of the Sociology of Deviance," in *Another Voice: Feminist Perspectives on Social Life and Social Science*, ed. Millman and Rosabeth Moss Kanter, pp. 251–79 (New York: Doubleday, 1975); and Richard Cloward and Frances Fox Piven, "Hidden Protest: The Channeling of Female Innovation and Resistance," *Signs* 4, no. 4 (1979): 651–69.

10. This may also be related to women's conditioned fear of violence: "The ratio of fearful females to males is between 2 to 1 and 3 to 1," according to Brian J. Jones, Bernard J. Gallagher, and Joseph A. McFalls, *Social Problems: Issues, Opinions, and Solutions* (New York: McGraw-Hill, 1988), p. 377.

11. The term "sick role" describes societal expectations for a person

viewed as ill; see Talcott Parsons, *The Social System* (New York: Free Press, 1951), pp. 428–79.

12. "Commissioning" reportedly means "approval of and solidarity with."

13. See Arlie Russell Hochschild, "The Sociology of Feeling and Emotion: Selected Possibilities," in Millman and Kanter, *Another Voice,* p. 290.

14. See Sacks, "Gender and Grassroots Leadership," pp. 80, 79.

CHAPTER V

1. The moral careers approach has been used to describe socially constructed careers in occupations (see Everett C. Hughes, "The Study of Occupations," in *The Sociological Eye: Selected Papers,* pp. 283–97 [Chicago: Aldine-Atherton, 1971]); medical school (see Howard S. Becker and Blanche Geer, "The Fate of Idealism in Medical School," *American Sociological Review* 23 [1958]: 50–56); mental asylums (see Erving Goffman, *Asylums* [New York: Anchor Books, 1961]); and faith development (see James W. Fowler, *Stages of Faith: The Psychology of Human Development and the Quest for Meaning* [San Francisco: Harper & Row, 1981]). See also Arlie Russell Hochschild, "The Sociology of Feeling and Emotions: Selected Possibilities," in *Another Voice: Feminist Perspectives on Social Life and Social Science,* ed. Marcia Millman and Rosabeth Moss Kanter, pp. 280–307 (New York: Doubleday, 1975); and C. Wright Mills, "Situated Actions and Vocabularies of Motive," *American Sociological Review* 5 (Dec. 1940): 393–94.

2. Those paths were constructed from themes that stand out in the case material; I do not intend them to represent fixed types of activism. Angela A. Aidala criticizes successor theory in "New Religions: A Test of the Successor Movement Thesis" (paper presented to the Association for the Sociology of Religion, San Francisco, 1989).

3. See George Herbert Mead, *Mind, Self, and Society* (Chicago: University of Chicago Press, 1934); Erik Erikson, *Childhood and Society* (New York: Norton, 1963); and Jean Piaget, *The Moral Judgment of the Child* (Glencoe, Ill.: Free Press, 1965).

4. See Carol Gilligan, *In a Different Voice: Psychological Theory and Women's Development* (Cambridge, Mass.: Harvard University Press, 1982); Nel Noddings, *Caring: A Feminine Approach to Ethics and Moral Education* (Berkeley: University of California Press, 1984), p. 8; and Arlie Russell Hochschild, *The Managed Heart: Commercialization of Human Feeling* (Berkeley: University of California Press, 1983).

5. See Arlene K. Daniels, "The Hidden Work of Constructing Class and Community: Women Volunteer Leaders in Social Philanthropy," in *Families and Work*, ed. Naomi Gerstel and Harriet Engel Gross, pp. 220–35 (Philadelphia: Temple University Press, 1987); Daniels, *Invisible Careers: Women Community Leaders in the Volunteer World* (Chicago: University of Chicago Press, 1988); and Susan A. Ostrander, *Women of the Upper Class* (Philadelphia: Temple University Press, 1984).

6. Many of the women had experienced changes in their religious outlook and affiliation, as noted below. In Appendix Table 1, four who switched between Catholicism and Protestantism as young adults after leaving a traditional church are classified according to their "religion of origin," since their early years more likely affected their faith development.

7. See Todd Gitlin, *The Sixties* (New York: Bantam Books, 1987). Marilyn Ferguson calls the 1960s the "Second American Revolution," when "members of the middle and upper classes . . . began to criticize existing institutions and speculate on a new society" (*The Aquarian Conspiracy: Personal and Social Transformation in the 1980s* [Los Angeles: Tarcher, 1980], pp. 125–26).

8. Ferguson's study of 1980s "New Agers" indicates that many similarly "preferred not to designate their positions on the political spectrum, saying that the old labels were no longer relevant" (*Aquarian Conspiracy*, p. 418).

9. Economist Hazel Henderson allegedly coined this maxim; see Harvey Wasserman and Marc Barasch, "Interview: Hazel Henderson," *New Age Journal*, March 1984, pp. 30–35, 88–95.

10. James A. Beckford, "Accounting for Conversion," *British Journal of Sociology* 29, no. 2 (1978): 260. See also Gregory B. Markus, "Stability and Change in Political Attitudes: Observed, Recalled, and 'Explained,'" *Political Behavior* 8, no. 1 (1986): 21–44.

11. Doug McAdam, John D. McCarthy, and Mayer N. Zald, "Social Movements," in *Handbook of Sociology*, ed. Neil J. Smelser (Newbury Park, Calif.: Sage, 1988), p. 713. See also David A. Snow, E. Burke Rochford, Jr., Steven K. Worden, and Robert D. Benford, "Frame Alignment Processes, Micromobilization, and Movement Participation," *American Sociological Review* 51 (1986): 464–81.

12. Murray Edelman, *Politics as Symbolic Action* (New York: Academic Press, 1971), p. 32.

13. See McAdam, McCarthy, and Zald, "Social Movements," p. 713.

14. See Fowler, *Stages of Faith*, pp. xii–xiii. See also Erving Goffman, *The Presentation of Self in Everyday Life* (New York: Doubleday, 1959).

15. See Anthony Oberschall, *Social Conflict and Social Movements* (En-

glewood Cliffs, N.J.: Prentice-Hall, 1973); and Mancur Olson, *The Logic of Collective Action* (Cambridge, Mass.: Harvard University Press, 1965).

CHAPTER VI

1. See Bennett M. Berger's study of structure and consciousness among commune members in *The Survival of a Counterculture: Ideological Work and Everyday Life among Rural Communards* (Berkeley: University of California Press, 1981).
2. See Doug McAdam, John D. McCarthy, and Mayer N. Zald, "Social Movements," in *Handbook of Sociology*, ed. Neil J. Smelser (Newbury Park, Calif.: Sage, 1988), pp. 704, 719.
3. These two also both recalled having socially active fathers, and their fathers' and husbands' occupations were notably identical.
4. The women who described family conflict over their activism were all laywomen except for Christine, the only married clergywoman.
5. See Myra Marx Ferree, "Sacrifice, Satisfaction, and Special Change: Employment and the Family," in *My Troubles Are Going to Have Trouble with Me*, ed. Karen Brodkin Sacks and Dorothy Remy, pp. 61–79 (New Brunswick, N.J.: Rutgers University Press, 1984).
6. Ibid., pp. 64, 76.
7. Familistic concepts contain "oppositional meanings and political potential" whose strength lies in their "multiple meanings" and "ability to bridge racial, gender, and occupational divisions"; see Karen Brodkin Sacks, "Gender and Grassroots Leadership," in *Women and the Politics of Empowerment*, ed. Ann Bookman and Sandra Morgen, pp. 77–93 (Philadelphia: Temple University Press, 1988).
8. See Robert Bellah, Richard Madsen, William Sullivan, Ann Swidler, and Steven Tipton, *Habits of the Heart: Individualism and Commitment in American Life* (Berkeley: University of California Press, 1985), p. 123.
9. See McAdam, McCarthy, and Zald, "Social Movements," pp. 703–4.
10. These included nine married laywomen (four Catholic and five Protestant), four nuns, and two clergywomen (one married). Jewish women discussed similarly politicized religious concepts. The Exodus narrative was the central biblical text cited to justify sanctuary. One discussed the importance of *pikuach nefesh*—saving lives—to Jewish sanctuary: "It's the only reason for violating rules on Sabbath—to save a life. One can work, turn off lights, drive—do all those things a Jew cannot ordinarily do on the Sabbath. That's what justifies this activism; it's saving lives." See Marc H. Ellis,

"Notes toward a Jewish Theology," in *Churches in Struggle: Liberation Theology and Social Change in North America,* ed. William K. Tabb, pp. 67–87 (New York: Monthly Review Press, 1986).

11. The base-community movement began in Brazil and involves church figures helping peasants to gain land reforms. Growing numbers of Catholics have allied themselves with the poor in a political struggle against ruling powers in Latin America, and many church members have been killed. Liberation theology has also met resistance within the Catholic church. Pope John Paul II has strongly opposed mixing politics with traditional church doctrine and has forbidden church officials to participate in social conflicts. The Vatican claims that some forms of liberation theology represent a fundamental danger to Catholic faith, threatening to divert attention from otherworldly concerns and embroil the church in political controversy. The liberation theology movement has continued to grow in Latin America, fueled by the belief that both Christian faith and a sense of human justice demand efforts to change the plight of the world's poor; see Leonardo Boff, *Ecclesiogenesis: The Base Communities Reinvent the Church* (New York: Orbis Books, 1986); Boff, *Church: Charism & Power: Liberation Theology and the Institutional Church* (New York: Crossroad, 1985); Blase Bonpane, *Guerrillas of Peace: Liberation Theology and the Central American Revolution* (Boston: South End Press, 1985); and Tabb, *Churches in Struggle.*

12. Elisabeth Schussler Fiorenza, "Feminist Theology as a Critical Theology of Liberation," in Tabb, *Churches in Struggle,* pp. 48–50. See also Darlene Nicgorski, "Women and Theology," *Basta!* Sept. 1987, pp. 34–37.

13. Fiorenza, "Feminist Theology," pp. 52–53.

14. See Marie Augusta Neal, *From Nuns to Sisters* (Mystic, Conn.: Twenty-Third Publications, 1989). Martha Long Ice documents this growing trend among clergywomen in *Clergy Women and Their Worldviews: Calling for a New Age* (New York: Praeger, 1987).

15. See Sue Tolleson Rinehart, "Toward Women's Political Resocialization: Patterns of Predisposition in the Learning of Feminist Attitudes," *Women and Politics* 5, no. 4, (1985–86): 11–26.

16. Liberal feminism "advocates such reforms as legal equality between the sexes, equal pay for equal work, and equal opportunities, but denies that complete equality requires radical alterations in basic social institutions," according to Mary Ann Warren, *The Nature of Woman: An Encyclopedia and Guide to the Literature* (Inverness, Calif.: Edgepress, 1980), p. 280.

17. Cultural feminism "changes the focus of the women's movement from winning . . . freedom to being a 'good person.' It promotes the therapy model of liberation . . . and replaces political organizing with moral rear-

mament," writes Sara Scott, "Holding On to What We've Won," *Trouble and Strife* 1 (Winter 1983): 25.

18. See Boston Women's Health Collective, *Our Bodies, Ourselves: A Book by and for Women* (1971; New York: Simon and Schuster, 1979).

19. Radical feminism holds that "women were historically the first oppressed group; that women's oppression is the most widespread [and] the hardest form to eradicate and cannot be removed by other social changes, such as the abolution of class society; that women's oppression causes the most suffering to its victims; and that women's oppression provides a conceptual model for understanding all other forms of oppression" (Alison Jagger and Paula S. Rothenberg, *Feminist Frameworks: Alternative Theoretical Accounts of the Relations between Women and Men,* 2d ed. [New York: McGraw-Hill, 1984], p. 86).

20. See Mary Daly, *The Church and the Second Sex: With a New Post-Christian Introduction by the Author* (1969; New York: Harper-Colophon, 1975).

21. Separatist feminism is defined by Marilyn Frye, *The Politics of Reality: Essays in Feminist Theory* (Trumansburg, N.Y.: Crossing Press, 1983), p. 96, as "separation . . . from men and from institutions, relationships, roles, and activities which are male-defined, male-dominated, and operating for the benefit of males and the maintenance of male privilege—this separation being initiated or maintained at will by women."

CHAPTER VII

1. See Janet Saltzman Chafetz and Anthony Gary Dworkin, *Female Revolt: Women's Movements in World and Historical Perspective* (Totowa, N.J.: Rowman & Allanheld, 1986), pp. 21, 23; and Ann Crittenden, *Sanctuary: A Story of American Conscience and the Law in Collision* (New York: Weidenfeld & Nicolson, 1988), p. vi.

2. See Christine Stansell, *City of Women: Sex and Class in New York, 1789–1860* (New York: Knopf, 1986), pp. 219–20; and Chafetz and Dworkin, *Female Revolt,* pp. 25–26.

3. Chafetz and Dworkin, *Female Revolt,* p. 23.

4. Ibid., pp. 24–26. See also Joseph R. Gusfield, *Symbolic Crusade: Status Politics and the American Temperance Movement* (Urbana: University of Illinois Press, 1963); Barbara Leslie Epstein, *The Politics of Domesticity* (Middletown, Conn.: Wesleyan University Press, 1981); and Ruth Bordin, *Women and Temperance: The Quest for Power and Liberty, 1873–1900* (Philadelphia: Temple University Press, 1981).

5. See Chafetz and Dworkin, *Female Revolt*, pp. 27, 29. See also Amy Swerdlow, "Ladies Day at the Capitol: Women Strike for Peace versus HUAC," *Feminist Studies* 8, no. 3 (1982): 498–520; and Hugh Mehan and John Wills, "MEND [Mothers Embracing Nuclear Disarmament]: A Nurturing Voice in the Nuclear Arms Debate," *Social Problems* 35, no. 4 (1988): 363–83.

6. See Joyce Rothschild-Whitt, "The Collectivist Organization: An Alternative to Rational-Bureaucratic Models," *American Sociological Review* 44 (1979): 509–27; and Rothschild-Whitt, "Conditions Facilitating Participatory-Democratic Organizations," *Sociological Inquiry* 46, no. 2 (1975): 75–86. Max Weber describes value-rational authority in *Economy and Society*, ed. Guenther Roth and Claus Wittich (New York: Bedminster Press, 1968), p. 24.

7. Rothschild-Whitt, "Collectivist Organization," pp. 521–22.

8. See Olive Banks, *Faces of Feminism* (New York: Basil Blackwell, 1981).

9. See Pauline B. Bart, "Seizing the Means of Reproduction: An Illegal Feminist Abortion Collective—How and Why it Worked," *Qualitative Sociology* 10, no. 4 (1987): 339–57.

10. On activists' character traits as predictors for activism, see Edward N. Mueller, "The Psychology of Political Protest and Violence," in *Handbook of Political Conflict*, ed. Ted Robert Gurr (New York: Free Press, 1980). On predisposing attitudes as predictors, see Clark McPhail, "Civil Disorder Participation: A Critical Examination of Recent Research," *American Sociological Review* 36 (1971): 1058–73. On the importance of cognitive processes to political activism, see Neil J. Smelser, *Theory of Collective Behavior* (New York: Free Press, 1962); Ralph Turner and Lewis Killian, *Collective Behavior* (Englewood Cliffs, N.J.: Prentice-Hall, 1972); Doug McAdam, *Political Process and the Development of Black Insurgency: 1930–1970* (Chicago: University of Chicago Press, 1982); and Karl Marx, *Selected Writings in Sociology and Social Philosophy*, ed. T. B. Bottomore, pp. 67–87 (New York: McGraw-Hill, 1956). See Bert Klandermans, "Mobilization and Participation: Social-Psychological Expansions of Resource Mobilization Theory," *American Sociological Review* 49 (1984): 583–600.

11. "This is all the more likely . . . when . . . women [are] financially dependent on men. Efforts to create groups or communities free from male influence . . . attest to the seriousness of the problem" (Doug McAdam, John D. McCarthy, and Mayer N. Zald, "Social Movements," in *Handbook of Sociology*, ed. Neil J. Smelser, [Newbury Park, Calif.: Sage, 1988], p. 704).

12. See Doug McAdam, "Recruitment to High-Risk Activism: The Case

of Freedom Summer," *American Journal of Sociology* 48 (1986): 64–90; David A. Snow and Cynthia L. Phillips, "The Lofland-Stark Conversion Model: A Critical Reassessment," *Social Problems* 27, no. 4 (1980): 430–47; E. Burke Rochford, Jr., *Hare Krishna in America* (New Brunswick, N.J.: Rutgers University Press, 1985); McAdam, McCarthy, and Zald, "Social Movements," p. 708; John Lofland, *Doomsday Cult* (New York: Irvington, 1977); and Howard Becker, *Outsiders: Studies in the Sociology of Deviance* (New York: Free Press, 1963).

13. See McAdam, "Recruitment," p. 70; John D. McCarthy and Mayer N. Zald, *The Trend of Social Movements in America: Professionalization and Resource Mobilization* (Morristown, N.J.: General Learning Press, 1973); Rochford, *Hare Krishna;* McAdam, McCarthy, and Zald, "Social Movements," p. 715; Jo Freeman, "The Origins of the Women's Liberation Movement," *American Journal of Sociology* 78, (1973): 792–811; and Anthony Oberschall, *Social Conflict and Social Movements* (Englewood Cliffs, N.J.: Prentice-Hall, 1973).

14. See McAdam, McCarthy, and Zald, "Social Movements," pp. 716–18; and Aldon Morris, *The Origins of the Civil Rights Movement* (New York: Free Press, 1984).

15. See Jo Freeman, *The Politics of Women's Liberation* (New York: David McKay, 1975); Kristen Luker, *Abortion and the Politics of Motherhood* (Berkeley: University of California Press, 1984); John D. McCarthy, "Pro-Life and Pro-Choice Mobilization: Infrastructure Deficits and New Technologies," in *Social Movements in an Organizational Society,* ed. Mayer N. Zald and John D. McCarthy, pp. 49–66 (New Brunswick, N.J.: Transaction Books, 1987); and Deena Weinstein, *Bureaucratic Opposition* (New York: Pergamon, 1979).

16. Mayer N. Zald and Roberta Ash describe social movement outcomes as demise, radicalization, schism, and movement organization becalmed; see their "Social Movement Organizations: Growth, Decay, and Change," *Social Forces* 44 (1966): 327–41. See also William Gamson, *The Strategy of Social Protest* (Homewood, Ill.: Dorsey Press, 1975); Dorothy Nelkin and Michael Pollak, *The Atom Besieged* (Cambridge, Mass.: MIT Press, 1981); McAdam, McCarthy, and Zald, "Social Movements," p. 727; Saul Alinsky, *Rules for Radicals* (New York: Random House, 1971); Leila Rupp and Verta Taylor, *Survial in the Doldrums: The American Women's Rights Movement, 1945 to 1960* (New York: Oxford University Press, 1987); and Doug McAdam, *Freedom Summer* (New York: Oxford University Press, 1988).

17. Armand L. Mauss, *Social Problems as Social Movements* (Philadelphia: Lippincott, 1975), pp. 64–66.

18. Chadwick F. Alger and Saul H. Mendlovitz, "Grass-roots Initiatives: The Challenge of Linkages," in *Towards a Just World Peace: Perspectives from Social Movements,* ed. Saul H. Mendlovitz and R. B. J. Walker (London: Butterworths, 1987), pp. 333–34.

19. See Peter Applebome, "In the Sanctuary Movement, Unabated Strength but Shifting Aims," *New York Times,* Oct. 27, 1987, p. 8.

20. See Tim Padgett, "Immigrant Advocates Protest End of Amnesty," *Chicago Sun-Times,* May 6, 1988, p. 35; *Basta!* June 1980, pp. 14–15. Approval rates for asylum cases for fiscal year 1988 were 3.2 percent for Salvadorans, 2.7 percent for Guatemalans, 5.8 percent for Hondurans, and 74.9 percent for Nicaraguans.

APPENDIX

1. Early on in the study I also had an information interview with four CRTFCA agency women, who gave generously of their time and supplied some back issues of *Basta!* (a CRTFCA publication) but declined personal interviews.

2. Temple Zion was in the germinal stage of becoming a sanctuary at the time of the study; it declared itself soon thereafter.

3. Christine was lay clergy (i.e., unordained), a co-minister with an ordained clergywoman; she resembled other women religious in her orientation and activities, and other laywomen in having a husband and children and in having left the church early and returned later to a socially active congregation, thus initiating her activism.

4. Women confirmed that most participants in the Chicago sanctuary network were white; I heard of only two women of color, one of whom was moving out of state and could not be interviewed.

5. See Ann Oakley, "Interviewing Women: A Contradiction In Terms," in *Doing Feminist Research,* ed. Helen Roberts (London: Routledge & Kegan Paul, 1981), pp. 30–61.

as a political process, 8–18, 21–24, 55; precedents for, 7–8; religious justification for, 7, 163–64, 198–99; size, 14–15. *See also* Future of sanctuary; Immigration and Naturalization Service (INS); Stages of involvement; Women in sanctuary
Social action committee: as a unit of action, 25, 33, 51–52; women's predominance on, 33
Social movements, women's historical roles and predominance in, 5–6, 189–90
Stages of involvement: learning about sanctuary, 34–37; declaring sanctuary, 37–40; preparing for refugees, 40–41; refugees' arrival, 41–44; monitoring, 45; institutionalizing procedures, 46; refugee turnover, 46–49; burnout, 49–51

Temple Israel: base-community format, 32; becoming a site, 37, 40–41; obstacles to sanctuary, 29–30; as a social action synagogue, 31; special catalysts, 35–36. *See also* Jewish sanctuary
Temple Zion. *See* Jewish sanctuary
Translating, 93–95
Travel to Central America: accompaniment and repopulation, 104–8; culture conflict, 108–13; personal witness, 104–6

University Church: becoming a site, 36–37; sanctuary longevity of, 51; as a social action church, 31, 33

Views of liberation, women's: feminism, 175; feminist theology, 176–77; laywomen, 177–82; liberation theology, 175–76; women religious, 182–86

Washington Church: becoming a site, 34–36, 38–41; Chicago's first site, 25; gendered conflicts at, 58–59; refugee turnover at, 46
Westminster Church: base-community format, 32; becoming a site, 32, 36–38, 40; Chicago's second site, 30–31; refugee turnover at, 46–49; as a social action church, 30–31, 33; unofficial support for, 45
Women in sanctuary: hidden work of, 5; impact of background of, 7, 115–18; laywomen versus women religious, 62–80, 187–88, 192–94; predominance of, 3, 7, 33; prior awareness of issues of, 18–21; as a rising class, 61, 83–84, 93, 117. *See also* Cognitive liberation; Social movements, women's historical roles and predominance in; Views of liberation, women's
Women's bilingualism. *See* Translating